The Shakespeare Authorship Mystery Explained

GEOFFREY EYRE

Mardle Publications

Also written by Geoffrey Eyre

The Case for Edward de Vere as Shakespeare

ISBN 978-0-9554608-4-5

The Shakespeare Authorship Mystery Explained

First published 2017 by Mardle Publications
www.mardlepublications.com

mardlebooks@gmail.com

Typeset by John Owen Smith, Headley Down

© 2017 Geoffrey Eyre

ISBN 978-0-9554608-8-3

Printed by CreateSpace

Contents

Quotations

All the Shakespeare quotations and name spellings have been taken from *William Shakespeare: The Complete Works*, edited by Wells and Taylor, Clarendon Press, Oxford, Second Edition 2005.

4

Preface

William Shakespeare – Man of the Second Millennium

1000 – 1999

In a poll organised by the BBC, William Shakespeare was chosen by the British nation as their Man of the Millennium, beating Sir Winston Churchill into second place. The 'Bard' was seen as a good choice, his world-famous name epitomising love of country and sturdy self-reliance. Shakespeare was the name most closely associated with the reign of Queen Elizabeth I and in a new Elizabethan age he was seen as an appropriate choice. Defeat of the Spanish Armada and the exploits of adventurous sea-captains made it an exciting time to be alive. The name 'Shakespeare' has ever since been identified with patriotism, with military and naval power, and with excellence in the performing arts.

But who, exactly, did the people choose? Or think they chose? These questions are not easily answered and lie at the heart of the authorship mystery.

Whoever wrote Shakespeare would have been born in the 16th century. The literary establishment has never wavered in its belief that Shakespeare wrote Shakespeare, this being the man who was born in Stratford-upon-Avon in 1564 and died there in 1616. The plays were not immediately popular and the restoration of the monarchy in the latter half of the 17th century ushered in a new generation of writers, and a more modern form of stage production. This began to change in the 18th century when strong stage performances by David Garrick in London led to a revival of interest in Shakespeare's plays. They also stirred the first rumbles of curiosity about the author, of whom surprisingly little was known.

In the 19th century interest in Shakespeare strengthened still further and gathered momentum with new editions of the plays, although with little additional information about the author. The long lapse in time and intervening events such as the civil war 1642-1651, and London's great fire of 1666, were seen as contributing factors to explain why so little was known of Shakespeare's life. The education act of 1870 ensured that by the end of the 19th century there was a literate population of readers and playgoers, with Shakespeare emerging as a clear favourite for their most esteemed author. The Victorian ethos of admiration for the self-made man elevated the 'Bard' to quasi-mythical status as the world's supreme literary genius.

In the early 20th century a few scholars began to break ranks by openly doubting that the Warwickshire man was the author of the plays. By this time Shakespeare had become a brand which was sold around the world, with considerable commercial benefit to the national economy. Yet many people at home and increasingly from abroad, from the United States of America in particular, were unable to reconcile the epic quality of the great Shakespearean tragedies with the small-town trader who was supposed to have written them. In the 21st century this remains the current position. The literary establishment (our teaching universities and sixth form colleges, the London and provincial theatres, the publishing houses, many critics and journalists), still stoutly defend the Warwickshire man as the author of the plays. This could also be said of the population at large who are mostly dismissive of any attempt to promote an alternative Shakespeare author.

Literary scholars have long wanted to be able to chart the evolution of Shakespeare's artistic development, to illuminate the darkness that has always surrounded the origins of the plays, and even more so of the sonnets. This has never proved possible, a matter of profound regret, since such knowledge is available for almost every other author of note, and from the earliest times, but is denied for Shakespeare the greatest of them all. The more the plays and poetry of Shakespeare are studied the more remarkable they become. Who could have written these extraordinary works of literature with their amazing felicity of language? Many would like to know but are baffled and frustrated by the lack of biographical details, not only for the man from Stratford-upon-Avon but for other writers considered as possible alternative authors of Shakespeare.

This short study is predicated on the assumption that the 'Mr. William Shakespeare' on the title page of the First Folio was the pseudonym of a writer whose identity has become irretrievably lost. It will attempt to explain how the mystery came about in the first place, how it was perpetuated, and the efforts made to identify the true author.

1 Historical Context

Shakespeare and the English language
The Fall of Constantinople
First printed books in English
Death of King Richard III
Columbus reaches America
The Protestant Reformation
Dissolution of the Monasteries
English Language for the English Church
Queen Mary Tudor
Queen Elizabeth I
Grammar and Spelling
Cecil House, London
Ovid's *Metamorphoses* and Holinshed's *Chronicles*
Elizabethan Acting Companies
Shakespeare Plays Privately Performed
Shakespeare Plays Publicly Performed
The Stationers' Company and the Revels Office
Henslowe's 'Diary'
The Rising of the North
Queen Elizabeth Excommunicated
The Dutch War of Independence
The Essex Rebellion

Shakespeare and the English Language

The themes and main story lines in the Shakespeare plays differ significantly from most other plays in the English language. Written at a period of history when the Middle Ages were drawing to a close, the plays retrospectively commemorate some of the feudalistic warrior kings who had ruled in Europe since the reign of Charlemagne. The fascination these plays have exerted on succeeding generations of readers and playgoers could be explained by the inherent sense of caste which underpins them. The emphasis is always on conduct, the need to behave honourably however fraught the situation, or whatever the sacrifice required. Strongly defined characters throughout the canon struggle with the conflictions of ambition, duty, loyalty and patriotism.

The primacy of Shakespeare in the global expansion of the English language cannot be over-estimated. The collection of Shakespeare plays known as the First Folio was published in 1623. In tandem with the King James Authorized Version of the Bible published in 1611 these two books set a standard of literary excellence which has never been matched, still less surpassed. Shakespeare's command of words and imagery, his grasp of history and the humanitarian cast of mind evident in the plays, still compel worldwide admiration.

It is almost beyond belief that the authorship of the Shakespeare plays should be in doubt but such has been the case for many years. Printing workshops and booksellers in Elizabethan and Jacobean London had not yet formed themselves into publishing houses and censorship was still enforced via the Lord Chamberlain's department. Bible translators, historians, pamphleteers and playwrights were all vulnerable in an age of political and religious turbulence. The penalties for provoking people in high places could be severe and many writers for this reason chose to publish anonymously or under a pseudonym.

To understand the Shakespeare authorship mystery it is helpful to be reminded of the historical context of the plays, and the sequence of events which influenced them. The fall of Constantinople in 1453 provides a starting point.

1453 – The Fall of Constantinople

The Ottoman conquest of Constantinople in 1453 brought the Roman Empire to an end after some 1,500 years. The overland trade routes into Asia were closed off and have remained closed ever since. Driven by commercial necessity to find alternative sea routes to China and the Far East the study of astronomy and mathematics became of prime importance to navigate the oceans safely. This rapid development of scientific method in northern and western Europe hastened the end of the Middle Ages.

1476 – First printed books in English

William Caxton's printing press was set up at Westminster in 1476. As well as a printer Caxton was also a bookseller and a translator of foreign books into English. He is credited with making the first attempts at standardising the spelling and structure of the English language. The power of the printing press to spread new ideas of freedom and justice was seen by church and state as potentially dangerous. Those in governance sought to control what was published through licencing and censorship.

1485 – Death of King Richard III.

The death of the last Plantagenet king brought to an end a long financially-draining internecine war. The first of the Tudor monarchs, King Henry VII, disbanded the old feudal militias as the first move in modernising the country. The new Tudor administration quickly rescued a failing economy by enforcing the collection of taxes and setting up an efficient government service. The Middle Ages in England came to an abrupt end.

1492 – Columbus reaches America

The discovery of the huge American land mass north and south had a lasting beneficial effect on the British economy. From being an offshore island on the far edge of western Europe the new Tudor government found itself ideally situated geographically between the old and new worlds. The pre-eminence of London as a great capital city accelerated the development of international trade. London was the seat of government, the financial centre and the country's main seaport. At a time of rapid change elsewhere the strong Tudor regime held the country well together.

1517 – The Protestant Reformation

Led by Martin Luther (1483-1546) and John Calvin (1509-64), the Protestant Reformation spread quickly across northern Europe. On 31 October 1517 Luther famously nailed his 95 theses on the door of All Saints Church at Wittenberg. Ostensibly as a protest against the remitting of sins for profit the new movement sought a profound and fundamental change in the way religion could be taught and practised within a western political system. It sought to replace the superstitious dread of an irascible extra-terrestrial deity needing to be constantly appeased with a more rational form of worship based on decorum in private and public life.

Many Protestant churches were established, including in England. Latin was the international language of scholarship but because it was so closely associated with Roman Catholicism all the Protestant churches switched to using vernacular languages for their religious services and prayer book literature. In England the vernacular language was English, a mainly spoken language at the time, and which would be barely comprehensible today.

The Dissolution of the Monasteries

The Act of Supremacy passed in 1534 made King Henry VIII the Supreme Head of the Church in England. This severed England from Papal authority in Rome, with far-reaching consequences. Between 1536 and 1541 the king ordered the disbandment of all Catholic religious communities in England, Wales and Ireland, and the confiscation of their buildings and financial assets. The brutality with which this was forced through fuelled extremism on both sides of the religious divide and left lasting bitterness.

The English Language for the English Church

King Edward VI – Reigned 1547-1553

In 1547 the staunchly Protestant young King Edward VI succeeded to the throne of England on the death of his father, King Henry VIII. Legislation in Edward's name was passed to make it compulsory for all church services to be held in English.

To serve this purpose university grammarians made haste to standardise the structure and spelling of English and to refine its pronunciation so that it could rival and then replace Latin. Which it did, with remarkable speed. The global march of the English language had been set irreversibly in motion.

Queen Mary Tudor – Reigned 1553-1558

Mary Tudor was the only surviving child of Henry VIII and Catherine of Aragon. She was married to King Philip 2nd of Spain and committed to restoring the country to Catholicism. Four days after her coronation on 30th November 1553 the new Queen Mary introduced legislation to repeal all the religious laws passed by her younger half-brother Edward VI. Starting in 1555 some two-hundred and eighty leading Protestants were executed in the next three years, including sixty women, most of them burned to death. Many Protestants fled abroad to escape the persecution, others did what they could to live within the new regime. Mary's death at the age of forty-two resulted in the Protestant Queen Elizabeth succeeding to the throne. Many of the old nobility still adhered to the Catholic religion and this made life difficult for the new young queen inheriting at the age of twenty-five.

Queen Elizabeth I – Reigned 1558-1603

Elizabeth Tudor was the daughter of King Henry VIII by his second wife Anne Boleyn. The marriage of her parents was annulled and Elizabeth declared illegitimate. When she was two and a half years old her mother was executed. Elizabeth as a Protestant was imprisoned by her Catholic half-sister Mary when she became queen in 1553. Elizabeth became queen when Mary died in 1558 and her first act was to establish an English Protestant Church with herself as Supreme Governor.

Elizabeth's precarious grasp on the monarchy was strengthened by her long association with William Cecil as her most astute and reliable adviser. Between them they saw off all their enemies at home and abroad and as Protestant rulers set up the Church of England. The Queen was much admired for her patriotism and liking for a show. At the halfway stage of her reign, the 1580s, there came a flowering of literary excellence which became known as the Elizabethan cultural renaissance. William Shakespeare became its most famous writer with Edmund Spenser, John Lyly, Philip Sidney and Christopher Marlowe contributing to this so-called golden age of literature. The Queen was a generous patron of the performing arts and paid well for herself and her court to be entertained. More than anyone else she created the circumstances which allowed the works of Shakespeare to be written.

Grammar and Spelling

The advancement of English was accelerated by the efforts of some distinguished Greek scholars at Cambridge University.

Thomas Smith	1513-1577	Queens' College
John Cheke	1514-1557	St John's College
Roger Ascham	1515-1568	St John's College
William Cecil	1520-1598	St John's College

They were able to use their knowledge of Greek to assimilate into English many words and expressions for describing abstract ideas and a wide range of human emotions. Under their guiding hands English was rendered capable of adaptation to any literary requirement. They shaped a language that would soon be enriched and made world famous by the writer known as William Shakespeare.

Cecil House, London

Sir William Cecil 1520-1598

Cecil House in the Strand was a huge double-courtyard brick-built palace, three storeys high with four corner turrets. The extensive grounds extended northward to Covent Garden and beyond. There was a paved tennis court, a bowling alley and an orchard, also a covered arcade and formal quadripartite gardens plus stables and tenement blocks to accommodate the huge number of servants and officials who worked there. Cecil House as the home of the sovereign's first minister could be seen as the equivalent of 10 Downing Street today. Sir William and his wife Mildred used the house to entertain foreign dignitaries, and on occasion to welcome the queen herself. Houses of this magnificence provide the setting for many Shakespeare plays.

Sir William Cecil also presided over the court of royal wards, set up to protect underage noblemen. In addition he provided board and private tuition for the sons of prominent members of the administration. Philip Sidney, nephew of Robert Dudley the earl of Leicester and the Queen's most privileged courtier, was one such pupil. For Sidney and his fellow scholars it would have been a prestigious upbringing. Cecil House also contained the largest library of books in London. When it was dispersed in 1678 it was found to contain many of the books used as source material for the plays of Shakespeare.

Two early books linked to Shakespeare

1567 – Ovid's *Metamorphoses*
translated from the Latin by Arthur Golding

The Roman poet known as Ovid was born in 43BC and died in 17AD. His epic poem *Metamorphoses* comprised 250 transformation stories divided into 15 books. They provide the single most influential source of information for the reworking of classical myths in western art and literature. Although no single plot originated from Arthur Golding's translation of Ovid, classical allusions are drawn from it in almost every Shakespeare play, for example the Pyramus and Thisbe story was used in *A Midsummer Night's Dream*.

Whoever wrote Shakespeare knew the *Metamorphoses* line by line.

1577 – Holinshed's Chronicles of England, Scotland, and Ireland

The historian Raphael Holinshed published the two-volume edition of his *Chronicles* in 1577. It provided source material for the History sequence of plays by Shakespeare, and to a lesser extent was drawn on for parts of *Cymbeline*, *King Lear* and *Macbeth*. An extended three-volume edition was published ten years later in 1587.

These books are linked because Arthur Golding (1536-1606) and Raphael Holinshed (1529-1580) were both members of Sir William Cecil's graduate family in residence at Cecil House in the Strand, in London. They would have had privileged access to his well-stocked library in a household where academic achievement was actively encouraged and highly regarded. The significance of these two books relative to the authorship mystery is the abundant source material they provided at a much earlier date than orthodox scholarship allows.

The Warwickshire businessman William Shakspere born in 1564 in Stratford-upon-Avon is still generally regarded as the author of the plays attributed to William Shakespeare. The earliest versions of these plays could have been written from the mid-1570s onward, with the bulk of the plays written between 1580 and 1600. References to these early versions are made by the English literary critics Richard Mulcaster, in *The First Part of the Elementary*, 1582, and Stephen Gosson in *Plays Confuted in Five Actions*, 1582. This would indicate that the surge in literary talent associated with the second half of Queen Elizabeth's reign was already launched and well under way at a time when Shakspere of Stratford was still a teenager. All this was going on in London long before his first visit to the capital at some time in the 1590s, the exact date being unknown.

This incompatibility of dates has always presented difficulties for an author not born until 1564. Scholars supporting the orthodox authorship position (Stratfordians) have mostly cited the latest possible dates of first performance or first publication for the individual plays in the Shakespeare canon. It is one of the reasons, among others, why some scholars eventually began to search for a more credible alternative author.

Elizabethan Acting Companies

These were originally touring family groups, travelling from town to town and castle to castle. The fear of contracting infectious diseases from strangers often made such troupes of entertainers unwelcome, and actors for that reason were considered members of a dubious profession. The rise of the professional theatre in the 1570s, and a new generation of university educated writers, helped to make acting a more acceptable vocation. These were the most prestigious companies

The Earl of Leicester's Men was founded in 1572 and merged with Lord Strange's Men after Leicester's death in 1588.

Lord Strange's Men was founded in 1582 and merged with the Chamberlain's Men in 1594 when Ferdinando Strange the 5th Earl of Derby died.

The most important company of actors in Elizabethan England was the Chamberlain's Men. This was founded in 1564 and was also known as Lord Hunsdon's Men, Henry and George Carey being father and son Lord Chamberlains. The main purpose of this company was to provide entertainments for the Queen and her courtiers in the royal palaces, mostly at Whitehall and Greenwich. When Queen Elizabeth died in 1603 the Chamberlain's Men became known as The King's Men.

Lord Howard's Men was renamed as the Admiral's Men when their patron Lord Howard of Effingham was promoted to Lord High Admiral in 1585.

William Stanley the 6th Earl of Derby kept on some of his brother's company of actors. These were formerly known as Lord Strange's Men, subsequently as Lord Derby's Men.

Edward de Vere the 17th earl of Oxford revived his father's company in 1580 and it was known as Lord Oxford's Men. This was finally merged with the earl of Worcester's Men in 1602. A troupe of singers and musicians known as Lord Oxford's Boys was also maintained by the earl.

Shakespeare Plays Privately Performed

The Shakespeare authorship mystery begins with a practical explanation, namely that the Shakespeare plays or earlier versions of them were mostly performed as private entertainments at one or other of the royal establishments. Queen Elizabeth was a generous patron who paid well for her courtiers to be kept entertained, rather than fighting duels or plotting against her. In addition to the royal palaces the plays of Shakespeare were performed in the privileged surroundings of the Inns of Court and the two universities.

Whitehall Palace	Gray's Inn	Oxford University
Greenwich Palace	Inner Temple	Cambridge University
Hampton Court	Middle Temple	Richmond Palace

Many of the early in-house productions at court would have been short plays known as Interludes. The more ambitious Masques could be on a lavish scale with music and sumptuous costumes. For these entertainments the courtiers were allowed to dress up and take speaking parts themselves.

Performances of plays at the Inns of Court would have been given to invited audiences of lawyers, merchants and senior government officials and administrators, members of the educated and increasingly influential middle class. The private nature of these gatherings, and the centuries which have since elapsed, could be a valid reason why so few precise records have survived.

Shakespeare Plays Publicly Performed

The plays of Shakespeare with their many classical allusions were less frequently performed in the public theatres, and references are scarce. London was the nation's principal seaport as well as its capital and financial centre, and as such had a rapidly expanding population. The playhouse known as The Theatre was commissioned in 1576 to meet the increasing demand for entertainment, followed by The Curtain a year later, both in the Shoreditch area of London. These were the more successful London theatres.

Blackfriars	Newington Butts
The Curtain	The Rose
The Theatre	The Globe

There were two separate Blackfriars Theatres, both based on the site of a former Dominican priory. The ground-level theatre was used by the Children of the Chapel Royal to rehearse and stage plays. In 1583 the sublease passed to Edward de Vere the earl of Oxford who employed his secretary John Lyly as his stage manager. Lyly's own plays were also performed in the first Blackfriars Theatre. The second and much modernised Blackfriars was owned by the Burbage family of actors and impresarios.

The Globe Theatre was built in 1599. An initial eighth share was taken by one 'William Shakespeare', a Warwickshire businessman. Almost nothing is known about this man apart from his name on legal documents, mostly in Stratford-upon-Avon. The original lease for the Globe was lost so it is not known how his name was spelled. In his home town of Stratford-upon-Avon it was spelled or abbreviated in many different ways but always lacking the medial 'e', for example as Shaxpere on his marriage licence, as Shagspere in the consistory court records, but mostly as 'Shakspere'. This suggests that it may have been pronounced as written, that is as Shackspere. Although extensive research later located men with a similar version of the Shakespeare name during the years when the works would have been written this was the only one which had a relevant connection. As a founding shareholder of the Globe Theatre, and with a similar sounding name, it is entirely understandable that twenty-four years later he was assumed to be the 'Mr. William Shakespeare' named on the title page of the First Folio when it appeared in 1623.

The conspirators of the Essex Rebellion arranged for Shakespeare's play *Richard II* to be performed at the Globe on 7th February 1601. This contained the deposition scene when King Richard was forced to surrender his crown to Henry Bolingbroke. The armed rebellion, more precisely an attempted palace coup, took place the following day. Queen

Elizabeth was childless with no clear line of succession, hence the link from the childless King Richard two hundred years earlier. The coup failed, Queen Elizabeth kept her throne, and the earl of Essex lost his head.

Only one other of Shakespeare's History plays was performed at the Globe and this was equally dramatic. In 1613, during a performance of *Henry VIII*, the roof caught fire and the Globe was burned to the ground.

The Register of the Stationers' Company

The Accounts of the Revels Office

The main sources of information on the English Renaissance theatre come from the Register of the Stationers' Company and the Accounts of the Revels Office, part of the Lord Chamberlain's department. Acting companies were required to obtain a licence from the Lord Chamberlain, application being made in the form of a prompt book. This named everything necessary to stage a performance, starting with the actors, managers and producers with their names and contact addresses. It also had to give some idea of the set and the costumes required, the exits and entrances of the players, and most importantly it had to include the script. A license cost seven shillings, a substantial sum at the time, but in return it afforded the acting company legal protection.

To grasp the complexity of the Shakespeare authorship mystery it is always helpful to bear in mind how far back in time the works were written. The plays themselves, or earlier versions of them, can be traced back to the late 1570s with the main body of work produced between 1580 and 1600. The plays appeared anonymously in single-edition quarto paperback format and did not name an author until 1598. This was for the play *Love's Labour's Lost*, with the name on the title page shown as W. Shakespere.

Life for writers and play producers was always challenging and often dangerous in an age of political and religious paranoia. Any form of writing deemed to contain seditious material could incur severe punishments, and frequently did so. The politician John Stubbs, an extremist Protestant, and his publisher William Page, were sentenced to death for issuing a pamphlet opposing the proposed marriage of Queen Elizabeth to the Catholic François Valois the duke of Anjou. The death sentences were commuted as an act of clemency and reduced to the more lenient punishment of amputation. On 3rd November 1579 both men had their right hands hacked off on a butcher's block, a meat cleaver smashed down by a mallet being the method of dismemberment.

As the author of politically sensitive plays, many of them featuring enforced regime change, disloyalty and the overthrow of anointed monarchs, whoever wrote the works attributed to William Shakespeare might well have considered it prudent to conceal his or her identity behind a pseudonym.

Henslowe's 'Diary'

Philip Henslowe 1550-1616

Much insight into the English literary resurgence in the latter half of Queen Elizabeth's reign is provided by the accounts of the theatre owner and manager, Philip Henslowe. Written in the form of a diary the entries span the years 1592-1609 and remain a valuable source of information on the theatrical history of the period. The 238 page diary was a substantial document written on good quality paper in book form. Used as a repository for theatrical information over an eighteen year period it was sufficiently robust to have survived prolonged examination by a succession of well-meaning scholars. It is now kept in the Dulwich College archive in south London.

Henslowe had a finger in many pies, including as a money-lender to writers and actors. His memoranda book shows records of box office receipts, salaries and loans, the purchase of stage properties and costumes, and more importantly from an authorship viewpoint, the payments made to writers. Twenty-seven of these are featured, among them some famous names, including Ben Jonson and Christopher Marlowe. The most notable omission is any mention of William Shakespeare, although some anonymous versions of plays with Shakespeare connections are mentioned. These are *Titus Andronicus, The Taming of A Shrew* (sic), *Hamlet* and *The Mawe*, which could refer to *Othello* (The Moor). Two History plays are mentioned. One is believed to refer to *Henry VI*, although which part is unknown, the other being *Henry V*.

The London theatres owned or managed by Henslowe were the transpontine Rose and Swan in Southwark, and Newington Butts a mile further south. The actor Edward Alleyn (1566-1626) was married to Henslowe's step-daughter Joan and they joined forces to build the Fortune Theatre in 1600. This was sited to the west of the Shoreditch locations of the Theatre and the Curtain and was timed to rival the Globe which opened in 1599. The Globe burned down in 1613 and in the same year Henslowe with a new partner (James Meade) built the nearby Hope theatre which also doubled up as a bear-baiting house. Henslowe died three years later, in 1616.

After Edward Alleyn's death in 1626 his papers, which included his father-in-law's book, were deposited at the school he had founded in 1619 at Dulwich. Originally to house and educate twelve poor boys it was known as The College of God's Gift, later as Dulwich College. The book now commonly referred to as *Henslowe's Diary* remained undisturbed in the College library for 154 years. This was until 1780 when the Irish barrister Edmond Malone, in his quest for information on the identity of William Shakespeare, tracked the book down to Dulwich College, which was much enlarged by this time.

In 1790 Malone removed it from the College library into his own possession where it remained until his death in 1812. Malone's disregard for the sanctity of documentary evidence by cutting out entries for use in his own edition of the Shakespeare plays greatly annoyed succeeding scholars. The missing items had been passed on to James Boswell the younger (1775-1822), Malone's literary executor. These were dispersed at a sale in 1825 and were not finally returned to Dulwich College until 1895. This enabled the scholar W. W. Greg (1875-1959) to publish a completed transcript of the full original text in 1904.

It is the absence of any reference to William Shakespeare by Henslowe which has intrigued literary scholars from Malone until the present day. In the eighteen years of busy theatrical transactions in London covered by the diary no one named William Shakespeare was recorded as a recipient of money, as a writer, as an actor, or even as a living person. One possible explanation is that Henslowe and Edward Alleyn were tied in with the Admiral's Men, the acting company most closely associated with the plays of Christopher Marlowe. Alleyne became rich and famous from his dramatic portrayals of Tamburlaine, Doctor Faustus, and Barabbas in *The Jew of Malta*. Shakespeare and the actor Richard Burbage were linked with the troupe known as the Lord Chamberlain's Men which existed mainly to provide entertainments for the royal courts. Burbage is not mentioned by Henslowe either, so professional rivalry could be a valid reason for the omission.

Even so it is puzzling. The name 'Shakespeare' has become synonymous with the explosion of literary talent in the latter half of Queen Elizabeth's reign, yet no one at the time seems to have been aware of any such person living and working among them. It is a big part of the Shakespeare authorship mystery. These were tumultuous times, historically, politically and geographically. The colonisation of the Americas, the expansion of populations in western Europe, the rise of nationalism underpinned by military might, all impacted on the Shakespeare plays. This included the continuing religious enmity between Catholics and Protestants, at home as well as abroad.

The Rising of the North – 1569-70

The long international reach of the Catholic Church, and the continued loyalty to it of influential noble families in Scotland and the north of England, were a threat to the Protestant regime in London. Queen Elizabeth and her close adviser Sir William Cecil were well aware how fragile was their hold on power at this stage of the reign. The Queen's right of inheritance was disputed on the grounds that the marriage of her parents Henry VIII and Anne Boleyn had been illegal under ecclesiastical law. Many considered that Mary Stuart, the exiled Queen of Scots, had a superior claim, her father James V of Scotland being the son of King Henry's sister Margaret Tudor.

Catholics resented the increasingly repressive nature of the Protestant enforcers led by Sir William Cecil and Sir Francis Walsingham and it was only a matter of time before an organised resistance movement mounted a challenge by force of arms. This manifested itself in the so-called 'Rising of the North' in November 1569. This was led by Charles Neville the 6th earl of Westmorland and Thomas Percy the 7th earl of Northumberland. These Catholic nobles began the process of attempting to depose Elizabeth by declaring for Mary Queen of Scots and defiantly holding a Mass in Durham Cathedral.

Two years earlier in 1567, at the age of twenty-four, Mary Stuart had herself been deposed as Queen of Scotland, with her thirteen month old son proclaimed as King James VI under a regency. Mary left the baby and fled south, seeking the protection of her first cousin once removed, Elizabeth the Queen of England. Ostensibly for her own safety Elizabeth had her cousin imprisoned in a succession of secure castles, at Bolton, Carlisle, Fotheringhay, Tutbury and Sheffield. Mary was in the strong position of having a son and heir, by this time three years old and safely resident in Edinburgh. She was also young enough to have more children if a husband of suitable rank could be found for her, a compelling argument in her favour after three successive childless monarchs, Edward VI, Mary Tudor and Elizabeth Tudor.

A complicating factor was the possibility of a marriage between Mary and Westmorland's Catholic brother-in-law, Thomas Howard the 4th duke of Norfolk. The thrice-widowed duke (England's only duke) was actively promoting and seeking support for such a match, offering himself as a moderate nobleman acceptable to most Protestants and thus capable of uniting the whole country. Released from her illegal marriage to the earl of Bothwell, long since exiled, Mary was also keen on the idea although anxious not to incur the displeasure of Queen Elizabeth by doing so openly. Catholic support for the proposed marriage from abroad made it an increasingly dangerous venture.

To combat the challenge from the north William Cecil appointed Thomas Radcliffe the earl of Sussex to the command of an army capable of swiftly crushing the rebellion. To demonstrate his commitment to the Protestant cause Cecil also sent both his sons. These were Thomas Cecil by his first wife Mary Cheke, and Robert Cecil by his second wife Mildred Cooke . His ward Edward Manners 3rd earl of Rutland was sent as well. Another of his young wards, Edward de Vere the 17th earl of Oxford, also followed the army north but several weeks later in 1570, having been incapacitated with an illness which had kept him housebound for several months.

Cecil was determined to put down the insurrection firmly and pressed the earl of Sussex, a battle-hardened campaigner, to show no mercy to the rebel army which had avoided defeat in a pitched battle by dispersal and flight north into Scotland. From London he insisted on the brutal retaliation which followed. Reprisals went on for many months as the rebel leaders were hunted down and punished one by one, with some 600 deaths claimed. Towns were burned and castles ransacked as a deterrent to any other dissident faction planning to confront the Protestant regime in London. Thomas Percy the earl of Northumberland was captured and taken to York where Queen Elizabeth ordered his execution. Charles Neville the earl of Westmorland escaped and made his way to Brussels where he died in poverty.

This was a turning point in her reign and Elizabeth's hold on power was never again challenged from within her kingdom. It also consolidated Sir William Cecil's position as her most reliable and trusted adviser. Neither of them had much affection for the old aristocracy which had consistently plotted against them since the Queen's accession eleven years previously. The Shakespeare connection is through the first part of the play *Henry IV*. This chronicles an earlier uprising by the northern Percy family and their supporters. It follows with uncanny accuracy the sequence of real life events which led to the suppression of the later rebellion 1569-70.

Queen Elizabeth Excommunicated

The harsh suppression of the northern insurgency extinguished any realistic prospect that Queen Elizabeth could be toppled by an armed force from within. But for the Queen and Sir William Cecil, now ennobled as Baron Burghley, there was unfinished business. This was the continuing presence on English soil of a credible alternative monarch in Mary Stuart. Her supporters still had lingering hopes of a palace coup financed by Catholics from abroad and this kept the Tudor oligarchy in London on a constant state of alert, fearing for plots and conspiracies.

The Protestant hardliners led by Burghley and Walsingham were uncompromising in their hostility to anyone suspected of being insufficiently supportive of their regime and never trusted Mary Stuart, keeping her under constant surveillance. Burghley's firm handling of the northern rebellion had triggered an angry response from the Vatican. Pope Pius V issued a Papal Bull (edict) dated 25th February 1570 with the title *Regnans in Excelsis*. This held Queen Elizabeth personally responsible for the ruthless suppression of the Catholic insurrection in the north of England and Scotland. He excommunicated her as being of illegitimate birth, and a heretic. The edict went further by warning that any Catholics who recognised her position as head of the church in England would be similarly expelled. At the same time absolution was offered in advance to any potential assassin, who would be seen as performing a dutiful act.

Suspicions that Mary and her followers were still conspiring with the duke of Norfolk to arrange a marriage between them led to the duke's arrest. Thomas Howard was the highest ranking nobleman in the land, the hereditary Earl Marshal and a cousin to the Queen whose grandmother had been Lady Elizabeth Howard, the mother of Anne Boleyn. Lord Burghley was determined that no such marriage would ever take place. By now appointed as Queen Elizabeth's principal secretary of state, and with his position at court consolidated by his forceful action against the northern rebellion, Cecil perceived the duke as a danger to the Protestant regime and sought his execution. Accused of scheming to marry Mary Stuart and making a bid for the throne, and of complicity in the so-called Ridolfi Plot to assassinate Queen Elizabeth in September 1571, the duke was beheaded on Tower Hill on 2nd June 1572 aged thirty-six.

Queen Elizabeth's disposal of this high ranking Catholic nobleman, the continued imprisonment of her cousin the Queen of Scots, and her assumption of the governance of the Church of England were not viewed kindly by the Vatican. In 1580 Pope Gregory XIII confirmed his predecessor's excommunication of Queen Elizabeth, again declared her a heretic and released her subjects from their allegiance to her. She was now in constant danger and her security chiefs Burghley and Walsingham uncovered many threats to her life, foiling several actual attempts. The most organised of these were the earlier Ridolfi Plot of 1571, the Throckmorton Plot of 1583, the Babington Plot of 1586 and the Lopez Plot of 1594.

The courtier Sir Francis Throckmorton tried to arrange for Queen Elizabeth to be assassinated at the same time as an invasion fleet financed by Spain would link up with Catholic supporters from within the kingdom. Sanctioned by the Vatican this complicated conspiracy was intercepted by Burghley and Walsingham with grim consequences for the perpetrators who were tortured and mostly put to death. Further investigation pointed to collusion by Mary Stuart herself and this led eventually to her trial in 1586, followed by a guilty verdict and her beheading on 8th February 1587 after eighteen and a half years of imprisonment.

The Catholic hierarchy regarded Queen Elizabeth and her commissioners as complicit in an act of political assassination when Mary was executed. As with the earlier death sentence on the duke of Norfolk the Queen wavered until she could be convinced that her own life was threatened before signing the death warrant. The throne of England was highly prized and as it was certain by this time that she would die childless the claimants began to declare themselves. Philip II of Spain, who had been married to Queen Mary Tudor, sought to restore the Catholic religion by a long-planned-for force of arms. The 120 strong Spanish invasion fleet set sail from Lisbon and Corunna in August 1588. Known as the 'Armada' from the Spanish word for a naval fleet, the plan was to link up with a land force from the Netherlands led by the duke of Parma.

This large-scale venture ended in failure. Appointed as Lieutenant and Captain-General of the Queens's Armies and Companies the earl of Leicester was successful in repelling the Spanish invasion fleet. Adverse weather conditions allowed the smaller but more responsive ships manned by the well-trained crews of Charles Howard (Lord Howard of Effingham) and Sir Francis Drake combined to scatter the enemy fleet, destroying some ships and forcing others up into the North Sea to be wrecked on the Scottish and Irish coasts.

This comprehensive victory made a heroine of the defiant Queen Elizabeth who had resolutely seen off all her enemies at home and abroad. It had taken thirty years to consolidate her hold on power but she had done it and in the process became one of the most famous women in world history. It was quite an achievement.

The Dutch War of Independence

This long-running conflict covered the period when the plays of Shakespeare were written, the last quarter of the sixteenth century and overlapping into the seventeenth century. Military and naval knowledge is evident in many of the Shakespeare plays, something hard to explain unless the author was writing from experience of active service, however limited. Orthodox scholarship maintains that the numerous soldiering and conflict scenes in the plays could have been lifted from translations of Greek and Latin drama.

This is possible but not convincing. The mustering of troops, the apprehension before a battle with its frightened soldiers, bullying corporals and nervous commanders all have a convincing authenticity when played out on the open stage. Add in the clamour and confusion of the actual fighting, the counting up of the dead and wounded after battle, the misery of defeat or the relief of victory, if taken together, make the case for an author who had himself witnessed armed conflict and experienced the throes of war at close quarters.

Spain under the Habsburg dynasty was the dominant military power in Europe and occupied the Netherlands which they subdivided into seventeen provinces. Differences in religion motivated the northern (Protestant) provinces to rise up against their Catholic occupiers, with a steady escalation of violence. This peaked in 1576 with the total destruction of Antwerp, burned to the ground by mutinous Spanish soldiers. This vicious onslaught against a civilian population became known as The Spanish Fury and struck fear into Protestant populations elsewhere. In their extremity the Dutch appealed to Queen Elizabeth for help and she responded by sending a small task force led by Robert Dudley the earl of Leicester.

This had no success against the much larger Spanish occupying army. Other members of Queen Elizabeth's court followed Leicester to the Netherlands in the hope of battlefield glory, among them Robert Devereux the earl of Essex, Edward de Vere the earl of Oxford, Peregrine Bertie Lord Willoughby d'Eresby and William Stanley later the earl of Derby. The professional soldiers Sir John Norris, Sir Horatio Vere and Sir Francis Vere with their modest forces were outnumbered in a long attritional struggle against the powerful Spanish army.

Leicester was appointed as Governor General of the United Provinces but lost the decisive Battle of Zutphen in September 1586. He was forced to resign and returned to London. This was the battle in which Leicester's nephew Sir Philip Sidney died of his wounds. Later casualties included Henry de Vere the 18th earl of Oxford, Robert de Vere the 19th earl of Oxford, Henry Wriothesley the 3rd earl of Southampton and his son James.

The Essex Rebellion

Between them Queen Elizabeth and Lord Burghley held the reins of power for forty years and accomplished much, their legacy a stable Protestant regime and a thriving sea-port economy. It was now twelve years on from the defeat of the Spanish Armada, the Queen's health was failing and the vexed question of the succession had become a matter of serious concern to senior members of the administration. James Stuart the son of Mary Stuart was the only contender with a legal claim and although the Queen resolutely declined to name him as her heir there was a tacit understanding from all factions of the court that he would succeed her as King James I, being already James VI of Scotland. How best to control him as a constitutional (politically powerless) monarch exercised the minds of those who would wield the executive power, in this case Robert Cecil. His father Lord Burghley died in 1598 but he had taken care to ensure that Robert would succeed him in office and so be in a position to negotiate with James Stuart from a position of strength.

A rival to this arrangement was another Robert, Robert Devereux the second earl of Essex (1565-1601), a former royal ward. He was a descendent of the Boleyn family and his stepfather had been the earl of Leicester, a senior courtier close to the Queen. Essex saw his own role as that of king-maker, the power behind the new king's throne. Handsome and self-confident, he was thirty-three to Robert Cecil's thirty-five and had greatly impressed the ageing Queen Elizabeth with his ability. Cecil suffered from scoliosis, curvature of the spine, but compensated for this disability by the subtle exercise of statecraft, and by long ties of loyalty to the crown. A turning point in the rivalry between these two ambitious young men came when news reached the court of a rebellion in Ireland led by Hugh O'Neill the earl of Tyrone. The Queen appointed Essex as Governor General of Ireland and provided him with the command of an army, his remit to crush the Irish rebellion with speed and finality. The earl set out from London on 27th March 1599 with every hope of a successful outcome to further his career prospects.

Surprisingly, Essex failed to deliver. Ignoring the Queen's implicit instruction to engage the rebels head-on and defeat them in a decisive on-slaught he confined his activities instead to a series of small inconclusive skirmishes. For whatever reason he dithered too long, squandered his resources and was reduced to agreeing exit terms favourable to the earl of Tyrone and his followers, in effect to have changed sides. He returned to London but the Queen was in no mood to overlook his dereliction of duty and had him imprisoned. This was later reduced to house arrest but with all his sources of income withdrawn he became increasingly impoverished and embittered, blaming his misfortunes on the perceived machinations of Robert Cecil.

There is a possible reference to Essex and his Ireland campaign in the Shakespeare play *Henry V*. Words spoken by Chorus at the start of Act 5 link King Harry's triumphant homecoming from France with the return of the earl of Essex from Ireland in September 1599.

> But now behold
> In the quick force and working-house of thought,
> How London doth pour out her citizens.
> The Mayor and all his brethren, in best sort
> Like to the senators of th' antique Rome
> With the Plebeians swarming at their heels,
> Go forth and fetch their conqu'ring Caesar in –
> As, by a lower but high-loving likelihood,
> Were now the General of our gracious Empress –
> As in good time he may – from Ireland coming
> Bringing rebellion broached on his sword.
> How many would the peaceful city quit
> To welcome him!
>
> 5.0.22-34

One of many peculiar features in the Shakespeare authorship mystery is the absence of references to contemporary events. Whether intentionally or by mischance, in the best part of a million words, there are no decisive clues. *Henry V* is generally agreed to have been written 1599-1600 so this reference to a successful campaign general returning from Ireland presents difficulties, bearing in mind that Essex's return was scarcely heroic. Charles Blount, Lord Mountjoy, replaced Essex as Governor General of Ireland and is a possible alternative candidate for the Chorus mention.

In London the continuing uncertainty over the succession made for fractious times, with shifting alliances as the courtiers jockeyed for position. The earl of Essex, still under house arrest, became a focus for dissent. He was able to gather around him a group of disaffected nobles and officials in an anti-Cecil faction, with the clear intention of mounting an armed coup. His second in command was the twenty-eight year old Henry Wriothesley, the third earl of Southampton (1573-1624), also a former royal ward. To avoid suspicion falling immediately on Essex their clandestine meetings took place in Drury House, Wych Street, Southampton's London home.

Whether it was a good idea or not the plotters paid generously to have the Lord Chamberlain's Men perform Shakespeare's play *Richard II* on 7th February 1601 at The Globe Theatre. This was on condition that the players included Act 4 Scene 1, the deposition scene. A common theme in the History plays is the need for loyalty and unity, stressing the adverse consequences which would follow from deposing an anointed sovereign. In a religious age the symbolism and mystique attached to the ceremonial anointment of a newly crowned monarch with holy oil was not lightly ignored. With good reason, as the deposition and subsequent murder of the childless King Richard II set in motion the long years of internecine conflict which became known as the Wars of the Roses, the rival factions of York and Lancaster.

Staging the play could have signalled that the childless Queen Elizabeth and her chief adviser Robert Cecil were likewise at risk. An anecdote of the Queen saying, 'I am Richard II, know ye not that?' has been many times repeated. The words were supposedly addressed to her archivist William Lambarde, Keeper of the Records in the Tower of London. (Chambers I, p 354). *Richard II* was a frequently performed play with the inference that the Queen was acutely aware of its relevance to her situation. Even after this length of time the re-enactment on stage of the humiliated Richard forced to hand over the crown and sceptre to his usurping cousin Henry Bolingbroke is still painful to watch. He parts with these symbols of kingship reluctantly and with bitterness, holding on to the crown until the last possible moment saying, 'Here, cousin, seize the crown' so that Bolingbroke has to physically wrench it from his grasp.

On the morning after the performance at the Globe, 8th February 1601, with some 200 followers, the two earls made their bid to seize control of the palace by force of arms, and to murder Robert Cecil in the process. The Cecils (William, Thomas and Robert) were noted as masters of subterfuge and surveillance. Robert had been kept well informed of the rebellion in advance of the event and issued a warrant to the mayor of London denouncing Essex and Southampton as traitors. When this was made known their followers dispersed and the coup quickly failed. The two main conspirators were condemned to death after a one-day trial in Westminster Hall, with Essex beheaded in the Tower on 25th February. This left Robert Cecil as the de facto interim head of state to negotiate a smooth transition of sovereignty to James Stuart after Queen Elizabeth died in 1603.

The Shakespeare History plays are unequivocal in their over-arching dire message to conspirators that no good comes to those who plot the downfall of others, of anointed sovereigns in particular. The epileptic Bolingbroke as Henry IV was repaid for his dethronement of Richard II by suffering an ignominious death, as described in painful detail in the second part of *Henry IV*. His insomniac lament that his poorest subjects can sleep peacefully in their beds while he, their king with his guilty conscience cannot, is dramatic writing of the highest quality.

> How many thousands of my poorest subjects
> Are at this hour asleep? O sleep, O gentle sleep,
> Nature's soft nurse, how have I frighted thee,
> That thou no more wilt weigh my eyelids down
> And steep my senses in forgetfulness?

Insomnia as a psychiatric condition occurs elsewhere in the canon, in Sonnet 27 for example (black night ... no quiet find) and again in Sonnet 28 (... debarred the benefit of rest). Macbeth is another character with a guilty conscience, and which also manifests itself as insomnia.

Methought I heard a voice call 'Sleep no more,
Macbeth does murder sleep' – the innocent sleep,
Sleep that knits up the ravelled sleave of care,
The death of each day's life

Considered as a component of the authorship mystery, and the commonly held belief that writers mostly write about what they know, whoever wrote Shakespeare would seem to have been familiar with troubled minds, including his own. In context with the deposition of King Richard II, and a parallel situation with the rapidly approaching end of the Tudor dynasty, the author of 2 Henry IV (3.1.34) sums it up in one neatly turned line.

Uneasy lies the head that wears a crown.

2 Shakespeare in Print

The First Folio
The First Folio Portrait
Images and Effigies
The Grand Censors and The Grand Possessors
The Missing Tributes
How authentic is the First Folio ?

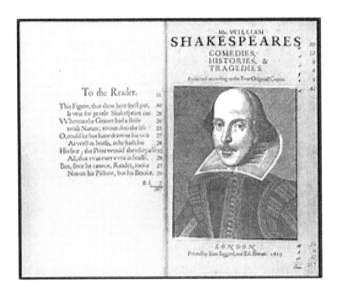

Mr. WILLIAM

SHAKESPEARES
COMEDIES,
HISTORIES, &
TRAGEDIES.
Published according to the True Originall Copies

The First Folio was published by Edward Blount in London and issued from the print workshop of William Jaggard on 8th November 1623. Great care had been taken in producing the Folio which was printed on high quality paper imported from France. The print run was believed to be 750 copies of which 233 remain in libraries and corporate collections around the world, although not all of them are complete.

No play included in the First Folio has ever proved to be entirely written by someone other than Shakespeare. No play omitted from the First Folio has subsequently proved to have been written entirely by Shakespeare. From which it could be deduced that the compilers of the First Folio knew which were the authentic texts and which not. This was a privately sponsored publication which would have needed considerable resources of time and money to bring to completion.

The long title is conventionally shortened to 'The First Folio'. It is referred to as the 'First' Folio because it was reprinted three more times, in 1632, 1663 and 1685. These later editions carried unverified material and it is the First Folio which defined the Shakespeare canon and continues to do so. Not all the plays had been previously printed but those which were had appeared one at a time in smaller quarto-sized paper-back editions. The thirty-six plays in the Folio were in three separately numbered sections as Comedies, Histories and Tragedies.

The anomalous case of *Troilus and Cressida* needs a word of explanation as it was included in the text but omitted from the Catalogue (list of contents). When first registered in 1609 it was described as a Comedy but on the title page it is referred to as a Tragedy. It is inserted in the Folio at the end of the Histories.

The Comedies
The Tempest
The Two Gentlemen of Verona
The Merry Wives of Windsor
Measure for Measure
The Comedy of Errors
Much Ado About Nothing
Love's Labour's Lost
A Midsummer Night's Dream
The Merchant of Venice
As You Like It
The Taming of the Shrew
All's Well That Ends Well
Twelfth Night, or What You Will
The Winter's Tale

The Histories
The Life and Death of King John
The Life and Death of Richard the Second
The First part of King Henry the Fourth
The Second part of King Henry the Fourth
The Life of King Henry the Fifth
The First part of King Henry the Sixth
The Second part of King Henry the Sixth
The Third part of King Henry the Sixth
The Life and Death of Richard the Third
The Life of King Henry the Eighth
(The Tragedy of Troilus and Cressida)

The Tragedies
The Tragedy of Coriolanus
Titus Andronicus
Romeo and Juliet
Timon of Athens
The Life and Death of Julius Caesar
The Tragedy of Macbeth
The Tragedy of Hamlet

King Lear
Othello, the Moore of Venice
Antony and Cleopatra
Cymbeline, King of Britain

Canonical plays not included in the First Folio
Pericles, Prince of Tyre
The Two Noble Kinsmen
The Reign of King Edward the Third
The Famous Victories of Henry the fifth

First edition plays that appeared in quarto prior to the First Folio of 1623

Titus Andronicus	1594	
Henry VI Part 2	1594	
Henry VI Part 3	1595	octavo
Edward III	1596	
Richard II	1597	
Richard III	1597	
Romeo and Juliet	1597	
Love's Labour's Lost	1598	
Henry IV Part 1	1598	
Much Ado About Nothing	1600	
A Midsummer Night's Dream	1600	
The Merchant of Venice	1600	
Henry IV Part 2	1600	
Henry V	1600	
The Merry Wives of Windsor	1602	
Hamlet	1603	
King Lear	1608	
Troilus and Cressida	1609	
Othello	1622	

On five quartos the title pages state that the texts had been edited, 'corrected and augmented', by the author but no further revisions occurred after 1604. The updated versions were for *Love's Labour's Lost, 1 Henry IV, Romeo and Juliet, Richard III* and *Hamlet*. The quarto editions of *King Lear, Troilus and Cressida* and *Othello* had all been previously registered. No new play can be positively dated later than 1604.

The inability of successive generations of researchers to locate the 'Mr. William Shakespeare' on the title page has provoked much scholarly debate and a great deal of controversy. No trace of a writer with this name has ever been found, thus prompting the supposition that it was a pseudonym, a pen name successfully used to conceal the identity of the actual author. It has proved to be an enduring mystery.

The First Folio Portrait

To the Reader.
This Figure, that thou here seest put,
    It was for gentle Shakespeare cut;
Wherein the Graver had a strife
    with Nature, to out-doo the life :
O, could he but have drawn his wit
    As well in brass, as he hath hit
His face, the Print would then surpass
    All, that was ever writ in brass.
But, since he cannot, Reader, look
    Not on his Picture, but his Book.
                                    B.I.

Martin Droeshout's depiction of Shakespeare in the front of the First Folio is so deeply embedded in our corporate subconscious minds that it is now impossible to disassociate it from any serious discussion of the plays or poetry. Ben Jonson's accompanying verse which was printed on the opposite page of the Folio includes some strange constructions and is worth a second read. He describes the Droeshout engraving as a 'Figure' rather than a portrait, that it was 'for' rather than 'of' Shakespeare, and includes the word 'gentle'. This could imply high social status rather than the possession of a placid nature.

The engraving itself shows a large mask-like face out of proportion with the body, which is much smaller. In an age when the Sumptuary Laws regulating appropriate dress were still enforced it is apparent that the man in the picture wears a richly embroidered doublet, a way of dressing that would only have been allowable for a person of the highest social status. The cut of the sleeves indicate that the sitter has his back to the artist. The ear partially shown on the left side of the face is more likely the right ear of the sitter and the strangely lifeless face mask appears to be attached to the back of his head.

The engraver Martin Droeshout was born in 1601 of Flemish parents resident in London. He would have been only fifteen when Shakspere died in Stratford-upon-Avon in 1616 so it is unlikely that the First Folio image was drawn from life. He received the commission to make the engraving at the age of twenty-one but it is not known who supplied him with a likeness from which to work. The First Folio engraving is another unsolvable component of the authorship mystery.

Images and Effigies

Subsequent publishers and illustrators of works by Shakespeare faced a common problem, namely that only two extant images of Shakespeare could be considered as sufficiently authentic and original to serve as models, and both were equally unattractive. The first of these was the copper engraving by Martin Droeshout on the title page of the First Folio, which showed the mask-like features of a bald-headed man. The second was the many-times altered funerary monument in Holy Trinity church in Stratford-upon-Avon which eventually morphed into the rubicund effigy of a middle-aged man.

The church effigy has been rarely used in sales literature and is not so readily identified with the Shakespeare name. There seems to be a general impression that it lacks the air of refinement appropriate for a man of letters. The Droeshout engraving although equally grotesque was more easily reworked to show an intellectualised and dignified version of the great author. Although unsatisfactory as a portrait it is the Droeshout image which has come to be synonymous with the name Shakespeare and has acquired worldwide recognition. With the same idea in mind several overpainted contemporary portraits later emerged, all touted as putative images of Shakespeare, with their supporters and doubters in equal numbers.

On 29th January 1741, a full-length informal statue of Shakespeare designed by William Kent and carved by the Flemish sculptor Peter Scheemakers (1691-1781) was unveiled in the Poets Corner section of the south transept in Westminster Abbey. Two years later in 1743 an almost identical statue was commissioned by Henry Herbert the 9th earl of Pembroke to stand in the entrance hall of Wilton House in Wiltshire. This statue was also designed by William Kent and sculpted by Peter Scheemakers. The main difference is that the Westminster memorial stands on a square plinth and the Wilton House counterpart stands on a circular plinth. Any significance for this discrepancy has never been established.

David Garrick the actor and theatre impresario was generous and sincere in his admiration for the author of the Shakespeare plays and sponsored an ambitious project to create a permanent monument dedicated to him. This materialised on the lawn of his house in Hampton, a shrine in the form of a classic temple with pillars, sited beside the River Thames. Installed in 1758, on the wall facing the entrance, there remains to this day a full-size statue of Shakespeare carved in Carrara marble by Garrick's fellow Huguenot, the sculptor Louis François Roubiliac (1702-1762). David Garrick's success had created a mass market for Shakepeare memorabilia. These were mainly busts and statuettes based on Scheemaker's statue in the Abbey.

In an age when portrait painters made a good living it is part of the Shakespeare mystery why no painting exists for the most famous man of the age. Such is the case. There is no authentic primary source that shows us the face of William Shakespeare.

'The Grand Censors' and 'The Grand Possessors'

The First Folio contained eighteen plays registered for the first time on 8th November 1623.

The Tempest	King John
Two Gentlemen of Verona	1 Henry VI
Measure for Measure	Henry VIII
Comedy of Errors	Coriolanus
As You Like It	Timon of Athens
The Taming of the Shrew	Julius Caesar
All's Well That Ends Well	Macbeth
Twelfth Night	Antony and Cleopatra
The Winter's Tale	Cymbeline

So many unregistered plays raise two fundamental questions relevant to the Shakespeare authorship. Where and by whom had these manuscripts been kept prior to their inclusion in the First Folio of 1623, and what became of them afterwards? To supply the correct answers would help solve the mystery since those who possessed them would surely have known the identity of the writer. No such answers can be found but there are interesting clues in the play *Troilus and Cressida*.

The earliest translation of Homer's *Iliad* into English was made by Arthur Hall of London in 1581. This translation was for the first ten books only but included the romantic story of Troilus and Cressida. Shakespeare's play of the same name was provisionally registered with the Stationers' Company on 7th February 1603. Some quarto editions appeared in 1609, one of which contained an address to the reader (*A never writer, to an ever reader*) asserting that *Troilus and Cressida* had never been publicly performed, which implied that it had been privately performed, most likely at one of the Inns of Court.

This strangely worded inclusion in the Preface (it was omitted from the First Folio) contains an intriguing reference to the 'grand possessors'. Who could they be? Strong candidates as custodians of the Shakespeare archive would be the two dedicatees, William Herbert the 3rd earl of Pembroke and his younger brother Philip Herbert the 1st earl of Montgomery. They were obsequiously addressed by Heminges and Condell in the front of the Folio as 'the incomparable pair of brethren'.

The *Troilus* appeal to the reader also referred to the 'grand censors'. William Herbert was the Lord Chamberlain 1615-1625 with censorship as his remit in regulating what was allowable in print or on the stage. The King's Men company of players, formerly the Lord Chamberlain's Men, were also on his payroll together with their copyright. This is the company which has always been most closely associated with Shakespeare, with the proviso that most of their performances would have been in the enclosed surroundings of the royal courts, the universities or the Inns of Court, rather than in the public theatres.

Censorship implies secrecy. The royal court was closely guarded then as now, the inner circle around the sovereign most of all, releasing as little information as possible to the outside world. This aura of state secrecy has hardly changed over several centuries and would apply to all governments everywhere, also to many large corporations who view concealment as a commercial necessity. If the actual and true Shakespeare author was protected within an enclosed system, and wished to remain anonymous by publishing under a pseudonym, this could go some way to understanding how the mystery came about in the first place and has remained un-disclosed ever since.

One explanation for the absence of Shakespeare's name from Henslowe's accounts book, his so-called 'diary', could be that the author occupied a privileged position, that he preferred to work alone and was able to do so separately from those writing for the public theatres. The absence of any recorded payments to the author known as William Shakespeare could be because he did not write for money. The implication is that he had sufficient wealth and status to create the circumstances conducive to writing, such as the provision of adequate free time, comfortable seclusion and protection from intrusion or distraction.

The accommodation for such a person would have been able to provide the ample desk and shelf space for storing working papers and manuscripts and any unregistered held-back plays. The seclusion and secrecy of this way of life could also explain why there were no literary tributes when he died, most likely because he was not primarily known as a writer. Nor apparently did people associate him with the published plays of Shakespeare so the mystery was set in motion and remains unresolved.

The Herbert family owned Baynard's Castle in London, a former royal palace, and Wilton House in Wiltshire. These are two possible locations where the Shakespeare archive may have been preserved for safe keeping, before and after the publication of the 1623 First Folio. By misfortune Wilton House was partly destroyed by fire in 1647 and Baynard's Castle was burned to the ground on the night of 3rd September 1666 during London's great fire. Not a single page of manuscript has survived, either of plays or poetry. Did they all go up in flames? It must be counted a minor miracle that the First Folio has come down to us intact when it could so easily have been lost. The 'grand possessors' deserve our thanks in overplus.

The Missing Tributes

If the whole of the Shakespeare authorship mystery can be reduced to just one question it is the absence of death tributes for either William Shakspere of Stratford-upon-Avon or the elusive actual author. Apart from an entry in the Stratford parish register Shakspere's death and burial in April 1616 passed without a single recorded mention, either in his home town, in London, or elsewhere. No tributes to him in prose or verse have ever been found.

The death a month earlier of the modestly renowned Francis Beaumont on 6th March 1616 was acknowledged by a generous quantity of valedictory praise followed by interment in Westminster Abbey. When Ben Jonson died the eulogies were so numerous they had to be made into a book. Yet for Shakespeare, nothing. Why was there no outpouring of grief from his fellow dramatists, no fulsome praise for a unique talent, and no lavish funeral in Westminster Abbey when the true author died?

During the years when the Shakespeare plays would have been written there were some twenty other playwrights active during the same period. In the small world of literary London they would surely have been known to one another, would have been aware of the quality of Shakespeare's work, and generous in their praise. Still alive on the day of Shakspere's death in April 1616 was his supposedly closest collaborator John Fletcher, as were George Chapman, Thomas Heywood, Ben Jonson, Thomas Lodge, John Marston, Thomas Middleton and Anthony Munday.

Michael Drayton could be added to the list. Although mainly considered as a poet he was paid by Henslowe as a scriptwriter, he had family ties with Stratford-upon-Avon and so could have been aware of Shakspere's death. Richard Field the printer of Shakespeare's two long narrative poems was another Stratford man on the scene. The lack of a single tribute from these or anyone else in the seven years between Shakspere's death in 1616, and the publication of the First Folio in 1623, is puzzling in the extreme.

The numerous print shops in London provided a commercial service to writers wishing to have their books printed and published. The best known of these bookseller publishers include William Aspley, Cuthbert Burby, John Busby, Thomas Fisher, Thomas Heyes, Arthur Johnson, Nicholas Ling, Thomas Millington, William Ponsonby, Edward White and Andrew Wise. The first edition printers were Thomas Creede, John Danter, James Roberts, Peter Short and Valentine Simmes. Ralph Crane (died 1630) is credited with preparing the transcripts that served as printer's copy for several Shakespeare plays including *The Tempest*, *The Two Gentlemen of Verona*, *The Merry Wives of Windsor*, *The Winter's Tale* and *Cymbeline*.

That none of these people left behind a record that would positively identify the author known as William Shakespeare is hard to understand. If to these are added the many published writers at work in Elizabethan London it is even harder to understand or explain that not one of them left a written record indicating knowledge of the real, live but elusive William Shakespeare. A man who cast no shadow.

The following list of writers concurrent with Shakespeare all have entries in dictionaries of literature. None of them unambiguously state that they were on back-slapping first name terms with the man himself, not even Ben Jonson. He was an abrasive literary critic whose strictures on Shakespeare as a literary dramatist are not in the least idolatrous, writing for example that 'he lacked art'. That they supped ale and traded Latin quips in the Mermaid Tavern conjures up a pleasant picture of London's two paramount wordsmiths but is an urban myth nevertheless. There is no evidence that the two men ever met, socially or otherwise.

Nor was there a David Garrick to resurrect Jonson's plays from obscurity. From this list of writers only Marlowe's plays are still performed. The contrast with Shakespeare is extreme. Almost all of the thousands of plays contemporaneously written are long forgotten and will never be seen on a stage again. The fame of Shakespeare overshadows the rest, by a multiple too large to calculate. Memorable quotations from his works are so numerous they would fill a book on their own. Many of them have been assimilated into the worldwide English language so that people quote from Shakespeare without realising it.

So how is it possible that we still do not know the identity of the man responsible for these commercially successful and highly regarded works of literary art? As mysteries go it remains a mystery still.

Francis Bacon	1561-1626
Richard Barnfield	1574-1627
Francis Beaumont	1584-1616
Nicholas Breton	1545-1626
George Chapman	1550-1634
Henry Chettle	1564-1606
Thomas Churchyard	1520-1604
Samuel Daniel	1562-1619
John Davies	1569-1626
John Day	fl. 1606
Thomas Dekker	1550-1632
John Donne	1572-1631
Michael Drayton	1563-1631
Edward Dyer	d. 1607
Richard Edwards	1525-1566
Abraham Fleming	1552-1607
John Fletcher	1579-1625
John Ford	fl. 1639
George Gascoigne	1525-1577
Arthur Golding	1536-1605

Stephen Gosson	1554-1624
Robert Greene	1558-1598
Fulke Greville	1554-1628
Gabriel Harvey	1550-1631
Thomas Heywood	1574-1641
Thomas Hoby	1530-1566
Ben Jonson	1572-1637
Thomas Kyd	1558-1594
Thomas Lodge	1558-1625
John Lyly	1554-1606
Christopher Marlowe	1564-1593
John Marston	1575-1634
Thomas Middleton	1570-1627
Anthony Munday	1553-1633
Thomas Nashe	1567-1601
Thomas North	1535-1601
Thomas Norton	1532-1585
George Peele	1558-1597
Henry Porter	d. 1599
Walter Raleigh	1552-1618
Barnaby Riche	1540-1617
Thomas Sackville	1536-1608
Mary Sidney	1561-1621
Philip Sidney	1554-1586
Edmund Spenser	1552-1599
Edward de Vere	1550-1604
William Warner	1558-1609
Thomas Watson	1557-1592
John Webster	1580-1625
George Wilkins	1576-1618
George Wither	1588-1667

How authentic is the First Folio ?

The satirist Ben Jonson is suspected of writing all or most of the adulatory verse and prose in the front of the Folio, much of it ambiguous or deliberately misleading. As an experienced writer for the stage he could have provided valued practical assistance in its compilation. The actors John Heminges (died 1630) and Henry Condell (died 1627) are also named in the prefatory material of the First Folio.

Heminges and Condell signed the long letter of dedication which is addressed to the brothers William and Philip Herbert, the earls of Pembroke and Montgomery respectively. The effusive wording of the dedication refers to the brothers as being of quasi-religious status. The address ends

> We most humbly consecrate to your highnesses these remains of your servant Shakespeare, that what delight is in them may be ever your lordships, the reputation his, and the faults ours, if any be committed by a pair so careful to show their gratitude both to the living and the dead.

TO THE MOST NOBLE
AND
INCOMPARABLE PAIRE
OF BRETHREN

WILLIAM
Earle of Pembroke,&c. Lord Chamberlaine to the Kings most Excellent Majesty,

AND

PHILIP
Earle of Montgomery,&c. Gentleman of his Majesties
Bed-Chamber. Both Knights of the most Noble Order
of the Garter, and our singular good
LORDS

The other named contributors of the commendatory verses were not famous literary men. These were Hugh Holland (died 1633), Leonard Digges (1588-1635) and James Mabbe (1572-1642), listed as I.M. Their fulsome praise for the author appeared seven years too late after his death in 1616. Even then they do not explicitly credit the Stratford man with the authorship of the plays, they do not mention any roles he may have played as an actor, nor do they offer any biographical information about him.

The two actors Heminges and Condell are put forward as the publishers of the First Folio but this must be considered as highly improbable if not deliberately untrue. Compiling and editing a book of this magnitude and importance would have necessitated literary expertise of the highest order, quite beyond the journeyman capabilities and financial resources of Heminges and Condell. Ben Jonson's involvement could be explained by having William Herbert as his literary patron. In addition to having the wealth to pay the cost of underwriting the First Folio publication the earl would have been able to call the tune as Lord Chamberlain, the arbiter of last resort in what could or could not be or performed on the London stage or published in print. The truly awful Droeshout portrait engraving, and the cringing flattery of the verses, are hard to reconcile with the contents of the book.

The second of the letters written in prose and signed jointly by John Heminges and Henry Condell is addressed *To the Great Varieties of Readers*. They make their intention plain, which is to part as many readers as possible from their money. Two urgent instructions to 'buy' are included in the first few strongly worded sentences. These compel admiration as an early example of the art and cut-throat business of book promotion.

> From the most able to him that can but spell: there you are numbered; we had rather you were weighed, especially when the fate of all books depends upon your capacities, and not of your heads alone, but of your purses. Well, it is now public, and you will stand for your privileges, we know: to read and censure. Do so, but buy it first. That doth best commend a book, the stationer says. Then, how odd soever your brains be, or your wisdoms, make your licence the same, and spare not. Judge your six-penn'orth, your shilling's worth, your five shilling's worth at a time, or higher, so you rise to the just rates, and welcome. But whatever you do, buy.

The Shakespeare scholar George Steevens (1736-1800) collaborated with Samuel Johnson in a joint 10 volume edition of Shakespeare's plays issued in 1773. Steevens was the first commentator to demonstrate that the Heminges-Condell letters in the First Folio were most likely to have been written by Ben Jonson, with some similarly worded examples. The dedication to Jonson's comedy *The New Inn* begins 'To the Reader ... If thou canst but spell ...'. In his *Discoveries* he writes '... .how odde soever mens brains or wisdoms are ...'. Jonson's Induction to *Bartholomew Fair* includes the words '... to

47

judge his six penn'orth, his twelve penn'orth, so to his eighteen pence'.

Obligatory to the orthodox Stratfordian authorship position is an acceptance that the First Folio prefatory prose and verse is genuine, that it should be taken at face value, and that it provides conclusive evidence that William Shakspere of Stratford-upon-Avon was also the poet and playwright known to the world as William Shakespeare. This is certainly the position staunchly defended for many years by our foremost Shakespearean scholars and editors. For this reason it has to be taken seriously.

3 The Life of William Shakspere

William Shakspere in Stratford-upon-Avon

William Shakspere was born in the small Warwickshire town of Stratford-upon-Avon in 1564 and died there in 1616. He was married in 1582 at the age of eighteen, had a daughter in 1583 and a twin son and daughter in 1585. Little is known about him apart from his name. This appears on a range of mostly hand-written legal documents such as parish registers and on the pages of his will. In the Stratford documents his name is never spelled as Shakespeare. The most frequent spelling is Shakspere, always lacking the medial 'e' so that it was most probably pronounced as Shackspere. No primary documents exist in the form of letters written by him, nor is there any record of a face-to-face encounter with him, or any mention of anything he may have said.

Neither of Shakspere's parents, John and Mary, nor his two surviving married daughters Susanna Hall and Judith Quiney, could read or write. The Shakespeare scholar Samuel Schoenbaum, in *Shakespeare: A Documentary Life*, publishes facsimiles of the marks made by John and Mary Shakspere on legal documents. On page 238 he doubts whether Susanna Hall could do more than sign her name, being unable to recognise her husband's handwriting when called on to do so. Judith Quiney signed twice with a mark when witnessing a deed of sale on 4th December 1611. (Shakespeare Birthplace Trust Records Office MS. ER 27/11). If judged by his six surviving signatures on legal documents, three of them on his will, William himself was at best only semi-literate, the lawyer or a clerk penning 'by me William' with the surname laboriously inked in from a copy.

The population of Stratford was under two thousand at the time when the Shakespeare plays would have been written. The town had been granted a Charter of Incorporation in 1553 and was administered by a self-electing body of twenty-four alderman presided over by a High Bailiff, the equivalent of a town mayor today. William's father John served as High Bailiff in 1568. Neither William nor John owned farmland yet both traded in farming commodities, John as a wool merchant, William as a trader in large quantities of grain. This would suggest that the family business was brokerage, buying and selling for profit, which in William's case extended to property investment, in London as well as in Stratford. Father and son also lent money at interest. Robert Bearman in his 1994 monograph *Shakespeare in the Stratford Records* quotes from Halliwell's *Life of William Shakespeare* that John Shakspere had been prosecuted for charging exorbitant rates of interest on his loans.

Apart from the registration details of himself and his immediate family no trace of William Shakspere has ever been found until he was almost thirty, and not much even then. There is no evidence that he received any form of education, nor is it known at what age he made his first business trip to London, or how long he stayed there. If he was leading a double life between Stratford and London he succeeded in this purpose as neither side seemed aware of the other.

William Shakspere died a rich man, a millionaire in modern terms, but how or where he obtained this wealth remains a mystery. If he made it in London he spent it in Stratford, acquiring land and property in his home town and elsewhere. Those who deny him the Shakespeare authorship talk him down as a country bumpkin but this is at odds with the facts. He traded large sums of money both in London and Stratford, and accumulated considerable amounts of land and property. He deserves to be taken seriously.

These are the document entries on which his name appears relating to his life in Stratford-upon-Avon, Warwickshire:

On 26th April 1564 the Parish Baptism Register of Holy Trinity Church, Stratford-upon-Avon, records the baptism of Gulielmus filius Johannes Shakspere, 'William son of John Shakspere'.

(Nothing known for the next eighteen years)

On 27th November 1582 the Worcester diocese episcopal register records the issue of a marriage licence to Willelmum Shaxpere and Anne Whately of Temple Grafton. Relatives of Anne Hathwey intervened to prevent this marriage and instead the consistory court records show that William Shagspere was married by special licence to the 'said Anne Hathwey of Stratford' on 28th November 1582. The groom was eighteen, the bride twenty-six. (E.K. Chambers, *William Shakespeare: A Study of Facts and Problems*, 41-42).

On 26th May 1583 the Stratford parish register records the baptism of Susanna, 'daughter of William Shakspere'. This would suggest that Anne Hathwey was three months pregnant on the day of her marriage and could have been the reason why the teenage Shaxpere's marriage to Anne Whately was cancelled when these exigent circumstances were drawn to the attention of the church authorities. His wife Anne outlived her much younger husband by seven years, dying in 1623 at the age of seventy-one.

On 2nd February 1585 the Stratford parish register records the baptism of Hamnet and Judith 'sonne and daughter to William Shakspere'. It is assumed but nowhere stated that they were twins. On 11th August 1596 the Stratford parish register records the death of Hamnet 'son of William Shakspere'. The boy was only eleven years old and his death must have caused his parents much sorrow. Why they had no more children is surprising since the marriage seems to have been amicable and enduring. One possible explanation is that there may have been gynaecological complications following the birth of Anne's twins in 1585.

(Another long gap with no information available)

In October 1596, while absent on a business trip to London, William Shakspere attempted to purchase a coat of arms for the Shakspere male line, his father having previously been denied. William's bid met the same negative response. The College of Arms archive contains three rough drafts for the Shakspere coat of arms. On the first version it is dismissed with the words 'Non, Sanz Droigt' legal French for 'No, Without Right' or 'merit'. On the second version appear the words 'Shakspear – the player'. When finally granted the motto is shown without the comma as Non Sanz Droigt 'Not Without Right'. (Chambers, 18-20). William's name does not appear on any surviving document connected with the coat of arms, only that of his father John.

Back home in 1597 William Shakspere purchased from Stratford resident William Underhill, a substantial property in the town. This was New Place which came with barns, orchards and a feature named the Great Garden. Its purchase established him as a leading citizen and rate-payer with influence in town affairs that lasted until the end of his life. He was aged thirty-three at the time but was already sufficiently wealthy to have money to invest. He consolidated his purchase of New Place by paying a fine, or 'final concord', a legal process known as 'exemplification' formally recording that the property had been properly conveyed. (Chambers, 95-96). In January 1598 he bought a load of stone from a neighbour named Chamberlin for ten pence and continued improving and maintaining this property until his death in 1616.

In February 1598 William Shakspere was listed by the Stratford Corporation as illegally holding the large amount of 80 bushels of grain at a time of shortage. (Chambers, 99). This was a serious matter. A succession of bad harvests beginning in 1595 had caused great hardship in rural communities, with famine conditions in some areas and the first stirrings of a countryside rebellion. To mitigate the suffering of the increasing numbers of destitute people the government in London instituted measures to investigate the hoarding of corn, a practice which was exacerbating the situation. Barley was more profitable if sold to the brewing industry for malting instead of used as food, with the implication that those hoarding grain were doing so in order to release it on to the market at inflated prices. Malnutrition in some areas was so severe that the government pressed for measures to outlaw hoarding, leading the Privy Council to describe hoarders as 'wicked people in conditions more like to wolves'. As one of the hoarders named in the Stratford Corporation's blacklist document 'Noate of corn and malt' Shakspere and his family could have been vulnerable at a time of civil unrest. (Bearman, pp. 26-31). Students of the Shakespeare plays find a parallel situation in the opening scenes of *Coriolanus* when the citizens of Rome take to the streets to protest against the grain shortages which were causing them great hardship.

Also in 1598 the food riots claimed another Stratford victim in Richard Quiney who acted as an agent for the Corporation in raising public money to provide aid, including from the government in London. His private business dealings soon became merged with the money raised to provide relief for the poor and when pressed by the Corporation to hand it over he was unable to stump up enough to evade arrest and prosecution. In desperation on 25th October 1598 he wrote a letter from the Bell Inn in

Carter Lane, London addressed to William Shakspere in Stratford pleading for a loan of £30, a sum large enough in those days to purchase a house. For whatever reason the letter although folded, sealed and addressed was never sent. It was found among Quiney's papers after his death. It remains the only recorded instance of a letter with authorship relevance. (SBT MS ER 27/4). In 1616 Shakspere's younger daughter Judith married Richard's son Thomas Quiney (1589-1662) .

In March 1601 the last will and testament of Stratford resident Thomas Whittington bequeathed to the poor people of Stratford forty shillings owed to him by 'Anne Shaxspere, wyf unto Wyllyam Shaxspere, and is due debt unto me'. (Worcestershire Record Office) Whittington was a shepherd in the employ of Anne's father-in-law John Shakspere but why she needed the loan in the first place and never repaid it is unknown.

In May 1602 Shakspere purchased from William and John Combe 107 acres of land in Stratford plus 20 acres of pasture, all for £320. In September the same year he purchased Chapel Lane Cottage in Stratford with a garden and a quarter acre of land. This was opposite his house New Place and was for the use of his younger brother Gilbert Shakspere. (SBT MS ER 27/1 and MS 28/1).

In July 1604 'Willielmus Shexpere' sued the apothecary Philip Rogers for 35 shillings and 10 pence plus ten shillings damages in an attempt to recover the unpaid balance on a sale of twenty bushels of malt and a loan made in March. (SBT MS ER 27/5).

In October 1604 an estate survey of Rowington Manor, which was eight miles north of Stratford, recorded that 'William Shakspere holdeth there one cottage and one garden by estimation a quarter of one acre and payeth rent yearly 2 shillings and sixpence'. (Public Record Office, E 178/4661).

In July 1605 Shakspere purchased tithes to the value of £440. This qualified him as a 'lay rector' for burial inside Holy Trinity church in Stratford. (SBT MS ER 27/2).

In 1606 an inventory of the estate of Stratford resident Ralph Hubaud, deceased, recorded 'There was owing by Mr. Shakspere thirty-one shillings'.

In 1607 Shakspere's elder daughter Susanna married Stratford physician Doctor John Hall. This marriage has significance on the Shakespeare authorship mystery for two reasons. Firstly, the canonical plays contain hundreds of references to a wide range of medical conditions. These have been thoroughly assessed by medically qualified writers and found to be accurate. Which forces the question, from where or from whom, did the author obtain his considerable medical knowledge if not from his doctor son-in-law? Secondly, Dr Hall kept meticulous records of his patients and their ailments. After his death these were found to contain anecdotal references to many of the notable residents in the area who had been his patients, one such being the locally born Michael Drayton. Hall enthuses that he 'was an excellent poet' but makes no mention of his supposedly famous father-in-law who was an even better poet.

In August 1609 Shakspere sued John Addenbrooke for debt. He failed to appear in court and the man who had stood surety for the loan, Thomas Horneby, was required to pay the debt instead. (SBT Misc. Doc, V116).

In 1611 a Stratford Court of Chancery Bill of Complaint adjudicated on a dispute among the holders of tithes, Shakspere being included as one such holder. (SBT Misc. Doc, X, 9).

In September 1611 Shakspere's name is included on a Stratford petition supporting a Parliamentary Bill for the 'Repayre of the highe waies'. (SBT Misc. Doc, 1,4).

In January 1613 the will of John Combe in Stratford contains a bequest of £5 to 'Mr William Shackspere'. (PRO, Probate 11/126).

In October 1614 the proposed enclosures of common land in the adjacent parish of Welcombe affected the value of Shakspere's tithes in Stratford and led to a covenant between him and another Stratford resident William Replingham. (SBT MS ER 27/3). Shakspere's name appears seven times in documents relating to the Welcombe land enclosures, from which as a landlord he would have expected to benefit.

Between November 1614 and September 1615 Stratford resident Thomas Greene made diary entries concerning his 'Cosen Shakspere' in relation to the land enclosures mentioned above. Greene was also the town clerk and kept meticulous records, including being summoned to London to present a petition against the scheme. (SBT Misc. Doc, XIII 27-9). Similar attempts to enclose common land were occurring all over Tudor England. An expanding population needing to be fed, combined with dwindling land resources, made a compelling argument in favour of conversion to arable farming. Many poor families were dependent on having access to common land and protested violently against the 'encroaching tyrants who grind the faces of the poor'. (Bearman, 49-59). William Shakspere could be included among those landlords pressing for the Welcombe enclosures but the negotiations were still ongoing when he died in 1616.

On 25 March 1616 Shakspere made his will, signing each of the three pages. The first signature is almost unreadable, the second is shown as Willm Shackspere, the third as William Shakspear. (PRO Principal Probate Registry, Prob 1/4). The will begins 'In the name of god amen I William Shackspere of Stratford upon Avon ...' On the last page of the will are the words '... the said William Shackspere' which would imply that the lawyer drawing up the will pronounced the name as it was spelled.

The will contains several undated interlineations (written between the lines) the most famous of which is 'Item I give unto my wife my second best bed with the furniture'. A similar apparent afterthought was leaving money to the value of twenty-six shillings and eight pence to buy rings for 'my fellows John Hemynge, Richard Burbage & Henry Cundell'. If genuine this would ratify his connection with the Globe Theatre in London and the acting company known as The Kings Men, formerly as

The Lord Chamberlain's Men. Whether this is sufficient to confirm him as an actor and dramatist is the question at the heart of the authorship mystery.

It must be considered as surprising that in his will he made no mention of owning a single printed book, no mention of valuable unpublished manuscripts in his possession, no shares from the Globe and Blackfriars theatres, nor any of the artefacts associated with writing such as a book case, a desk, pens, ink and paper. His readiness to litigate in pursuing debts or to defend his business interests in Stratford did not apparently extend to London where his plays were routinely pirated. During his retirement years in Stratford he staged no plays nor wrote one line of text. At no time did he claim to have been the playwright known as William Shakespeare, nor after his death did members of his family make such a claim on his behalf, or attempt to obtain commercial benefit from the plays.

The leading historian in Elizabethan London was William Camden (1551-1623). As an antiquarian and topographer he visited all parts of the British Isles, including Stratford-upon-Avon. His findings were published in a great work with the title *Britannia*. The entry for Stratford singles out for special mention Hugh Clopton who left the town at a young age to make his fortune as a retailer in London. He became Master of the Worshipful Company of Mercers and was Mayor of London in 1491. Subsequently he was a generous civic benefactor to his home town of Stratford. No mention is made in *Britannia* of anyone in Stratford named William Shakespeare.

On 25 April 1616 the burial register of Holy Trinity Church, Stratford-upon-Avon, records the burial of 'Will Shakspear gent'. An unidentified grave slab in the chancel close to the wall monument is believed to be his last resting place. His death passed without a single recorded mention, either in Stratford, in London, or elsewhere. Nor was any commendatory verse penned in his honour, a surprising omission. Nothing of a literary nature connecting this man to the works of Shakespeare has ever been found in Stratford-upon-Avon.

Shakespeare signatures

a) Willm Shakp   Bellott-Mountjoy deposition 12th June 1612
b) William Shaksper   Blackfriars Gatehouse conveyance
                                                     10th March 1613
c) Wm Shakspe   Blackfriars mortgage   11th March 1613
d) William Shakspere   Page 1 of will   25th March 1616
e) Willm Shakspere   Page 2 of will   25th March 1616
f) William Shakspeare   Last page of will   25th March 1616

[a]

[b]

[c]

[d]

[e]

[f]

William Shakspere in London

How many William Shakespeares were there in Elizabethan and Jacobean London, either as actors, writers or theatre owners? Of only one can we be certain, this being the Warwickshire man whose name was mostly spelled as 'Shakspere'. His business interests in London were centred on the murky world of the entertainment, gambling, bear-baiting and sex trade industry located on the south bank of the River Thames. Many of the properties used as brothels, big houses some of them, were owned by the diocese of Winchester, with their many prostitutes jocularly referred to as the 'Winchester geese'. There was money to be made in these dubious surroundings and as William Shakspere of Stratford-upon-Avon died a rich man this could have been where he made it.

The original tripartite lease for the Globe Theatre between the landowner Sir Nicholas Brend and six shareholders was signed on 16th May 1599. The Burbage brothers Richard and Cuthbert took half the shares, the rest were split between John Heminges, Augustine Phillips, Thomas Pope and William Shakespeare. William Kemp was proposed as the seventh partner but sold his share in advance to the four minority holders. The original lease has never been found so it is not known how the Shakespeare name was spelled. It is only referred to in a Court of Requests action in 1619, *Witter versus Heminges and Condell*. 'Shakespeare's Globe' could be more accurately referred to as the 'the Burbages' Globe', to accompany Henslowe's Rose and Langley's Swan as theatre owners on the south bank of the River Thames.

Shakspere's involvement beyond staking some money in the new theatre can only be guessed at. As a 'sharer' he could have had access to the players of the Chamberlain's acting company, may have befriended some of them, perhaps loaned them money. Was he a player himself? This seems unlikely given that he could barely write his own name, unless it was as a walk-on extra. No documentary evidence has ever been found to name him in cast lists for any play in any theatre, nor for any payment made to him as an actor or a writer.

Whoever wrote the plays had a commanding grasp of all the varied requirements for successfully staging a theatrical performance but there is no evidence that the Stratford man had ever acquired this high level of commitment and expertise. Even so the name 'William Shakespeare' has become indelibly associated with the Lord Chamberlain's Men and the Globe Theatre. However tenuous the link it must be conceded that those supporting the orthodox authorship attribution to the Stratford man have the majority opinion on their side.

The first recorded mention of the name in London came on 3rd March 1595 when the accounts of the Queen's treasurer records a payment to 'William Kemp, William Shakespeare and Richard Burbage, servants of the Lord Chamberlain ... for two several comedies or enterludes shewed by them before her majestie in Christmas tyme … viz St Stephen's day and Innocent's day'.

In November 1596 a Queen's Bench court order issued Writs of Attachment (restraining orders) against William Shakespeare and Francis Langley to keep the peace, after complaints against them of physical intimidation. Two accomplice women were included in the order, they were named as Anne Lee and Dorothy Soer, about whom nothing is known. Francis Langley (1548-1602) was active in theatrical affairs as an owner and manager, opening the Swan Theatre in 1585, in Southwark. He was also involved in money-lending and prostitution but died heavily in debt. His nefarious reputation and apparently close association with Shakspere must be considered when seeking the man who wrote some of the world's most widely admired love poetry.

A year later in November 1597, Shakspere is named in the King's Bench Subsidy Roll as a tax defaulter in Bishopsgate ward, assessed at five shillings. He could not be traced and was recorded as 'either dead, departed or gone out of the ward'. (Public Record Office 179/146/354). He was still on the unpaid list in 1598 and is again named in the King's Rembrancer Subsidy Roll as a tax defaulter, this time for an annual assessment of thirteen shillings and four pence. (PRO 179/146/369. In 1599 and 1600 he was again listed as a tax delinquent, with a note that he had moved into Sussex.

In May 1603 a Privy Seal warrant authorised by King James allowed 'William Shakespeare … and the rest of their Associates freely to use and exercise the Arte and faculty of playing Comedies Tragedies histories Enterludes moralls pastoralls Stageplaies and such … for the recreation of our loving Subjectes as for our Solace and pleasure …' (Privy Seal Office 2/22).

In 1604 members of the King's Men, naming Shakespeare as one of themselves, were granted four and a half yards of scarlet cloth for a Royal procession by the Master of the Wardrobe. (PRO LCD 2/4(5) f78).

(A long gap with no recorded mention)

In May and June of 1612 William Shakspere appeared as a court witness in a civil dispute over an unpaid dowry bond (Bellott v Mountjoy). Although the case was heard in London he was described in the transcript as a 'gentleman of Stratford'. He made a deposition, signing as 'Willm Shakp'. This was the first of his six extant signatures.

In March 1613 William Shakspere, William Johnson, John Jackson and John Hemming purchased the Blackfriar's gate-house from Henry Walker for £140. The conveyancing indenture and the mortgage document contain the second and third Shakspere signatures, written as William Shakspe and Wm Shakspe. (British Library, MS. Egerton 1787).

In April 1615 a Court of Chancery bill of complaint lists Shakspere, with others, seeking access to the Blackfriars property documents. In May 1615 a court plea includes Shakspere's name in a list of shareholders for the Globe Theatre and the Blackfriars gate-house.

These few references warrant a question: was it possible for the provincial businessman William Shakspere to have pursued a secondary parallel career in London as the classically educated poet and dramatist known to the world as William Shakespeare? The literary establishment (academe, criticism, publishing, theatre) continues to maintain that such was the case. To express doubt about this openly can still prejudice a student or jeopardise an academic career. The print media and the nation generally also favour the orthodox view and can be hostile to those who suggest otherwise.

4 Launched

Pestilence and Civil War
Nicholas Rowe
David Garrick
Edmond Malone
Edward Dowden
Delayed First Performances
The Elementary Education Act 1870
Early Doubters
Delia Bacon

Pestilence and Civil War

The plays contained in the First Folio of 1623 were disadvantaged by appearing at a time when the public health of the city of London was greatly at risk, and was a serious concern for the authorities. Recurrent outbreaks of smallpox and the plague led to the closure of all places of assembly and entertainment, mainly the bull and bear baiting houses, but also the public theatres. These remained closed during the civil war 1642-1651, and throughout the puritan regime which followed. This dislocation of time and literary reputation goes some way to explain how the Shakespeare plays stayed under the radar for so long, to use a modern expression.

When King Charles II and his court returned from exile in 1660 they brought with them their experiences and admiration of the flourishing French theatre. Founded in 1630 the *Academie Française* had raised all forms of art and drama to a level of sophistication where Paris and Versailles rather than London could be claimed as the high-watermark of modernising western civilisation. Very soon London had caught up, with enclosed theatres and moveable scenery. More significantly women actors for the first time began to play female roles.

Periods of repression are customarily followed by periods of licence. Released from the constraints of the puritan era a new generation of dramatists changed the way in which plays could be written and performed on the London stage. Restoration drama with its often sexually frank dialogue was much to the public taste, particularly those plays of a bawdy nature classed as Comedies. The standard of writing was high and many of the plays were enduringly popular.

Although the more wordy and poetic plays of Shakespeare were also performed during this long period they had not yet made the breakthrough that was to come later with David Garrick. Often abridged and adapted, they languished by comparison. Bearing in mind that the greater proportion of the plays were written 1580-1600 the distance back in time was already starting to be measured in centuries.

Nicholas Rowe

In 1709 there was a new edition of the plays. The publisher was Jacob Tonson (1655-1736). He had obtained a copyright on the plays of William Shakespeare by buying up the rights of the heirs of the publisher of the 1685 Fourth Folio. The new edition in six volumes was based on the text of this Folio and edited by Nicholas Rowe (1674-1718), the first occasion on which the name of an editor had appeared on a collection of works by Shakespeare. It was also printed in quarto as a more reader-friendly size than the larger formats of the Folios.

Rowe was a versatile literary man. (In 1715 he succeeded Nahum Tate as Poet Laureate). He had written plays of his own and his skilled and sensitive editing of the Shakespeare plays was acknowledged with generous praise by other editors later in the century. In *The Works of Mr. William Shakespear; Revis'd and Corrected* he modernised the punctuation and spelling, including names, and provided cast lists for every play. His practical knowledge of the stage helped him to divide the plays into scenes and acts, including directions for the entrances and exits of the players. Rowe's edition included a frontispiece engraving for each play and also provided illustrations. These were based on contemporary stage performances of the plays, showing that they were performed in modern costumes.

All these innovations made the plays more accessible to the general public and widened their appeal. They ensured that David Garrick thirty years later would inherit a receptive audience for his large-scale stage presentations. Rowe's edition influenced other editors for the rest of the 18th century but as it was based on the less reliable Fourth Folio subsequent scholars and editors in the 19th century reverted to the definitive text of the First Folio.

There was another first for Rowe's edition because it included a biographical note of the author, the first to do so. Its title was *Some account of the life, &c. of Mr. William Shakespear*. The ageing actor Thomas Betterton (1635-1710) had been tasked with researching the life of the Warwickshire businessman who had purchased a small share in the newly built Globe Theatre in London. This was in 1599, a distance back in time of 110 years.

Betterton made it to Stratford-upon-Avon but found no Shaksperes living there. This was because William had died in 1616 with no male heir and the last remaining descendants of his two daughters had died out fifty years and more in the past. Any hope of finding information of value to a biographer had to be abandoned. Nothing was found in Stratford-upon-Avon which remotely connected William Shakspere to the plays of William Shakespeare. Even Shakspere's house known as New Place, and where he spent the last nineteen years of his life, had been demolished in 1702 so the trail had come to an end.

The most Betterton could report back to Rowe were the basic registration dates of the man himself and his immediate family. Shakspere's only son had died in 1596 at the age of eleven. His daughter Susanna married John Hall in 1607 and had one child, Elizabeth, in 1608. Although Elizabeth was married twice (in 1626 to Thomas Nash and in 1649 to John Bernard), she never had any children. Shakspere's other daughter Judith married Thomas Quiney in 1616 and had three sons, one of whom died in infancy. The other two sons both died unmarried in 1639.

Betterton was able to confirm to Rowe that the Shakespeare monument in Holy Trinity Church was still in its place, and as yet unchanged from its original appearance. This was because the new edition of the plays contained an engraved plate of the monument copied from William Dugdale's *The Antiquities of Warwickshire* published in 1656. The engraving had been made by Wenceslaus Hollar from Dugdale's original drawing of the monument made in 1634. It showed an elderly man clasping a woolsack, and with a few minor discrepancies was accurately copied by the engraver Michael Van Guchts for Rowe's new edition of the plays. It now shows a writer with a quill pen.

Betterton writes of William Shakspere

> He was buried on the North side of the Chancel, in the Great Church at Stratford, where a Monument, as engraved in the Plate, is placed in the Wall.

In common with many later researchers Betterton was puzzled by the lack of any evidence of a cultured upbringing or classical education for the future world-famous poet and playwright, or indeed for any form of education however basic. He could only wring his hands and suppose that the young William must have gained his learning somewhere else, otherwise he would not have been able to write his great works of literature. In stark contradiction, and with no apparent doubts or misgivings that he might have been researching the wrong man in the wrong place, he relates an unedifying anecdote

> He had, by a Misfortune common enough to young Fellows, fallen into ill Company; and amongst them, some that made a frequent practice of Deer-stealing, engaged him with them more than once in robbing a Park that belonged to Sir Thomas Lucy of Cherlecot, near Stratford and was prosecuted by that gentlemen, as he thought somewhat too severely , . . and was obliged to leave his Family and Business in Warwickshire and shelter himself in London.

Betterton is also the source for believing that the earl of Southampton as the dedicatee of Shakespeare's two long poems *Venus and Adonis* and *The Rape of Lucrece*, made a gift of a thousand pounds to this erstwhile rural thief fleeing jurisdiction.

> There is one Instance so Singular in the Magnificence of this Patron of Shakespear's, that if I had not been assured that the Story was handed down from Sir William Davenant ... I should not have ventured to have (it) inserted, that my Lord Southampton, at one time, gave him a Thousand pounds, to enable him to go through with a Purchase which he heard he had a mind to.

In summing up at the end of the introductory essay Rowe regretted that his emissary Betterton had been unable to find any credible evidence for the Shakespeare authorship. Betterton offers his own apology

> This is what I could learn of any Note, either relating to himself or his Family. The Character of the man is best seen in his Writings.

Subsequent hopeful researchers making the long journey from London to Stratford-upon-Avon similarly returned empty-handed, prominent among them the lawyer Edmond Malone. Betterton's meagre haul remained all that could be retrieved by way of a biography of Shakespeare for another hundred years. But his prescient conclusion that the answers to the authorship mysteries had to be found from within the works themselves proved in time to be the most fruitful line of research.

David Garrick

The actor and theatre impresario David Garrick (1717-1779) had the rare ability of making an art form commercially successful. London's growing wealth had created a prosperous and discerning bourgeoisie that liked to dress up for an evening spent in the pleasant surroundings of a theatre. Garrick's talent lay in understanding how this well-to-do and well-educated audience would prefer to be entertained and set about providing exactly the kind of serious drama they would appreciate.

The plays of Shakespeare fitted the bill exactly and soon began to receive the overdue acclaim they deserved. From the 1740s onward David Garrick devoted his career to reviving and revitalising these plays, with his own strong performances as Richard III and King Lear much admired. Audiences then as now were fascinated by the lives of the royals, their love affairs and their family feuding. It was a rich seam which Garrick mined assiduously for the rest of his life.

In 1769 (five years too late) Garrick became involved in planning a 'Stratford Jubilee' to commemorate the 200th anniversary of the author's birth in 1564. The event was washed out by torrential rain and restaged at Drury Lane Theatre in London where it ran for over ninety performances. Garrick wrote an Ode to introduce performances of the Jubilee, declaiming the lines himself to music written by Thomas Arne. The Ode referred to the author of the plays as 'our matchless Bard', the first use of the infamous sobriquet. Contemporary accounts suggest that the proceedings were more a celebration of Garrick rather than Shakespeare but the exercise had succeeded in its purpose by launching 'The Bard' to worldwide fame.

Garrick had provided the country with its National Poet, doubling up as its National Hero when a string of victories over Napoleon and the French later established Britain as the dominant naval and military power of the age. Shakespeare became linked with national prestige and patriotism, a link which has been strongly maintained until the present day.

Edmond Malone – 1741-1812

Edmond Malone was an Irish barrister resident in London. Family money allowed him to retire early and he devoted the rest of his life to studying the plays of Shakespeare, which had been popularised by the efforts of David Garrick. In 1778 Malone issued an essay with the wordy title

*An attempt to ascertain the order in which the plays
attributed to Shakspeare* (sic) *were written*

The task he set himself proved not to be possible. It defeated Malone as it defeated many later generations of scholars, and continues to do so. The reason being that the plays had been so extensively revised that it was not possible to tell early from late with any degree of certainty. It was not therefore possible to chart the writer's artistic development, the underlying purpose for writing the essay. Sequencing the plays was agreed to be a legitimate area of enquiry but one which foundered on the awkward problem of the authorship. It still awaits a resolution.

In 1790 Malone issued his own edition of the Shakespeare plays, in ten volumes. In the introduction to the first volume he set himself a second task which likewise proved not to be possible. He stated his intention to write 'a uniform and connected narrative' of Shakespeare's life. Following the lead of a previous editor, Nicholas Rowe, he directed his research to Stratford-upon-Avon. The Warwickshire businessman's purchase of a share in the Globe Theatre in 1599 was well authenticated and Rowe's acceptance that the Stratford man and the 'Mr. William Shakespeare' on the First Folio title page were one and the same remains to this day the orthodox position.

No one at that time would have thought it necessary to seek elsewhere for a more credible author of the famous plays and Malone understandably centred his biographical research on Stratford-upon-Avon. Having received parish registers and other documents through the post he finally visited the small country town in 1793, a time lag of 194 years since the Stratford man's investment in the Globe Theatre in London. Malone received willing help from the town's civic officials, being allowed 'a complete rummage through all their papers'. Garrick's earlier attempts to stage a Jubilee had given the Stratford burghers a lively appreciation of the commercial benefit that could be generated by the town's association with the famous dramatist known as William Shakespeare, hence the licence given to Malone to ransack their local archive.

He retrieved some previously unknown records of the Stratford man's business dealings, property speculation and debt recovery litigation but found nothing which associated him with any literary activities, either in his home town, in London, or elsewhere. A state of affairs which remains unchanged to the present day. Malone never proceeded with his projected biography of the Stratford man but nine years after he died his literary executor James Boswell (the son of Samuel Johnson's biographer) used Malone's notes to write a short biography himself. It was issued in 1821 as a preface to the *Third Variorum edition of the Works of Shakespeare.*

The reason why Malone abandoned his plans for writing a 'a uniform and connected narrative' of Shakespeare's life has never been made known and is now unlikely to be found. As a lawyer with a professional ability to assess evidence he may have finally realised that, like Thomas Betterton before him, he was looking for the wrong man in the wrong place.

Edward Dowden – 1843-1913

Shakespere: (sic) *A Critical Study of his Mind and Art*

The next major review of the chronology of Shakespeare's plays came in 1874 with a book written by another Irish scholar, Edward Dowden. He was born in Cork and went on to become Professor of English Literature at Trinity College, Dublin. He sorted the plays into four phases under the titles 'In the workshop', 'In the World', 'Out of the depths' and 'On the heights'.

These or similar divisions would apply to the practitioners of many art forms, in essence they represent First attempts, Growing mastery, Full maturity and a Valedictory final phase. By the third edition of Dowden's book in 1881 he had extended these literary groupings from four to twelve but with no more success. Even so Dowden's preferred chronology influenced many later scholars, notably E. K. Chambers in 1930 and Wells and Taylor in 1987.

The grit in the oyster for all literary analysts trying to date and sequence the plays of Shakespeare is the incompatibility of the Stratford man's birth in 1564 with the publishing data that exists. This information is not extensive and often open to interpretation but nevertheless puts the escalation of literary talent in the second half of Queen Elizabeth's reign back into the 1580s. There is no record of a Shakspere visit to London until the mid or late 1590s by which time many of the early anonymous versions of the plays had already appeared in print. It should always be kept in mind that some influential sources were available well before the 1590s.

1560 The Geneva Bible, the primary Protestant Bible
1564 François de Belleforest, *Histoires Tragiques*
1565 Plutarch's *Lives* in the French translation by Jacques Amyot
1567 Ovid's *Metamorphoses* translated into English by Arthur Golding
1573 *Cardanus Comforte* translated from the Italian by Thomas Bedingfield
1577 Holinshed's *Chronicles*, with a second enlarged edition in 1587
1580 Michel de Montaigne, *Essais*

Allusions, topicality and source material for example would allow a date of 1587 for *Hamlet*, the most famous of the plays. It is hard to believe that a young countryman with little in the way of formal education could have written this play in his early twenties. Editors have always tried to dodge this awkward problem by assigning the latest possible dates to individual plays. *The Tempest* is usually given the date 1611 but all the major source material was available by 1580 and the structure, content and language

69

also suggest an early date of composition. The First Folio is only roughly chronological but *The Tempest* comes first which supposes that the compilers may have also considered it an early play.

Some dates of first performance or first publication exist for the plays but few can be stated with certainty and no date of first writing is known for any of the plays. The frequent use of these sources in the plays of Shakespeare indicate a writer competent in languages other than English, notably in French, Italian and Latin.

Delayed First Performances

The Shakespeare plays were abridged and adapted by the provincial theatres and touring companies and so went through many hands, changing as they went. They were modernised, bowdlerised and some were provided with family-friendly happy endings. These well-meaning generations of actors, editors, stage managers and directors could collectively in some small way be considered as co-authors of Shakespeare and they certainly contributed to the success and popularity of the Shakespeare brand.

Several of the plays had to wait until after the restoration of the monarchy in 1660 before receiving their first full-text performance, and some of these were delayed for a surprising length of time.

1674	*Timon of Athens*
	Thomas Shadwell, in one of the Inns of Court
1737	*King John*
	Shakespeare Ladies Club, Covent Garden, London
1740	*As You Like It*
	David Garrick, Drury Lane Theatre, London
1741	*All's Well That Ends Well*
	Goodman's Field Theatre, Whitechapel, London
1762	*Two Gentlemen of Verona*
	Benjamin Victor, Drury Lane Theatre, London
1839	*Love's Labour's Lost*
	Elizabeth Vestris, Covent Garden, London
1849	*Antony and Cleopatra*
	Samuel Phelps, Sadler's Wells, London
1898	*Troilus and Cressida*
	First with full text in Munich, Germany
1928	*The Two Noble Kinsmen*
	An Old Vic Production, London
2002	*King Edward III*
	Royal Shakespeare Company, at The Swan.

There was another production of *Edward III* in 2016 by the Hudson Shakespeare Company, New Jersey, USA.

The Elementary Education Act 1870

The National Education League led by the Liberal member of parliament William Foster had long campaigned for the mass education of all children between the ages of 5 and 12 in England and Wales. Although idealistic, intended for the good of the children, it received wide support because it was perceived as beneficial for the export of manufactured goods to have a literate workforce. The Act was strictly implemented and achieved its aim with little resistance because the facility for reading books was pleasurable as well as commercially expedient. A mass readership was soon created and the plays and poetry of William Shakespeare reached a new and ever widening level of popularity in the 1880s, and beyond into the next century.

At school, and in amateur dramatic societies in every part of the country, people of all age groups were able to share in the Shakespeare experience. Men from all walks of life could recite from the plays, with the patriotic speeches from *Henry V* and the 'sceptred isle' John of Gaunt speech from *Richard II* being particular favourites. Many people grew up with the feeling that they knew Shakespeare personally and were proud that a man of the people could write drama that was the envy of the world. He was elevated to cult status, embodying all that was finest in the national character. He was the 'Soul of the age!' to quote Ben Jonson's First Folio tribute.

Although this adulation was deserved, and to be welcomed, it had the parallel effect of exposing the plays to a more intense and critical scrutiny. Many ordinary readers and playgoers found it increasingly hard to reconcile the epic grandeur of the plays with the money-making and debt collecting exploits of the affluent burgher who was supposed to have written them. By all accounts an astute trader and good family man but scarcely credible as the author of plays featuring the lives of so many royal and noble characters.

This gathering disquiet over the authorship did not play well at any level of society. The lack of proof that anyone other than Shakespeare wrote the plays, and the unwavering support of the teaching universities, entrenched the orthodox position. Any hint of a suggestion that they might be worshipping the memory of the wrong man was met with fierce resistance, not just from the literary establishment but from the population at large. Many who had grown up to venerate and cherish 'The Bard' felt it as an affront, unpatriotic, sacrilege even, and resisted any attempts to convince them otherwise. This attitude still prevails.

Early Doubters

No person in history can have been the subject of such exhaustive research as the author known as William Shakespeare. For diligence and accuracy the Clarendon Press folio edition of Samuel Schoenbaum's *Shakespeare : A Documentary Life* published in 1975 is an invaluable resource. Dr Robert Bearman the former head of archives at the Shakespeare Institute is the author of *Shakespeare in the Stratford Records* (1994). Between these two books and the Public Record Office all that is ever likely to be known about William Shakspere of Stratford-upon-Avon has long since been published. Yet after all this research nothing links him to the plays, and paradoxically serves to disqualify rather than confirm him as the author.

The first authorship doubters were puzzled by the awkward break at the end of the supposed author's literary career. Fifteen quarto editions of Shakespeare plays were printed between 1594 and 1604 but then came to a stop, only two more appearing in print before Shakspere's death in 1616. (*King Lear* in 1608 and *Troilus and Cressida* in 1609, but both previously registered). No new play can be found to date definitively after 1604. This left a vacuum of empty years to be filled, obliging Stratfordians to fall back on the unconvincing excuse of early retirement. Why a successful middle-aged writer should leave London and resume his former uninspiring way of life in Stratford-upon-Avon was hard to understand, hence the lingering doubts.

Regrettably for all concerned Shakspere's conduct in the latter part of his life was not consonant with that of a refined man of letters. Back home in Stratford-upon-Avon it was one petty law suit after another, squabbles with neighbours, listed as a grain hoarder at a time of national shortage and active in a shady campaign to enclose common land. These are hardly the activities of a high-minded music-loving poet and playwright and it is understandable why the early doubters began the search for a more credible alternative author of the plays attributed to William Shakespeare.

Delia Bacon – 1811-1859

The inability of doubters to produce a credible alternative author blunted much of the early rumblings of disquiet over the Shakespeare authorship. How much did Ben Jonson know? How many were paid to keep quiet? With careers and reputations at stake few of the people qualified to do so risked a challenge. Bearing in mind as always that the plays of Shakespeare were still many years away from their worldwide fame and that any surviving manuscripts may have been treated less reverently than they would be today.

The first doubter to publish a full-length closely-argued attempt at unravelling the authorship mystery was a self-educated American woman named Delia Bacon. After a prodigious amount of research, and having to overcome opposition and prejudice from the literary establishments of the day, she finally published in 1857 a book with the title *The Philosophy of the Plays of Shakspere Unfolded*. This was almost seven hundred pages in length and the labour of writing it impoverished her and ruined her health. She died two years later at the age of forty-eight.

In her book Delia Bacon reasoned that the depth of erudition evident in the plays could only have originated from the greatest intellects of the time working together in pursuit of a new system of philosophy based on social reform. The writers she considered most likely to have collaborated in producing the works of Shakespeare were Francis Bacon (no relationship claimed), Edmund Spenser and Walter Raleigh. Even if with caution, her research and findings were considered sympathetically by other American writers, among them Nathaniel Hawthorne, Walt Whitman, Mark Twain, Ralph Waldo Emerson and Henry James. In republican America there were fewer feathers to be ruffled by doubting the Shakespeare authorship, a situation which remains unchanged to the present day.

Although her research did not provide the answers she hoped for it was Delia Bacon who had uncorked the bottle and let loose the code-breakers, the conspiracy theorists, the forgers, the cranks and the hopelessly misguided. Even if not entirely single-handed she was responsible for much of the spilled ink shed by future generations of literary sleuths. All seeking the eternally elusive Mr. William Shakespeare of First Folio fame.

5 The Knowledge

Out-topping knowledge

The poet Matthew Arnold in his early sonnet with the title '*Shakespeare*' described him as 'Out-topping knowledge'. Thomas Carlyle in his book '*On Heroes and Hero-Worship*' published in 1841, wrote 'Shakespeare is the greatest of intellects'. These endorsements from two great scholars merit our attention because the wide sweep of learning evident in the plays is central to the authorship mystery and cannot be ignored.

Experts called on to arbitrate in their various subjects have mostly concluded that the writer's grasp across many areas of knowledge was genuine rather than superficial. The terminology of many occupations and professions is used accurately and organically as naturally arising from the subject matter, rather than as add-ons for effect or vanity. Libraries were few and far between in Elizabethan England. Books were expensive, highly prized and closely guarded so to acquire this amount of learning narrows the field when searching for an alternative author.

Two other highly respected scholars, Geoffrey Bullough (1901-1982) and Kenneth Muir (1907-1996) have between them listed some three hundred sources with documentable links to the Shakespeare plays and poetry. Professor Bullough's eight-volume *Narrative and Dramatic Sources of Shakespeare* was published by Columbia University between 1957 and 1973. Professor Muir's *The Sources of Shakespeare's Plays* was published by Methuen in in 1977. Muir writes in his introduction

> Shakespeare ... used translations when they were available; but he did not use them slavishly, and there is plenty of evidence that he read Latin works of which there was no translation. Of modern languages Shakespeare acquired some knowledge of French, Italian, and perhaps a smattering of Spanish. He could certainly read French ... He could have read Boccaccio in a French translation; but he appears to have read Geraldi Cinthio's *Hecatommithi* and Ariosto's *Orlando Furioso* in the original Italian.

Muir strongly supports the man from Stratford-upon-Avon as the author of Shakespeare but citing him as a reader of Italian *commedia erudita* collides abruptly with the few known facts about his life. He would have needed to visit Italy to read these books in their original language and no record exists that he made such a journey, or had been educated to the level where he could appreciate them sufficiently to use them as source material for *Othello* and *The Tempest* respectively. But since the connection is valid it prompts the suspicion that the fruitful journey to Italy must have been made by someone other than the Stratford businessman.

A selection of the topics and areas of expertise distributed through the texts of the plays and poetry would include knowledge of ancient and modern history, both correctly grounded in the geography of the world as then known. Scriptural references are numerically second only to allusions drawn from the classical world and its literature. Astronomy, ships, sailing and navigation, descriptions of storms and the fear of drowning if taken together would indicate an author with considerable seafaring experience.

Familiarity with courtly protocol, including in French and Italian courts, also heraldry, diplomacy, the manners and etiquette of the nobility, and the formal mode of speech in which the main characters address one another would all suggest that this was the top level of society where the author was most at ease. An over-arching broad interest in philosophy, government and politics reveal an author with a well-developed analytical and critical capability. Music, including its composition, musical instruments and teaching, singing and dancing, all feature prominently. These interests and activities are associated with the court and upper class society, where such accomplishments were most highly practised and regarded.

The plays contain numerous references to cultivated herbs and plants, with scenes set in formally designed gardens. Only in the great houses of the wealthy were these horticultural interests pursued and practised, which would place the author as a man familiar with these privileged surroundings. Martial arts, falconry in particular, is a field of expertise mostly exclusive to the landed gentry. Military and naval warfare figure in many plays, as might be expected in an age of conflict. These are written in sufficient detail to suggest an author who had himself experienced travelling with an army and had witnessed armed combat.

Law and medicine are two main areas of knowledge in which the author seems to have been exceptionally well informed. These and some other topics featured in the plays are now considered in more detail.

Geographical Locations

A good atlas and some map pins are needed to plot the plays of Shakespeare. Thirty of the 40 canonical plays are set wholly or partly outside the British Isles, mostly in the countries bordering the Mediterranean, the Adriatic and in Asia Minor. This has a direct bearing on the Shakespeare authorship since the natural and obvious question to ask is whether this familiarity with the history, topography, law, customs and politics of foreign lands could be acquired entirely by reading books and studying the classics, or whether the writer may have actually visited these countries to learn such things for himself? It is still a valid question.

These are the thirty plays with offshore content

All's Well That Ends Well	Roussillon near Lyons; Paris, Florence, Marseilles
Anthony and Cleopatra	Rome in Italy and Alexandria in Egypt
As You Like It	The Ardennes area of north-eastern France
The Comedy of Errors	Ephesus, ancient city on the west coast of Turkey
Coriolanus	Rome
Cymbeline	Partly in Rome
Edward III	Partly in France
Hamlet	Elsinore Castle, Denmark
Henry V	Partly in France
Henry VI Part 1	Partly in France
Henry VI Part 3	Partly in France
Julius Caesar	Rome
King John	Partly in France
Love's Labour's Lost	Navarre, Northern Spain
Measure for Measure	Vienna
The Merchant of Venice	Venice
A Midsummer Night's Dream	'A wood near Athens' but Italian in character
Much Ado about Nothing	Messina, Sicily
Othello	Venice and Cyprus
Pericles	Antioch, Syria ; Tyre, Lebanon
Romeo and Juliet	Verona, Italy
The Taming of the Shrew	Padua, Italy
The Tempest	A volcanic island in the Tyrrenean
Timon of Athens	Athens
Titus Andronicus	Rome
Troilus and Cressida	Troy, legendary city in North West Turkey
Twelfth Night	Illyria, an ancient Balkan region
Two Gentlemen of Verona	Verona and Milan

Two Noble Kinsmen	Athens
The Winter's Tale	Bohemia, modern day Czech Republic, once extending to the Adriatic coast near Venice.

First-hand knowledge of northern Italy is implicit in the plays, for example the writer knew of the existence of the network of canals on the Lombardy Plain, and that it was possible to be shipwrecked on the Adige, the river which runs through Verona. And that it was also possible, as in *The Two Gentlemen of Verona*, to make the journey from Verona to Milan, two inland cities, entirely by boat. In the first act of *Romeo and Juliet* ('In fair Verona, where we lay our scene'), Romeo's mother asks his friend Benvolio if she has seen her son and receives the reply (1.1.118-120)

> Where, underneath the grove of sycamore
> That westward rooteth from this city side
> So early walking did I see your son.

Sycamore trees still grow outside the western walls of the city. Richard Roe includes a photograph of them in his book *The Shakespeare Guide to Italy* published in 2011.

Othello, subtitled *The Moor of Venice* is set partly in Venice and partly in Cyprus. The need to resist an imminent danger from the Ottoman Turks in the eastern Mediterranean necessitated Othello's urgent posting to Cyprus. Queen Elizabeth and Lord Burghley were always alert to threats against trade and were also worried by the Ottoman Turks who were steadily encroaching westward into Europe. The Ottomans were a Sunni regime, simultaneously infiltrating eastward into Persia. As a counter-balance to this danger the diplomat Sir Anthony Shirley (1565-1635) and his younger brother Robert Shirley were sent as envoys to broker alliances with the Shia states making up Persia, the modern Iran. They went with an offer to supply arms to Persia and to provide military training as the most immediate means of containing their mutual enemy, the Ottoman Turks.

There is a reference to this Persian association in *Twelfth Night*. One of the conspirators, Fabian, does not want to miss the humiliation planned for Malvolio   2.5.173-74

> I will not give my part of this sport for a payment of thousands to be paid from the Sophy.

This is believed to be a reference to the generous cash award paid to Anthony Shirley by the Shah of Persia, Abbas I, known to westerners as the 'Sophy'. The founder of the Shafavid branch of Islam was Sheikh Safi, anglicised as Sophy, a name applied to all subsequent leaders.

A reference to military prowess at the Persian court comes at 3.4.271-72 in the same play

Sir Toby They say he has been a fencer (swordsman) to the Sophy.
Sir Andrew Pox on't. I'll not meddle with him.

In so far as the personality traits of a writer can be deduced from his or her published texts the writer of Shakespeare had an insatiable curiosity about all matters great and small. Not much escaped this author's sharp inquisitive eye. A fascination with foreign clothes and commodities, or anything strange or exotic, soon found their way into a speech. 'All the perfumes of Arabia will not sweeten this little hand,' grieves Lady Macbeth. Hamlet commiserates with the recently arrived company of travelling players when referring to an unappreciative audience. 'The play, I remember, pleased not the million. T'was caviar to the general'. Caviar, obtained from sturgeon caught in the Caspian Sea was a luxury product imported from Persia.

On a wider geographic scale Shakespeare was aware of the existence of large countries elsewhere in the outside world, and even if he never visited them he still knew enough about them to provide a quotable phrase. In the second part of Henry IV the ensign Pistol states, 'I speak of Africa and golden joys' (2.3.101). Titania challenges Oberon, 'Why art thou here, come from the farthest step of India' (*A Midsummer Night's Dream* 2.1.68-9). In Act 2 of *Much Ado About Nothing* Benedick offers to run an errand for Don Pedro 'to the Antipodes … or the farthest inch of Asia'. In *The Merry Wives of Windsor* Pistol boasts, '… the world's my oyster, which I with sword will open'. 2.2.4-5.

In *The Two Gentlemen of Verona*, Julia the dark complexioned lover of Proteus is described as 'but a swarthy Ethiop' (2.6.26). Hermia is similarly disparaged by Lysander in *A Midsummer Night's Dream* 3.2.266. He goes on to call her a tawny Tartar, referring to a central Asian people of Mongol origin. In *Love's Labour's Lost* the male lords dress up in traditional Russian costume to amuse the ladies. In the banter that follows Rosaline says to Biron, 'Why look you so pale? Sea-sick I think, coming from Muscovy'. (5.2.392-93). Attempts by merchants to navigate a north-east passage to Cathay (China) were unsuccessful but in the process they found a way of accessing Persia via Archangel, the Volga and the Caspian Sea.

The Merchant of Venice is one of Shakespeare's most cosmopolitan plays. Shylock the Jewish financier, the Prince of Aragon and the Prince of Morocco emphasise the racial mix of this thriving ancient seaport city with its proximity to Asia Minor. The Prince of Morocco contrasts 'the watery kingdom' of Venice with the Hyrcanean deserts of eastern Persia and 'the vasty wilds of wide Arabia' (2.7.41-2). Bassanio ticks off the countries where Antonio's merchant shipping fleet puts into port

From Tripolis, from Mexico, and England,
From Lisbon, Barbary and India

Nearer to home the map pins for the British Isles would be scattered the length and breadth of the country. The denouement in *Macbeth* takes place in Perthshire 'when Great Birnam Wood' finally meets 'high Dunsinane Hill'. The Northumberland village of Holmedon (Humbleton) was a battlefield site in *2 Henry IV*. King Richard in *Richard II* was imprisoned in Pontefract Castle in Yorkshire. The advancing earl of Richmond in *Richard III* camps out at Haverfordwest in Wales. King Harry in Southampton sorts out the traitors before embarking for France and Agincourt. (2.2.88). King John loses his baggage train in The Wash 'devoured by the unexpected flood', and the Venetian merchant Antonio's ship is believed wrecked on the Goodwin Sands off the east coast of Kent. Warwickshire receives a mention. In the second part of *Henry VI*, Kenilworth Castle is touted as a possible refuge for King Henry and Queen Margaret, fleeing after the Jack Cade rebellion. 4.4.38.

Astronomy

The entrance to the modern world, known as the Scientific Revolution, was opened by Nicolaus Copernicus (1473–1543), a mathematician and astronomer born of German parents but resident in Poland. Working as an independent scholar with little university support or sophisticated optical equipment he developed the theories on which all subsequent research into astrophysics has been based. The heliocentric nature of the solar system with orbiting planets was outlined in his main work, anglicised as *On the Revolutions of the Celestial Spheres*. It was published in 1543, the year of his death.

Although resisted by the Vatican his conclusions were favourably received in England under succeeding Tudor administrations. The awareness of the huge landmass on the other side of the Atlantic Ocean, the 'New World', had repositioned Britain from an offshore island on the outer fringes of Europe to the centre of the world map, providing unrivalled opportunities for trade and development. Commercially driven maritime exploration was facilitated by the new Copernican mathematics, used to navigate the oceans safely. In a superstitious age where most knowledge was still derived from the ancients who believed in witchcraft, ghosts and astrology the arrival of strict scientific method changed for ever the way in which the world was perceived by its intellectual elite, which at this time would have included Francis Bacon and the writer known as William Shakespeare.

John Dee (1527-1609) was the oceanographer most trusted by the Queen and Lord Burghley. Dee's protégé Thomas Digges (1546-95) was the principal promoter of the Copernican theory in Elizabethan England and he is credited with constructing an early form of telescope. The word 'telescope' had not yet been invented and Digges referred to his invention as 'perspective glasses'. References in his writings to the 'blastments' (craters) on the moon and the red spot on Jupiter are considered insufficient to support a claim that he invented the telescope before Galileo. His main claim to fame was his independently researched conclusion that contrary to the findings of Copernicus (and before him, Aristotle) the universe was not a finite entity bounded under a fixed canopy. Instead he was the first astronomer to argue for a limitless cosmos in all directions, and with no boundaries. This frightening concept of our tiny planet being adrift in an infinite space surrounded by countless millions of similar celestial moving objects was hard to comprehend at the time, and in many ways still is. Shakespeare foreshadowed quantum physics with his neatly summed up paradox that the microscopically small and the infinitely large are constructed in the same way. Hamlet says, 2.2.256-57

I could be bounded in a nutshell (atom) and count myself a king of
infinite space

Other references to astronomy in Shakespeare included this one on the
fixed orbits of the planets, spoken by Ulysses in *Troilus and Cressida*
1.3.85-88

> The heavens themselves, the planets, and this centre,
> Observe degree, priority and place.
> Infixture, course, proportion, season, form,
> Office, and custom, in all line of order:

Hamlet's love letter to Ophelia quoted by Polonius implies
knowledge that the sun is stationary 2.2.116-19

> Doubt thou the stars are fire;
> Doubt that the sun doth move;
> Doubt truth to be a liar;
> But never doubt I love.

Again in *Hamlet* the soldier Bernardo's description of a bright star has
been identified as a supernova observed in 1572 by the Danish astronomer
Tycho Brahe 1.1.34-6

> When yon same star that's westward from the pole
> Had made his course t'illume that part of heaven
> Where now it burns …'

Sonnet 116 quotes the Pole Star as a fixed point for trigonometric
calculation

> O no, it is an ever fixed mark
> That looks on tempests and is never shaken;
> It is the star to every wand'ring barque,
> Whose worth's unknown although his height be taken.

In *Timon of Athens* (4.3.439-40) Shakespeare shows that he is aware that
the moon shines by reflected light:

> The moon's an arrant thief,
> And her pale fire she snatches from the sun.

Hamlet sums it all up succinctly in 1.5.168-69

> There are more things in heaven and earth,
> Horatio, than are dreamt of in our philosophy.

Money

'Thou whore of mankind', snarls Timon, delivering his verdict on gold, the commodity for which the world long ago sold its soul. (*Timon of Athens*, 4.3.43) . The possession of money and the influence it can exert in the conduct of human affairs is well understood by the Shakespeare author. Those who lack it envy those who have it, and in a play this provides ready-made creative tension. Money and its purchasing power is something everyone understands, and is always of interest. Shakespeare's general knowledge included coinage. These are some examples.

English money was reckoned in pounds, shillings and pence, with 12 pence to a shilling and 20 shillings to a pound. The gold 'noble' was worth 6 shillings and 8 pence, a third of a pound, and used by Shakespeare for most of the English based plays. The fateful quarrel in *Richard II* which triggered the events leading to the king's downfall was over money. Bolingbroke accused Mowbray of misusing military funds to the value of 8,000 nobles by spending them on 'lewd employments'. (1.1.87-91)

The 'crown' which was worth 5 shillings, a quarter of a pound sterling, was also used for the Wars of the Roses plays. This was an anachronism as the gold crown was not introduced until 1526 long after the end of the conflict. It was the standard coin in use during the times when the plays would have been written.

The gold crown was superseded by the 'angel', so called because it showed the Archangel Michael defeating a dragon, a reference from the Book of Revelation. King John was an early dissenter from a European union led by the Vatican. After waging war in France he plans his return to England. In jocular punning mood he instructs the Bastard, (3.3.6-8)

> Cousin, away for England! Haste before,
> And ere our coming see thou shake the bags
> Of hoarding abbots: imprisoned angels set at liberty

This was also wrong historically, as there was no gold coinage in thirteenth century England. In *The Merchant of Venice*, a play in which money figures prominently, the Prince of Morocco faced with a choice of a gold, silver or lead casket to win Portia's hand in marriage unwisely opts for gold   (2.7.55-60)

> They have in England
> A coin that bears the figure of an angel
> Stamped in gold, but that's insculpted upon;
> But here an angel in a golden bed
> Lies all within. Deliver me the key.
> Here do I choose, and thrive I as I may.

The author would seem to be familiar with past coinage, its worth and appearance. *The Comedy of Errors* is another play about money, in this case involving angels and ducats as well as a gold chain. Trade wars between Syracuse in Sicily and Ephesus in Turkey explain the tension underlying the comedy in this fast-moving play.

One of the young gentleman scholars in *Love's Labour's Lost*, Longueville, joins in the sneering at the *Nine Worthies* pageant put on for their entertainment. He describes one of the participants as having 'The face of an old Roman coin, scarce seen'. Mark Antony in *Julius Caesar* reads out the terms of Caesar's will. 'Under Caesar's seal he gives to every Roman citizen seventy-five drachmas'. (3.2.235) This is of interest because the Greek drachma from Plutarch was quoted, not the Latin denarius of equivalent value which appears in North's translation of Plutarch.

In the more contemporary settings of the Italian plays it is the Venetian gold ducat which has the most references. Antonio the merchant in *The Merchant of Venice* offers a pound of his flesh to Shylock as surety against a loan of 3,000 ducats. Shylock's distress when his daughter Jessica decamps with family money and jewellery is mocked by Antonio's friend Solanio (2.8.15-16)

> My daughter! O, my ducats! O, my daughter!
> Fled with a Christian! O, my Christian ducats!

The most familiar foreign coin in circulation in Tudor England was the French *écu à la couronne*. It was known as the 'French crown' and distinguished by its yellow colour. Bottom in *A Midsummer Night's Dream* offers to discharge his part 'in your French-crown-coloured beard, your perfect yellow'. (1.2.86)

In *Timon of Athens* the monetary unit is the silver 'talent', although this refers to weight rather than value. The exiled half-naked Timon leaving his cave in the woods with a spade begins digging and finds something better than silver (4.3.25-26)

> What is here?
> Gold? Yellow, glittering, precious gold?

Another silver coin the 'thaler' (anglicised as 'dollar') originated from the Kingdom of Bohemia in 1525. It was legal tender in Scotland and is referred to in Macbeth.

> the Norways king craves composition;
> Nor would we deign him burial of his men
> Till he disbursèd at St Colum's inch
> Ten thousand dollars to our general use.

86

The Portuguese gold coin known as the 'crusado' is named in *Othello*. Desdemona is worried by the loss of her handkerchief (3.4.25-26)

> Believe me I had rather lost my purse
> Full of crusados.

A missing handkerchief that had dire consequences.

The Acting Profession

Orthodox Stratfordian opinion has always been on safe ground by asserting that the author of Shakespeare must also at some point in his career have been an actor. Theatrical imagery is abundant throughout the plays and is used with such telling authenticity that it would be perverse to deny that the author was writing from anything other than first-hand stage experience. How he acquired it is not known but since the indicators point to a palace insider as the writer known as William Shakespeare this would provide a valid explanation.

Queen Elizabeth liked to be entertained and it is known from the Revels Office records that lavish productions were staged at court to mark great state occasions. To perform an elaborate Masque would be an opportunity for sumptuous costumes with the latest in music, song and dance. This form of amateur dramatic entertainment was mainly confined to the houses of the nobility and the royal courts. For young courtiers this was a chance to dress up and take part, with advancement opportunities for those demonstrating talent in the performing arts. Given that the Shakespeare authorship mystery by its very nature invites speculation it may be permitted to suggest that the nurturing of his theatrical expertise could have originated in the masked and gowned extravaganzas in the royal courts.

No other writer has lauded the profession of acting so forcefully, or championed its ability to re-interpret the great deeds of history. In *Hamlet* the prince effusively welcomes the touring company of players (Act 2, Scene 2) and himself declaims part of a speech from their repertoire. Hamlet then instructs Polonius, Denmark's chief minister, to treat the actors with the dignity that he considers their due. 'Do ye hear? – Let them be well used, for they are the abstracts and brief chronicles of the time. After your death you were better have a bad epitaph than their ill report while you live'. (2.2.526-29). 'Use them after your own honour and dignity.' (2.2. 534). In the next act, when they are about to perform *The Murder of Gonzago* to a court audience, Hamlet directs how he wishes them, in exact detail, to present their play and deliver their lines. (3.2.1-35).

Consider also these words spoken by Cassius after the violent assassination of Julius Caesar. (*Julius Caesar* 3.1.112-14).

> How many ages hence
> Shall this our lofty scene be acted over,
> In states unborn and accents yet unknown!

In other words the ability to retell history, to make great men live again, to glorify their noble deeds and high aspirations, are skills greatly to be admired and actors therefore worthy of professional respect.

The Classical World

Look here upon this picture, and on this,
The counterfeit presentment of two brothers.
See what a grace was seated on this brow –
Hyperion's curls, the front of Jove himself,
An eye like Mars, to threaten or command,
A station like the herald Mercury
New lighted on a heaven-kissing hill
Hamlet 3.4.52-58

Although there are numerous classical allusions to be found dispersed through the corpus, with a scholarly consensus that they are used accurately and in context, they do not actually seem to have had much effect on the substance of the writing itself. Ovid's *Metamorphoses* in the 1567 translation by Arthur Golding is the source most commonly quoted for classical references but no single plot originated from the author's obviously close acquaintance with this long translation. The poet and critic Ezra Pound (1885-1972) praised the Golding translation for its narrative quality, saying he considered it 'the most beautiful book in the English language'. (*The ABC of Reading*, 1934).

That Shakespeare was most closely associated with the theatrical company known as Lord Chamberlain's Men is not disputed but as the name suggests their primary duty and source of income was to provide entertainment for the royal courts. The Queen and her immediate entourage were educated to a high standard, in languages most particularly, and so would have picked up the classical allusions in the plays. French was the language of diplomacy, Latin was the entry-level qualification for employment in the government service. English was gaining ground but graduates who sought to win royal approval needed to be proficient in these two essential languages. Ability to read classical literature in Greek as well as Latin was part of the Tudor meritocracy. The noted Greek scholar Roger Ascham (St John's College, Cambridge), became Princess Elizabeth's Greek and Latin tutor in 1548.

In Shakespeare the term 'classical' refers to plays whose subject matter has been drawn from classical sources and whose scenes are laid in ancient times. The question of how far classical mythology was based on reality is a difficult one with no generally agreed answer. Many of the myths could have originated from a grain of truth, now lost. Did the Trojan War actually take place? Probably not but it inspired some remarkable literature and has had a lasting influence.

A collected edition of Seneca's plays translated by Thomas Newton appeared in 1581 and so could have been drawn on by Shakespeare. The character of Lady Macbeth may well have been based on Seneca's *Medea*.

(Alternatively on Catherine de Medici, mother of King Henri III of France). In *Henry V* the king's tour of the English camp before the battle of Agincourt could have come from reading Tacitus, the *Annals*. This relates how Germanicus, a provincial governor and general in the reign of Tiberius, similarly infiltrated army ranks to gauge the level of morale before a battle. Bolingbroke suffering the pain of exile in *Richard II* is referenced from Cicero's *Tusculan Disputations*.

Troilus and Cresida and *Titus Andronicus* are plays which have much in common with the classical tradition and consequently have a high number of allusions. Ovid's *Metamorphoses* was the main source for Shakespeare's classical references, mostly from Arthur Golding's 1567 translation, although Latin scholars can pick up examples which derive from the original rather than the translation. *Antony and Cleopatra, Love's Labour's Lost, A Midsummer Night's Dream, Cymbeline, Coriolanus,* and *Romeo and Juliet* are plays also rich in classical allusions.

Antony and Cleopatra and *Julius Caesar* owe much to Thomas North's 1579 translation of Plutarch's *Lives*. North's translation was not directly from the original but from the 1565 translation into French by Jacques Amyot. North's version has been much praised for the style and clarity of its prose in English, from which was taken Shakespeare's description of Cleopatra's royal barge

> The barge she sat in, like a burnish'd throne
> Burned on the water: the poop was beaten gold;
> Purple the sails, and so perfumed that
> The winds were lovesick with them; the oars were silver,
> Which to the tune of flutes kept stroke, and made
> The water which they beat to follow faster,
> As amorous of their strokes. For her own person,
> It beggared all description: she did lie
> In her pavilion, cloth of gold, of tissue –
> O'er-picturing that Venus where we see
> The fancy outwork nature: on each side her
> Stood pretty dimpled boys, like smiling Cupids,
> With divers-coloured fans, whose wind did seem
> To glow the delicate cheeks which they did cool,
> And what they undid did.

Antony and Cleopatra 2.2.198-212

Shakespeare's play *Titus Andronicus* is seen as closest to the ethos to the classics, with the names of some minor characters drawn from Plutarch – Aemilius, Lucius, Marcus, Martius, Sempronius. In *The Comedy of Errors* the plot of the twins is derived from the *Menaechmi* of Plautus, the only Shakespeare play sourced from a comedy in Latin. The main plot of the *The Merry Wives of Windsor* features multiple suitors for Anne Page, with each of her parents favouring a different suitor, neither of which is chosen.

This engaging state of affairs is taken from *Casina*, a play by Plautus not at that time available in translation.

Othello's speech (3.3.456) beginning 'Like to the Pontic Sea', referring to the flow of water from the Black Sea, is taken from Pliny the Elder's *Natural History*. The source material for *Othello* would allow a date of composition for 1588 in which case the references would have been derived from the original in Latin as Philemon Holland's translation was not published until 1601. Ulysses' speech on degree (*Troilus* 2.3.193-98) is taken from Homer, the *Iliad*.

August Schlegel (1767-1845) achieved fame and success with his translations of Shakespeare's plays into German. These were so highly rated and taken up that Shakespeare was awarded the status of a German national poet, with admirers including Goethe and Beethoven. Schlegel's nephew Felix Mendelssohn composed the incidental music for *A Midsummer Night's Dream*, now as famous as the original play. Comparing Shakespeare to the classics Schlegel wrote of *Macbeth* 'since Aeschylus nothing so grand and terrible has ever been composed'. (*Lectures on Dramatic Art and Literature*, 1809).

The massive amount of research material on Shakespeare aggregated over very many years is impressive. Scholars of international renown have devoted their lives to trawling bygone literature in the hope of finding a word or phrase that can be linked to the plays. Although well-intentioned this exhaustive research reached the point where it became counter-productive, diminishing the author's reputation by creating the impression that he was a serial plagiarist and plunderer, incapable of original thought and dependent on others to provide inspiration. It is true for example that to write *Troilus and Cressida* he borrowed from Homer, Boccaccio and Chaucer but the resultant powerful masterwork was the product of his own creative genius.

Italian Comedy in Shakespeare

Discussing the Shakespeare authorship prompts many questions, most of them unanswerable, one of which is why there are so many Italian settings for the plays. No evidence has ever been produced to show that the Stratford man visited Italy or could read books written in Italian for which no translations into English had been made in his lifetime. Early biographies of the 'Bard' passed lightly over this considerable difficulty, implying either that it was of minimal significance or that to avoid treading on sensitive toes the settings had been tactfully transferred abroad, so that for Venice or Egypt or Denmark we should understand that the real location was actually London and therefore no first-hand knowledge of foreign parts was required.

When this explanation became increasingly hard to sustain some biographies began to consider the possibility that during Shakspere's so-called 'lost years' (his twenties) he might actually have visited Italy or learned to speak Italian. It was thought likely that he would have known John Florio (1553-1625) who was born in London of Italian parents and wrote a series of manuals for the study of Italian. Florio dedicated his Italian-English dictionary to Henry Wriothesley, the 3rd earl of Southampton, and this could have provided the connection because Shakespeare's two long narrative poems *Venus and Adonis* and *The Rape of Lucrece* were similarly dedicated to the earl. Florio himself was never known to have visited Italy but Stratfordians insist that the author could have obtained sufficient knowledge from him to account for the Italian content of the plays. Wells in his 2002 *Shakespeare: For All Time* and Wood in his 2003 *In Search of Shakespeare* simply ignore the problem of why there is so much Italian knowledge in the plays and mention Florio only as the translator of Montaigne's *Essays*.

Thirteen plays are set in Italy. Of these *Antony and Cleopatra, Coriolanus* and *Julius Caesar* are drawn from the classics. *Titus Andronicus* is set in Rome, the sources include Plutarch but otherwise remain vague. Other plays are set in the Italy of the period. Those from northern Italy are *Romeo and Juliet*, set in Verona, *Two Gentlemen of Verona* set partly in Verona and partly in Milan, *The Taming of the Shrew* in Padua, *The Merchant of Venice* in Venice, and *Othello*, subtitled *The Moor of Venice* partly in Venice and partly in Cyprus. *Much Ado About Nothing* is set in Messina in north eastern Sicily. *All's Well That Ends Well* is set partly in Florence.

A Midsummer's Night's Dream has the direction 'a wood near Athens' but is Italian in character. Richard Roe in his book *The Shakespeare Guide to Italy* argues for the small walled city of Sabbioneta as the setting for the play. Sabbioneta is some twenty-five miles southwest of Mantua and is described in tourist brochures as *La Picola Atena*, 'Little Athens'. Richard Roe also identifies the island Vulcano as the location for *The*

Tempest. This island is situated in the Tyrrhenian Sea about twenty miles north of Sicily and contains geographic features such as the sulphurous lakes and other evidence of ongoing volcanic activity mentioned in the play.

The texts of these plays contain references from books written in Italian for which no translations existed at that time. Bocccaccio's novella *Tito and Gisippo* is one example, cited by Geoffrey Bullough in his *Narrative and Dramatic Sources of Shakespeare* as a main source for *Two Gentlemen of Verona*. This text was not translated into English until 1620. Italian literary influence extends to the more serious plays, not just the comedies. Italian authors whose *commedia erudita* is considered by experts to have provided source material for Shakespeare, but which were not available in translation at the time, included Ludovico Ariosto (*The Tempest* and *The Taming of the Shrew*), Matteo Bandello (*Romeo and Juliet* and *Twelfth Night*), Giraldi Cinthio (*Othello* and *Measure for Measure*) and Ser Giovanni Fiorentino (*The Merchant of Venice* and *The Merry Wives of Windsor*).

Of particular interest is the influence of the form of Italian theatre tradition known as Commedia dell'Arte. The name apparently implies that it is a professional enterprise, literally 'show-business', with lively and colourful routines performed by versatile and accomplished actors, women as well as men. Although sometimes referred to disparagingly as 'street theatre' the small troupes of ten or a dozen performers preferred to be invited into large houses or a court to ensure a captive audience and to collect ticket money. The performances were not scripted and there was no stage director. Although the players were familiar with their roles the main requirement was for improvisation and spontaneity. Masked and costumed stock characters could be readily identified by the audience. Unmasked were the young lovers, and the basic plot situations usually revolved around their efforts to become better acquainted while the other characters did their best to keep them apart.

Whoever wrote Shakespeare must at some point have witnessed performances featuring these stock characters, if not in Italy perhaps at home in England. In 1573 a company of Italian actors toured the country but the nearest recorded performance to Stratford-upon-Avon was at Nottingham, sixty-eight miles to the north. If the nine year old William Shakspere had been taken to see the Italian actors they must have made a lasting impression on him as characters and situations derived from Commedia dell'Arte feature in several plays, most noticeably in *The Comedy of Errors*, *The Two Gentlemen of Verona*, *The Tempest* and *Love's Labour's Lost*.

Disagreeable old men feature prominently in Italian comedy. Known as 'Vecci', they often come in pairs and are usually intent on spoiling everyone else's fun, their daughters' fun in particular. Capulet and Montague in *Romeo and Juliet* would be one such pair, also Theseus and Egeus in *A Midsummer Night's Dream* and Brabantia and the Duke in

Othello. Vecci can be rich but are always miserly, often lecherous, or like Polonius in *Hamlet* senile and interfering. By tradition upper class speaking parts were in the Tuscan dialect and all the lovers were star-crossed, not just Romeo and Juliet. Other pairs would be similarly doomed, either by family enmity or incompatible social status. These include Silvia and Julia in *Two Gentlemen*, Helena and Hermia in the *Dream*, Katherine and Bianca in *The Shrew*, and Viola and Olivia in *Twelfth Night*. Shakespeare more than any other dramatist of the time used these *Commedia* pairings to provoke comic interplay such as cross-dressing and plot complication.

Zanni (Zany) characters are the distinguishing feature of Comedia dell'Arte. They are servants but always up to mischief. They caper, sing and play musical instruments and generally misbehave with anarchic energy. Feste the singing jester in *Twelfth Night* would fill the role of a Zanni character. The Dromio twins in *Comedy of Errors*, Speed and Launce in *Two Gentlemen*, Grumio and Curtis in *The Shrew*, and of course Bottom and his bumbling cronies in the *Dream*, would be other examples in Shakespeare. Servants can be loyal, as in Juliet's Nurse and Portia's Nerissa but also duplicitous as Borachio in *Much Ado*, Panthino in *Two Gentlemen*, Stephano and Trincolo in *Tempest*. Dogberry the incompetent official in *Much Ado* and Autolycus the talkative rogue in *Winter's Tale* would qualify as Zanni characters. The boastful but cowardly soldier *Il Capitano* would be Paroles in *All's Well*, Armado in *Love's Labour's Lost*, Sir Andrew Aguecheek in *Twelfth Night*, Falstaff in *Merry Wives* and *Henry IV*, Bardolph, Pistol and Nym in *HenryV*. Il Dottore (doctor) would include frauds and pedants such as Holofernes in *Love's Labour's Lost* and Sir Hugh Evans in *Merry Wives*.

The pan-European Renaissance originated in northern Italy, making it the favoured destination for those fortunate enough to be able to afford the time and expense of travelling there and back safely, which was not guaranteed in dangerous times. During the period when the plays would have been written, the end of the sixteenth and the beginning of the seventeenth century, many wealthy citizens and some members of Queen Elizabeth's court are known to have made the continental journey. From among this company could have come the writer of the plays of Shakespeare which are set in and around Italy.

Shakespeare's Clowns, Fools and Jesters

'Motley's the only wear' says Jaques in *As You Like It* (2.7.34). House-holds wealthy enough to support a jester were expected to do so, and these would include most of the settings for Shakespeare's plays. Rich families wanted to be entertained and a good court jester could keep everyone amused in a kind of perpetual background cabaret of dancing, juggling, pratfalls and waspish wit. Being constantly funny is hard work and the penalties for doing or saying the wrong thing in efforts to amuse could be severe. ('Take heed sirrah – the whip'. *King Lear* 1.4.104).

Dimwitted country bumpkin characters such as William in *As You Like It* and Costard in *Love's Labour's Lost* could only marginally be described as clowns. The singing rogue Autolycus in *The Winter's Tale* would qualify as a Shakespeare clown, and was given a good part to play. The Dromio twins in *The Comedy of Errors* clown to great advantage as servants in an amusing play. Launce and Speed in *The Two Gentlemen of Verona* are another pair of shifty servants. The porter in *Macbeth* and the two grave-diggers in *Hamlet* also act clownishly. Pompey in *Measure for Measure* acts as a domestic fool even though employed in a brothel. Lavatch in *All's Well* is another domestic fool but one with many bitter things to say. He is still less malevolent than Thersites in *Troilus and Cressida*, the least amusing of all the Shakespeare characters who could be classified as court jesters. Many a true word is spoken in jest and those who employed them were well aware that they were hearing unpalatable truths about themselves.

It was possible on the Elizabethan stage for a jester to become wealthy and famous, Richard Tarleton being the best known of his generation. Tarleton had no connections with Shakespeare and was not an associate of the Lord Chamberlain's Men, who became the King's Men under James I. Their top funny man was William Kemp. He too was a clever actor whose clowning stopped just short of buffoonery. Parts such as Bottom in *The Dream* and Falstaff in *Merry Wives* and the *Henry IV* plays could have been written with him in mind. Kemp was one of the original stakeholders in the newly built Globe Theatre but sold his shares in advance and left the company.

His place was taken by Robert Armin whose acting and singing skills and more cerebral nature are reflected in the calibre of the writing in the plays recognised as among Shakespeare's finest. In these the role of Fool, or Jester, was elevated to match the intellectual level of the main characters. They become participants as well as observers, assimilated into the drama while acting as its interpreter to the audience. Touchstone in *As You Like It* and Feste in *Twelfth Night*, are two of Shakespeare's most accomplished jesters. They were given a licence to be familiar with their betters but were skilled in knowing how far to go and no farther. The countess Olivia sums it up neatly. 'There is no slander in an allowed fool, though he do nothing but rail'. (*Twelfth Night* 1.5.89.90).

Modern society has more than its fair share of 'allowed fools'. Cartoonists and satirists of varying degrees of malice have punctured the mighty since the first journals and daily newspapers became part of everyday life. In film, television and theatre the traditions of slapstick comedy live on. Mockery of those rarely able to answer back has spawned the chat show format where nothing and no one is sacred. Poking fun at politicians and the royal family is a career path with a long and ignoble tradition. Those who wear the cap and bells today may be better educated and better paid than the Fools in Shakespeare's time but for most it still remains a demeaning profession.

In his touching devotion to his master the Fool in *King Lear* shares in the most poignant and tragic of all Shakespeare's relationships between master and servant. It is mutual. In the storm scene Lear comforts the younger man. 'How dost, my boy? Art cold?'. Only Cordelia is equally attentive and supporting of her father, although she and the Fool are never on stage together. Through his hour by hour descent into squalor and madness the loyalty of Lear's Fool remains steadfast. He is never given a name, appearing in the cast lists only as Lear's Fool. His remit was to act as Lear's spiritual alter-ego of conscience and reason in the most extreme of adverse circumstances for a humiliated king. Eventually they become separated but as he lies dying Lear's last thought is for his faithful companion, 'And my poor fool is hanged'. (5.3.300).

A case could be made that the character of Hamlet in *Hamlet* is Shakespeare's ultimate court jester, given a whole play in which to air his prejudices against the world in general and his relatives in particular. Whether or not his hallucinatory episodes are genuine or feigned his behaviour becomes increasingly chaotic and disruptive. Dressed in black for the king's wedding Hamlet casts himself as the villain of the piece and acts it out to the bitter end with glee and relish. A spectacularly violent scene of family annihilation winds up the action of Shakespeare's most famous play. Whoever wrote *Hamlet* certainly knew how to put on a show.

Shakespeare's Legal Knowledge

Sir George Greenwood (1850-1928) was a Middle Temple barrister who became a Member of Parliament (for Peterborough) as he neared retirement. As a practising lawyer he was intrigued by the legal content of the Shakespeare plays. Between 1908 and 1925 he wrote several books on the Shakespeare authorship mystery, mostly to demonstrate that the legal knowledge in the plays could only have been written someone who had trained in the law. *Shakespeare's Law* published in 1920 was his main work on this subject.

In addition to the books he was a prolific writer of letters to newspaper editors and had many articles published, all in support of his basic premise that the man from Stratford-upon-Avon could not have been the author of the plays. Surprisingly he never himself championed the cause of any of the main contenders. In 1922 he collaborated with Thomas Looney to found the Shakespeare Fellowship which has survived in various forms until the present day.

That legal terms or 'legalese' occur throughout the Shakespeare corpus is not controversial, they are too numerous to miss. The compilation by B J Sokol and Mary Sokol, *Shakespeare's Legal Language: A Dictionary*, runs to 500 pages. (London, The Athlone Press, 2000). Hamlet's graveside humour that the latest skull unearthed might be that of a lawyer would be one such example. 'Where be his quiddits now, his quillets, his cases, his tenures, and his tricks?' (*Hamlet* 5.1.96-109). Another mordant joke comes in Part 2 of *Henry VI* when Dick the butcher delivers his solution to the troubles of the day, 'The first thing we do let's kill all the lawyers'. (*2 Henry VI* 4.2.78).

The point at issue with those scholars defending the orthodox position is whether or not the lawyer jargon in the plays is used accurately. They maintain that similar usage of legal terms can be found in the works of contemporary writers, with equal levels of accuracy, and therefore Shakespeare's knowledge of the law was not exceptional and consequently had no bearing on the authorship. Whether this claim stands up to close scrutiny is another matter but Sir George Greenwood would seem to have the most widespread support for his contention that the legal terms were precisely used and in context. He maintained that Shakespeare was able to achieve this because these legal phrases were an integral part of his vocabulary and flowed out naturally as and when required by the exigencies of the plot.

The inference to be drawn from Greenwood's conclusions is that the actual writer of the plays could only have come from the echelon of society which sent its well-tutored sons to university as preparation for a professional career, including in the law. In England this would have required enrolment at one of the London Inns of Court. William Cecil, himself a lawyer (Gray's Inn), was Master of the Court of Wards, an elite institution preparing young men and boys of suitable social standing for a career in the government service. These fortunate students would from an early age have become familiar with the legal mind and the formal manner of speech. We hear it in every play.

Shakespeare's Medical Knowledge

Accounting for the medical knowledge in the plays has always been a problem, not just for those championing the case for the Stratford man but for all the other candidates caught up in the authorship mystery. At the time when the plays would have been written in the late sixteenth century, bridging over into the seventeenth, medical practice was still based on the ancient Greek model of Hippocrates and the second century teaching of Claudius Galene. He was also Greek but practised in Rome and through numerous treatises propounded a theory of medicine that remained unchanged for some 1,500 years.

The Renaissance brought new ideas to medicine, as it did to other fields of knowledge, but met stiff resistance. The Swiss-born physician Philip von Hohenheim (1493-1541), better known as Paracelsus, pioneered a new form of medical practice based on pharmacology. This required the administration of drugs for specific conditions, including calming medication for mentally disturbed patients. Paracelsus found a few willing disciples in London alert to the therapeutic potential of chemical compounds for conditions otherwise resisting treatment. Apothecaries prospered by morphing into dispensing chemists but Galenic practitioners diagnosing 'humours' and letting blood were not easily dislodged and the pace of change was slow.

So from where did Shakespeare obtain the extensive medical knowledge evident in the plays? Medical literature in English was almost non-existent at this time, nor was there a comprehensive history of medicine available in English until 1699 when a translation of Le Clerc's *L'Histoire du Phsyique* was published. Translations of books written in foreign languages began to appear in the 1580s, mostly from French and Italian originals. The best known and most influential of these was *The Newe Jewell of Health* translated by George Baker from the writings of Konrad Gesner at Zurich University. Baker was appointed as Queen Elizabeth's Sergeant-Surgeon, and after her death kept on as the King's Surgeon. In 1597 he was elected as Master of the Worshipful Company of Barber Surgeons so he was the top doctor at the time when the plays were written. There is a scholarly consensus that *The Newe Jewell of Health* could have been a main source of Shakespeare's medical knowledge.

The Scottish surgeon R. R. Simpson writing in 1959 identified over 700 documentable allusions to medical conditions in his book *Shakespeare and Medicine*, some of them of an abstruse nature implying advanced knowledge. For example a reference to the *pia mater* in *Love's Labour's Lost*. The term *pia mater* is applied to the innermost layer of the meninges, the membranes surrounding the brain and spinal cord. The eccentric scholar Holofernes boasts (4.2.66-71)

This is a gift that I have, simple, simple – a foolish extravagant spirit, full of forms, figures, shapes, objects, ideas, apprehensions, motions, revolutions. They are begot in the ventricle of memory, nourished in the womb of *pia mater*, and delivered upon the mellowing of occasion.

The reference to 'the ventricle of memory', has also been identified as strangely prescient. Shakespeare's apparent knowledge of specialised areas of neuro-surgery has aroused the curiosity of psychiatrists because the left ventricle is now implicated in the function of short term memory loss. The Australian psychiatrist Doctor Aubrey C. Kail wrote a comprehensive study *The Medical Mind of Shakespeare* in which he expresses surprise that for someone with no history of medical training the many references in the plays are not only extensive and accurate but contained medical knowledge only recently available at the time when the plays would have been written.

This applies most intriguingly in references to the circulation of the blood. The physician William Harvey (1578-1657) is credited with the first full explanation of how the arterial blood is pumped around the body by the opening and closing of valves. His paper was delivered to the College of Physicians in April 1616. He continued his experiments and in 1628 published his major work on the subject, *Exercitatio Anatomica de Motu Cordis et Sanguinis in Animalibus*, which roughly translates as 'On the Motion of the Heart and Blood'. His discovery that the pulsation of blood through the arteries to the brain was dependent on the contractions of the left ventricle was a major breakthrough in the study of the human heart. Opposition from the medical profession obliged him to publish his book abroad, in Frankfurt. The first translation into English (from the Latin) was not published until 1653. Harvey's findings were still not accepted at the time of his death in 1657.

This makes all the more remarkable references in Shakespeare's plays to the flow of blood around the body. While not suggesting that the author engaged in scientific experiments or undertook research it does argue for someone acquainted with current thinking on medical matters, including the human anatomy. These are some of the quotes

Coriolanus 1.1.138 Menenius
    Because I am the store house and the shop
    Of the whole body. But, if you do remember,
    I send it through the rivers of your blood
    Even to the court, the heart, to the seat of the brain;
    And through the cranks and offices of man
    The smallest nerves and small inferior veins

Julius Caesar 2.1.288-90 Brutus to Portia
    You are my true and honourable wife,

As dear to me as are the ruddy drops
That visit my sad heart.

2 Henry IV 5.2.129-30 Prince Harry
The tide of blood in me
Hath proudly flowed in vanity till now.

Hamlet 1.5.63-68 The Ghost describes how he was murdered by his
    brother
        in the porches of my ear did pour
The leperous distilment, whose effect
Holds such an enemy with the blood of man
That fast as quicksilver it courses through
The natural gates and alleys of the body

Measure for Measure 2.4.20 Angelo
Why does my blood thus muster to my heart?

Romeo and Juliet 4.2.95-97 Friar Laurence to Juliet
Take thou this vial, being then in bed,
And this distilling liquor drink thou off,
When presently through all thy veins shall run
A cold and drowsy humour; for no pulse
Shall keep his native process, but surcease

King John 3.3.43-45 King John
Or if that surly spirit, melancholy,
Had baked thy blood and made it heavy, thick,
Which else runs trickling up and down the veins

Aubrey Kail in *The Medical Mind of Shakespeare* devotes a whole chapter to *Timon of Athens* and the ravages of syphilis. This harsh play charts the rapid mental deterioration of the title character from ruinously profligate benefactor to pitiful beggar in the late stages of syphilis. The latter half of *Timon* is written in a seething welter of unflinching disgust. Formerly known as 'general paralysis of the insane', Timon's syphilitic afflictions are so accurately and painfully described that the writer must have seen sufferers for himself. Just as leprosy was brought to western Europe by returning Crusaders so syphilis was believed to have been brought back by returning sailors from the expeditions of Christopher Columbus. In common with other large towns and cities London offered hot tubs where victims could inhale mercury vapours to alleviate the symptoms.

In reproaches to two prostitutes Phrynia and Timandra for spreading the disease, Timon lists some of these symptoms

                    Consumption sow
In hollow bones of man, strike their sharp shins.
And mar man's spurring. Crack the lawyer's voice,
That he may never more false title plead
Nor sound his quillets shrilly. Hoar the flamen
That scolds against the quality of flesh
And not believes himself. Down with the nose,
Down with it flat; take the bridge quite away
Of him that his particular to foresee
Smells from the general weal.
Make curled pate ruffians bald
And let the unscarred braggarts of the war
Derive some pain from you.

Doctor Kail explains these veiled symptoms as the hollowing bones of the cranium, painful nodes on the shin bones, venereal ulceration of the larynx, white scaly skin eruptions and the loss of the nasal bones, one of the most hideous disfigurements of chronic syphilis. Last in the list come impotence and baldness which Kail states were only recently observed to be symptoms of syphilis at the time when the plays would have been written.

An earlier psychiatrist, Sir John Bucknill (1817-1897), was fascinated by the plays and impressed by their forcefulness of language, most of all by the 'extent and exactness' of their psychiatric knowledge. He wrote three books on the Shakespeare plays, *The Psychology of Shakespeare* published in 1859, *The Medical Knowledge of Shakespeare* in 1860 and *The Mad Folk of Shakespeare* in 1867. In addition he founded the *British Journal of Psychiatry* in 1853. It is still published monthly.

In *The Medical Knowledge of Shakespeare* he expresses astonishment that the author's descriptions of the 'diseases of the mind' were comparable with 'the most advanced science of the present day'. This is almost a quote from *Macbeth* (5.3.43-45). Macbeth asks the doctor why he cannot alleviate his wife's insomnia and hallucinations

        Canst thou not minister to a mind diseased,
        Pluck from the memory a rooted sorrow,
        Raze out the written troubles of the brain?

Bucknill writes that Shakespeare used medical terms with 'scientific strictness'. In *The Psychology of Shakespeare* he deals with specific characters in the plays and writes long case-study notes about them, calling them 'psychological essays'. These include studies of Constance, Hamlet, Jaques, King Lear, Macbeth, Malvolio, Ophelia and Timon.

Bucknill concentrates on mental illness, and the characters who suffer from depression or dementia. He writes

That abnormal states of mind were a favourite study of Shakespeare would be evident from the number of characters to which he has attributed them. On no other subject has he written with such mighty power.

Characters with a case history of mental disorder come to a long list, with depression as one of the most common conditions. Antonio (*Merchant of Venice*), Hamlet, Jaques, Orsino, Richard II, Romeo and Timon would serve as examples of characters suffering severe depression. Suicides include Brutus, Cassius, Cleopatra, Mark Antony and Romeo. The somnambulist Lady Macbeth goes mad, as does Ophelia. Those who hallucinate or see apparitions in dreams and visions include Brutus, Calpurnia, Hamlet, Queen Katherine, Macbeth, Posthumus and Richard III.

King Henry IV dies following an epileptic fit (*2 Henry IV*, 4.3.110-11).

> … my brain is giddy. O me! Come near me now. I am much ill.

Other characters afflicted with epilepsy include Julius Caesar, Macbeth and Othello. In the whole of literature there is no more harrowing study of an elderly man in mental distress than Shakespeare's King Lear. Symptoms of senile dementia are exhibited by King John and Shylock. Also Polonius, who struggles with short term memory loss (*Hamlet* 2.1.49-51).

> And then, sir, does a this – a does –
> what was I about to say? By the mass, I was about to say something.
> Where did I leave?

Yet Sir John Bucknill could not explain how the son of a 'wool-comber' (his term for John Shakspere) acquired such extensive medical knowledge. He concluded that Shakespeare must have been 'an insatiable devourer of books', which he says at that time would have needed to include medical treatises written in French. It never seems to have occurred to Sir John that someone other than the son of the 'wool-comber' might have written these extraordinary plays.

Shakespeare's Musical Knowledge

There is no religious music in Shakespeare, all the songs and settings are secular and sung in English. They contribute hugely to the success of the plays. To open a play with the words, 'If music be the food of love, play on,' as Shakespeare does in *Twelfth Night*, would suggest an author who was knowledgeable about music and alert to the many ways it could enhance a stage performance. Apart from *King John* and the third part of *Henry VI* all the plays have a musical content, mostly manifested as songs, of which there are just over a hundred. Other types of vocal music that appear in the plays include ditties, rounds, catches (an elementary form of canon), part-songs and serenades.

The ability to sing, or to play a musical instrument, was considered a legitimate accomplishment for the wealthy and their families, women as well as men. An example of music teaching comes in the third act of *The Taming of the Shrew* where Bianca, the supposedly docile younger sister of Katherine the Shrew, proves to be a spirited student playing off her two male teachers, who are also rivals for her affection. How to tune the lute, master the fingering, and learn the gamut (musical scale) are stage business smoothly inserted into the play as a seduction scene conducted with the best of good manners.

Many other Shakespeare plays are set in the grand houses of the wealthy where the presence of servants and the provision of music is an integral part of daily life. In *Troilus and Cressida* the character Pandarus accompanied by a servant are joined by Paris and Helen. They arrive 'attended by musicians'. Called on by Paris and Helen to sing, Pandarus commands a musician 'Give me an instrument'. This would most likely have been a lute and he accompanies himself in an erotic and cynical song beginning with the words 'Love, love, nothing but love'. Throughout the play Pandarus is portrayed as corrupt and deceitful so the song is in character. This would apply to most of the other songs in the Shakespeare canon which merge seamlessly into their plots and story lines.

In *Richard III* the recently crowned King Richard in his opening monologue refers disparagingly to those who caper nimbly in a lady's chamber 'to the lascivious pleasing of a lute'. Although mainly used for accompanying singers the lute could produce a sweetly melodic sound as a solo instrument. The lute remained the most favoured instrument for secular music until the end of the century when it was superseded by the viol in the early 1600s. The viol was played like a cello between the legs and could be bowed as well as plucked. There are many references to lutes in Shakespeare but mentions of viols are scarce, twice in *Pericles*, and once in *Richard II* 'an unstringed viol' (1.3.156). This could suggest that the greater part of the Shakespeare oeuvre had been written by the end of the sixteenth century.

Of the hundred or so songs in Shakespeare's plays nearly all were original, although some of the drinking songs in the Falstaff scenes bear resemblance to popular songs of the period. Many of the songs have become independently famous and profit from being sung by the professionally trained voice. 'Under the greenwood tree' and 'It was a lover and his lass' as examples, both from *As You Like It*. 'Sigh no more, ladies' in *Much Ado About Nothing*, 'Take, O, take those lips away' from *Measure for Measure*, 'O mistress mine' from *Twelfth Night* and 'Full Fathom Five' from *The Tempest* are some of the best known, and are regularly performed in song recitals.

In the plays the songs are mostly performed by the servant classes, men and boys, with the men designated in cast lists as fools, as in Lear's Fool, or clowns (Feste) or a rogue (Autolycus). The bawdy drinking songs in *Twelfth Night*, *Othello*, and *The Tempest* would suggest an author familiar with convivial low life in downtown Elizabethan London and elsewhere. The main male characters never sing but some of the most poignant songs are performed by aristocratic women. Ophelia when deranged is given some deeply moving lyrics to sing. In the first quarto of *Hamlet* the stage direction is given as 'Enter Ophelia playing on a lute, and her hair down, singing'. Desdemona's 'Willow' song just before her murder can be heart-breaking. Shakespeare's was an all-embracing talent.

The music of this Renaissance period bears little resemblance to the baroque and classical music which followed. Apart from trumpets and drums none of the modern musical instruments were available to professional musicians of the period. The entrance of a noble character on to the stage is presaged by a blast on the trumpet, mostly appearing in the directions as a 'Flourish'. These could be augmented for special occasions with drums and the addition of a hautboy, (an ancestor of the oboe). Othello bids farewell to war by listing the sounds he will never hear again, ' … the neighing steed and the shrill trump / the spirit-stirring drum, th'ear-piercing fife' (3.3.356-57).

Stage directions in *Romeo and Juliet* (1.5) help to set the scene where the lovers meet, 'Music plays, and the masquers, guests and gentlewomen dance'. In *The Merchant of Venice* the young aristocrat Lorenzo elopes with Jessica and arriving at Portia's house after the trial they speak words of love to one another in poetic language. The stage directions help to create the mood, 'Musician's arrive', followed by 'Musicians play'. Lorenzo takes advantage of the moment to beguile Jessica with words (5.1.54-57).

> How sweet the moonlight sleeps along this bank!
> Here will we sit, and let the sounds of music

> Creep in our ears. Soft stillness and the night
> Become the touches of sweet harmony

Trumpets, cornettos, and wailing hautboys presage bad news, for example in the banqueting scenes in *Titus Andronicus* and *Macbeth*. 'Hautboys play' is the stage direction that precedes the dumb show in *Hamlet*, the turning point of this most famous of all plays, capturing as it does 'the conscience of the King'. By contrast softly played viols, lutes and citterns (an elementary form of guitar for strumming an accompaniment to singers in a consort) are used therapeutically to induce calm and spirituality, for the benefit of young lovers most particularly.

Only two of Shakespeare's 154 sonnets have a musical content, Number 8 which is one of the so-called 'Procreation' group of sonnets, and Number 128 which is one of the so-called 'Dark Lady' group of sonnets. The musical imagery in 128 is highly sensuous, erotic even, but also carefully controlled, revealing little while hinting much. The writer recalls his feelings at watching a woman playing a keyboard instrument. This was most likely a virginals, in which the metal strings are plucked by wooden keys mounted on jacks. He remembers wistfully being aroused by the swaying of the woman's body as she used the keyboard, with the implication that she did so knowingly to ensure his attention, with the further implication that they were or had been lovers.

Sonnet 128

> How oft, when thou, my music, music play'st
> Upon that blessed wood whose motion sounds
> With thy sweet fingers when thou gently sway'st
> The wiry concord that mine ear confounds,
> Do I envy those jacks that nimble leap
> To kiss the tender inward of thy hand
> Whilst my poor lips, which should that harvest reap,
> At the wood's boldness by thee blushing stand!
> To be so tickled they would change their state
> And situation with those dancing chips
> O'er whom thy fingers walk with gentle gait,
> Making dead wood more blest than living lips.
>> Since saucy jacks so happy are in this,
>> Give them thy fingers, me thy lips to kiss.

The poem also holds out the possibility that they were not alone at these recitals which would most likely have taken place in the intimate setting of a small salon with other people present. It offers a rare and tantalising glimpse of how the real-life Shakespeare may have appeared to others in a gathering of friends. But who were they seeing? And by what name was he known to them? It is an enduring mystery.

Prayer Books and Bibles

As with religious art and architecture, those who fashioned the Book of Common Prayer, or made the translations of the Bible into English, considered it a privilege to serve their religion in this way and were motivated to do so to the highest possible standard. This devout piety was the midwife of some impressive literature. The Bible translations and the Anglican prayer book both have an association with the First Folio of Shakespeare which appeared soon afterwards. This is because all three contained texts which were intended to be performed: from the pulpit, from the altar and choir stalls, and from the stage.

The pleasing cadences of sound produced by these literary master-works when read aloud, chanted, sung or spoken by actors, lay in their rhythmic rise and fall as measured by the length of a human breath. This performance-based textual phrasing will always set these famous books apart as special and different. English as a dynamic and ever-evolving language has moved on since then but the high-minded timeless elegance of the King James Bible and the Book of Common Prayer will endure into the foreseeable future.

Thomas Cranmer (1489-1556) was responsible for compiling the first Book of Common Prayer. This was during the reign of King Edward VI, following the break from Rome. Banned during the reign of Mary Tudor the 1552 Cranmer version was reissued by Queen Elizabeth with some changes and again revised with additions by King James in 1604. The Anglican prayer book included the forms of service for morning and evening prayer, the Litany, and Holy Communion, the orders for baptism, confirmation, marriage, and the funeral service. It also set out the epistle and gospel readings for the Sunday communion service. Old Testament and New Testament readings for daily prayer were specified, as were the Psalms and canticles that were provided to be said or sung between the readings. After major revision in 1662 the Book of Common Prayer was again reissued and this edition remained the official prayer book of the Church of England for over three hundred years. A modernised version 'Common Worship' is now more widely used.

Richmond Noble, an American biblical scholar (Richmond Samuel Howe Noble, died 1940), in his 1935 book *Shakespeare's Biblical knowledge and the use of the Book of Common Prayer*, drew attention to the number of allusions drawn from the Psaltery. This refers to the 150 Psalms which form part of the Church of England's *Book of Common Prayer*. Noble extends this knowledge to the Latin titles of the psalms, which are still printed in the standard version of the prayer book. He speculated that Shakespeare may have acquired his excellent grasp of Latin more readily as a chorister than as a pupil at the Stratford-upon-Avon grammar school.

In Reformation Europe translating the Bible was a dangerous occupation, viewed with suspicion by the state as well as the church. A notable casualty was William Tyndale whose printed translation into English spread unwelcome ideas of social change across Europe, incurring the wrath of King Henry VIII in the process. Tyndale fled to the continent but was hunted down, imprisoned near Brussels, tried for heresy, then strangled and his body burned. Another translator, Myles Coverdale, spent much of his life in exile and so escaped the fate of Robert Barnes and Thomas Cranmer who were burned and Thomas Cromwell who was beheaded.

The so-called Matthew Bible was named after the translator Thomas Matthew and published in 1537. This was the first Bible in English to be translated from the original languages of Hebrew for the Old Testament and Greek for the New Testament, rather than taken from the increasingly unreliable Vulgate editions in Latin. No such person as Thomas Matthew existed, the real translator John Rogers prudently using Thomas Matthew as a pseudonym. This did not save him and he was 'tested by fire' at Smithfield on 4th February 1555, the first of Mary Tudor's many Protestant Martyrs.

Protestant exiles during Mary's reign made their way to Geneva in Switzerland and in 1560 produced a Bible in English which was then actively promoted and widely distributed. The printer and bookseller William Seres held a licence from Lord Burghley to sell religious books from a stall in St Paul's churchyard and this was the version of the Bible which was most widely available at the time when the plays of Shakespeare were being written. It was the first Bible to be printed in a Roman font and the first to be given numbered verses. The ease of reference this provided made it enduringly popular. It also contained maps, illustrations, indexes and scriptural study guides although some of these were removed in later editions.

Another American researcher, Professor Naseeb Shaheen of the University of Memphis, in his 800 page book *Biblical References in Shakespeare's Plays,* demonstrates how important the Scriptures were as a literary source for the author, second only to classical mythology in the number of allusions drawn on for the narrative poems and the plays. The various Bibles available at the time differed sufficiently from one another to be identifiable as sources in the many biblical references. Whoever wrote Shakespeare knew his Bible well, both Old and New Testaments.

Also the Apocrypha. At the trial scene in *The Merchant of Venice* when the case seems to be going his way Shylock praises Portia as 'a Daniel come to judgement'. When Portia grants him his pound of flesh but denies him 'one drop of Christian blood' Graziano taunts him with a counter-judgement from 'a second Daniel'. This is a reference from the *Book of Susanna,* one of the apocryphal books of the Old Testament. A woman falsely accused of adultery and condemned to death is reprieved by the intervention of a youthful advocate named Daniel and it is the accusers who suffer the punishment. (The Apocrypha was not officially excluded until 1885, reducing the Bible from 80 to 66 books). In the same play Shylock quotes from the New Testament with a reference to the Gadarene Swine. (1.3.31-2).

When King James succeeded to the throne in 1603 the Anglican clergy campaigned for a new Bible to replace the so-called 'Bishops Bible' of 1568, as new translations had become available. A fifty strong team of divines laboured for many years to produce what they considered to be the definitive edition of the Bible and it became known as the King James Authorized Version. This was published in 1611 and became the most widely produced book of all time, with over a billion copies printed worldwide. Even so the Protestant Geneva Bible was not easily displaced, it remained popular for many years and was the more widely used of the two in America.

Before Shaheen's scrupulous research, Noble also differentiated quotations which can be matched to the individual translations of the Bible available to Shakespeare. He expresses surprise that these do not include either the Douai Bible of 1609 or the Authorized Version of 1611. The Douai Bible was printed abroad (in Reims) by English Catholics in support of the Counter-Reformation. The inference to be drawn from Noble's observation is that the author of Shakespeare had either stopped writing or had died before the Douai of 1609 or the King James of 1611. This would apply to two of the contending alternative authors, Christopher Marlowe who died in 1593 and Edward de Vere the earl of Oxford who died in 1604.

Although the Shakespeare author was clearly familiar with all this Christian literature, and could quote and refer to it accurately, there is a surprising lack of religiosity in the plays. Mostly they are secular in approach, either to the exercise of governance or the administration of justice. As one who could see into the minds of men and women better than most, and could write about them sympathetically, the author comes across as mostly tolerant and forgiving in his accounts of human behaviour in all its many forms.

6 The Poetry

Pallas Athena
Venus and Adonis
The Rape of Lucrece
Willobie His Avisa
The Sonnets

Pallas Athena – The Spear Shaker

In Greek mythology Athena was the daughter of Zeus the mightiest of the gods and Metis the wisest of the gods, combining in herself their qualities of warlike strength and intellectual creativity. With Zeus and Apollo she forms the supreme triad in Greek mythology.

Athena's birth was dramatic, she burst from the head of Zeus with a terrifying battle cry, clad in full armour with helmet, shield and spear. Images of the goddess as warrior queen show her dressed in a Spartan tunic and cloak, wearing a gold helmet (it conferred invisibility) and carrying a round shield with the ugly decapitated head of Medusa in the centre (as a deterrent). More to the point she brandished a spear. A giant statue of Athena on top of the Acropolis (now lost) could be seen at a distance by homecoming Athenians from the sea, her golden helmet and the tip of her spear being first to catch the sunlight. One of the explanations for her adopted descriptive name 'Pallas' was its derivation from the Greek *pallein*, to brandish. (*The Penguin Book of Classical Myths*).

Most educated men in Elizabethan England, particularly those attending court, would have been familiar to some extent with popular Greek mythology, in which case the term 'shake-spear' would have triggered an image of Pallas Athene and her brandished spear. After this lapse in time it can only be a matter of speculation why the pen name 'William Shakespeare' was chosen but the link to Athena is well made. As the goddess of warfare she has always embodied male as well as

113

female attributes. As the exemplar of all intellectual pursuits, with a special care for oratory, poetry and philosophy, she would have been a natural choice for the polymath author of so many erudite plays. William (Wil-helm) might also suggest that her gold helm of invisibility would equate with anonymity, making it an even more apt choice as a pseudonym to front the plays and poetry.

Venus and Adonis

To the
Right Honourable Henry Wriothesly,
Earl of Southampton and Baron of Tichfield.
Right Honourable,

I know not how I shall offend in dedicating my unpolished
lines to your lordship, nor how the world will censure me for
choosing so strong a prop to support so weak a burden: Only,
if your honour seem but pleased, I account myself highly
praised, and vow to take advantage of all idle hours, till I have
honoured you with some graver labour. But if the first heir of
my invention prove deformed, I shall be sorry it had so noble a
god-father, and never after ear so barren a land, for fear it
yield me still so bad a harvest. I leave it to your honourable
survey, and your honour to your heart's content: which I wish
may always answer your wish, and the world's hopeful
expectation.
Your honour's in all duty,
William Shakespeare.

Henry Wriothesley the earl of Southampton was only nineteen when the long narrative poem *Venus and Adonis* was published in 1593. This was the first occasion on which the famous name of William Shakespeare appeared in print, although it should be noted, not on the title page but under the dedication. The much-quoted phrase 'the first heir of mine invention' in the dedication is unlikely to mean that it was the writer's first efforts at writing poetry but it could indicate that it was the first occasion on which the invented pen-name 'William Shakespeare' was openly used for a work of literature, all previous publications by the same author having been issued anonymously. It was used again for a second long poem *The Rape of Lucrece* a year later but after that not until Lord Burghley's death in 1598.

Without deducing too much from too little the felicity of language in this long narrative poem has to be considered as part of the authorship mystery. Few would disagree that this carefully constructed poem originated from the mind and pen of an experienced writer, one who was already a master of his craft, and certainly much older than the teenaged dedicatee Henry Wriothesley. The poem describes how the lovely Venus with her imploring outstretched arms tries to seduce the awkwardly seated Adonis, who leans away from her. In refusing to lay aside his hunting spear, or release the leashes from his dogs, he rejects her sexual advances, preferring to hunt for a wild boar instead. He is gored by the boar and dies, so the poem has a tragic outcome.

The poem is based on an Ovidian myth taken from Book 10 of the translation of the *Metamorphoses* by Arthur Golding. The excerpt is of 75 lines so the author of the poem expanded as well as adapted the myth in which Venus the goddess of love predicts but cannot prevent the death of her mortal lover, Adonis. The familiar Shakespearean anguish over unrequited love, as most famously expressed in the sonnets, is here reversed, since it is the woman and not the man who is rejected. A link could be made with Silvia in *The Two Gentlemen of Verona* who has to woo and pursue her reluctant and inept lover Valentine. The high quality of the writing in *Venus and Adonis* has always been admired for the intense mood of sensuality it conveys to the reader. The sensitive handling of erotic material and the descriptions of sexual excitement are nicely done. Urbane and sophisticated in tone, it also shows sympathy for the poignancy of unattainable love.

From an authorship viewpoint this deftly written narrative poem provides a benchmark of excellence relative to the date of 1593. Any play or part of a play or poem tested against *Venus and Adonis* could be roughly assessed on a 'before or after 1593' comparison for dating purposes. A virulent strain of the plague kept the London play-houses shut during the years 1592-94 so this long poem of 1,194 lines published in 1593 found a receptive home readership and went through many editions. It has never been out of print.

In Italy the peak year for the plague was 1576. One of the casualties, on 27th August that year aged eighty-eight, was the artist Tizianio Vecellio, anglicised as Titian. He had painted a series of Ovidian myths, including *Venus and Adonis.* This has resonance for the authorship debate since there is a strong possibility that the author of the poem had seen a version of this famous painting on view in Titian's studio, at his house in the northern Venetian suburb of Biri Grande.

The acknowledged original of the Titian art work *Venus and Adonis* is held in the Museo del Prado in Madrid. It depicts a bare-headed Adonis without his red hunter's cap and was painted in 1553 for Philip II of Spain to mark the occasion of his marriage to Mary Tudor, and sent ahead to London. When Philip left London in 1555 the painting went with his other possessions to the Low Countries, then under the control of the Spanish Habsburgs. A year later it reached the Prado where it has remained ever since.

Titian made five autograph replicas of Venus and Adonis (as distinct from copies made by students). Only one of these, the fifth, showed Adonis wearing the peaked cap referred to in Shakespeare's poem.

Line 339   And with his bonnet hides his angry brow
Line 1081   Bonnet or veil therefore hence no creature wear

This last replica was painted for the Holy Roman Emperor Charles V to hang in his picture gallery in Prague. It then passed into the ownership of Queen Christina of Sweden who brought it with her to Rome after her abdication in 1654. Successive royal owners took it to Paris and St Petersburg after which it was returned to Venice. As an item in the Torlonia collection it finally ended up in 1892 at the Palazzo Barberini in Rome, where it is currently still on view.

For anyone who has studied Shakespeare's poem, and then viewed the Barberini painting in Rome, or seen a full-length print of it, the correlation between the two is so remarkable that the only explanation which serves is for the author of the poem to have seen the painting for himself. After Adonis has met his death, shafted by a boar, Venus tearfully laments that he will no longer need the cap which protected his beautiful face from the wind and sun. The bright sun can be seen breaking through clouds in the top right corner of the painting and in lines 1087–88 she describes the peaked cap

> And therefore would he put his bonnet on,
> Under whose brim the gaudy sun would peep.

The Rape of Lucrece

To the
Right Honourable Henry Wriothesly,
Earl of Southampton and Baron of Tichfield.

The love I dedicate to your lordship is without end; whereof
this pamphlet, without beginning, is but a superfluous
moiety. The warrant I have of your honourable disposition,
not the worth of my untutored lines, makes it assured of
acceptance. What I have done is yours; what I have to do is
yours; being part in all I have, devoted yours. Were my worth
greater, my duty would show greater; meantime, as it is, it is
bound to your lordship, to whom I wish long life, still
lengthened with all happiness,

Your lordship's in all duty,

William Shakespeare.

The wording of the second dedication like the first is breezily self-confident while being at the same time ever so slightly condescending. This adds to the mystery which surrounds much of Shakespeare's work, his poetry in particular. These dedications are not obsequious appeals for cash from a journeyman wordsmith to a wealthy nobleman. It is Southampton himself who is being talked down to, which again is a problem, suggesting that the author was not only much older but of equal or higher status than the earl, in a society where high birth was venerated.

In the earlier dedication to *Venus and Adonis* the author promised to honour the earl next time with 'some graver labour'. This duly materialised a year later in 1594 with *The Rape of Lucrece*, a much more serious composition based on historical fact rather than classical myth. Sourced from Ovid's *Fasti*, his 'Book of Days', and from similar accounts by the historian Livy, Shakespeare's long poem relates the events leading to the downfall of the Tarquin dynasty and its replacement by the Roman Republic.

Sextus Tarquinius the third son of King Lucius Tarquinius is sexually aroused when his companions describe the beauty and purity of Lucretia, the wife of his cousin Collatinius. Failing to seduce her he resorts to force. Shamed, she stabs herself to death. Outraged by the rape, her husband's friend Lucius Junius Brutus rouses the common people and in 509 BC the king is overthrown and the monarchy replaced with a republic. *The Rape of Lucrece* was commercially successful with several editions published prior to the Restoration of 1660, after which it fell out of favour, in common with much other Elizabethan literature.

Shakespeare's ability as a dramatist to conjure great literature from small amounts of unpromising material is a remarkable feature of his writing. *The Rape of Lucrece* foreshadows Shakespeare's powerful full-length dramas set in ancient Rome, *Coriolanus* and *Julius Caesar* among them, featuring the dynastic struggles of the ruling families. History brought to life. More than this, the mental anguish suffered by Tarquin leading up to the rape is a precursor for the suicidal despair which haunts the great tragic characters in *Hamlet, King Lear, Macbeth* and *Othello*.

In another Shakespeare play, *Cymbeline*, the traducing of an innocent woman's reputation is a parallel theme. The duplicitous Giacomo boasts to the somewhat naive Posthumus that he would be able to seduce his wife Innogen. He infiltrates her bedchamber, smuggled inside a chest, and although he does not violate her body he is afterwards able to convince Posthumus that he did so (2.2.12-14).

> Our Tarquin thus
> Did softly press the rushes ere he wakened
> The chastity he wounded

The raped and mutilated Lavinia in *Titus Andronicus* is revenged by her family members. Her uncle Marcus makes the connection to Lucretia, '… that chaste dishonoured dame.' (4.1.89). As a poet and dramatist Shakespeare unflinchingly explores these adult themes and emotions emanating from the darkest corners of the human mind.

Willobie His Avisa

Willobie His Avisa is a long rhymed poem divided into seventy-two cantos. It was registered with the Stationers' Company on 3rd September 1594. It has been much studied because it contains oblique references to the authorship of Shakespeare's plays. The two long poems *Venus and Adonis* and *The Rape of Lucrece* written by William Shakespeare remain inextricably linked by their dedications to Henry Wriothesley, the third earl of Southampton. The initials WS and HW used in *Willobie His Avisa* by inference would seem to refer to Shakespeare and Southampton although this is by no means certain.

Avisa is the central character in the poem, ostensibly 'a chaste and constant wife' but one who nevertheless enters into an extra-marital relationship. Although deadly dull and poorly written this poem was reprinted six times between 1594 and 1635, which included being suppressed in 1599, with copies confiscated and burned. Why so unpopular with the authorities and so eagerly sought after by the reading public? The answer lies in the age-old battle between the ruling elite who wish to keep their affairs private and the unquenchable public interest in royalty and the goings-on at court. In this case both sides must have known something that we can only suspect at this distance in time, namely that the promiscuous Avisa was a woman near the queen, although not the queen herself.

Why the subterfuge? Because any writer found guilty of defamatory or seditious material could expect severe punishment, and not just a hefty fine but mutilation, dismemberment, even death. A pamphlet lampooning Queen Elizabeth or accusing her of sexual misconduct would be risky, to say the least, so it is understandable that the authorship of *Avisa* seems to have been deliberately obfuscated. Made-up names and misleading sets of initials would have effectively reduced the risk of being singled out for punishment.

The first recorded use of the name Shakespeare by anyone other than the author occurs in *Avisa*. It appears in the introductory poem regretting the scarcity of faithful wives, and is hyphenated as 'Shake-speare'. The quotation refers to Shakespeare's long poem *The Rape of Lucrece*, also published in 1594. The Roman consul Collatinius was the husband of Lucretia. She was raped by her husband's cousin Sextus Tarquinius, with far-reaching consequences.

> Though Collatine have deerely bought,
>   To high renowne, a lasting life,
> And found, that most in vaine have sought,
>   To have a Faire, and Constant wife,
>   Yet Tarquyne pluckt his glistering grape,
>   And Shake-speare, paints poor Lucrece rape.

The soldier-poet George Gascoigne (1535-1577) is credited with an early version of the poem in 1577, the same year as he died. The 1594 version was issued and probably written by Gascoigne's stepson Nicholas Breton. He named Henry Willobie as the author, with an introductory poem by Hadrian Dorrell. No trace has ever been found for anyone named Dorrell but there is an apparent identity borrowing for Willobie as there was a real life Henry Willobie (1574-1596). He entered St John's College, Oxford, completed his degree in 1595 and died at the age of twenty-two.

Breton updated *Willobie His Avisa* which was originally about Queen Elizabeth and her suitors. He made it topical, added some subtle allusions and changed the focus to indicate Elizabeth Trentham as Avisa. Elizabeth Trentham the second wife of Edward de Vere the earl of Oxford came from Staffordshire to be one of Queen Elizabeth's Maids of Honour. She was almost thirty before she became the new countess of Oxford, and was in her early thirties when she gave birth to Henry de Vere the future 18th earl of Oxford.

The literary device of writing in a moralistic and disapproving tone while at the same time slipping in salacious titbits of court gossip worked as well then as it does still. In the poem WS and HW are on friendly terms, with WS giving HW advice on how to seduce Avisa in a *ménage à trois* love triangle. Generations of literary scholars have trawled the Shakespeare sonnets, literally word by word, frustrated that the secrets they contain remain so obstinately concealed. *Willobie His Avisa* in a behind-the-hand stage whisper to the reader implies that the Countess and the much younger earl of Southampton shared an adulterous relationship, with baby Henry the Oxford son and heir born as the result.

Avisa may have been influenced by the anonymous play *The Taming of A Shrew*, also published in 1594. This resurfaced later in the 1623 First Folio as *The Taming of The Shrew* set in the Italian city of Padua but telling a similar story. A wealthy woman of strong character (Katherine) finally marries, but to an impoverished young nobleman (Petruccio) who makes no secret that he is in urgent need of a rich wife. 'I come to wive it wealthily in Padua.' (1.2.74). Substituting the heiress Elizabeth Trentham and the insolvent Edward de Vere makes a persuasive comparison. Portia and Bassanio in *The Merchant of Venice* would make a similar pairing. George Gascoigne's play, *The Supposes*, performed at Gray's Inn, is also considered to be among the sources for the later *The Taming of The Shrew*. This Italian style play was derived from Ludovico Ariosto's prose work *Suppositi*, supplying Lucentio and Bianca as a sub-plot.

If WS was Shakespeare the question may be asked, who then was the cuckolded husband of Elizabeth Trentham? As with other fleeting references to a real live author they stop just short of telling us what we want to know.

The Shakespeare Sonnets

```
TO.THE.ONLIE.BEGETTER.OF.
THESE.INSVING.SONNETS.
Mr. W. H. ALL.HAPPINESSE.
AND.THAT.ETERNITIE.
PROMISED.

BY.

OVR.EVER-LIVING.POET.

WISHETH.

THE.WELL-WISHING.
ADVENTVRER.IN.
SETTING.
FORTH.


T. T.
```

The world of literary scholarship remains permanently intrigued by the Shakespeare sonnets, guessing that they conceal a mystery yet to be discovered. Even if considered independently of the plays these 154 short poems would still be a significant literary offering. Many writers have established a reputation on less. That the identity of the person responsible for these literary masterworks should remain obscured is hard to understand or explain. Yet such is the case and the sonnets, so frankly written, so personal in content, keep their secrets still.

And of secrets there are many. The earliest mention of the sonnets is by Francis Meres in his 1598 book *Palladis Tamia* (translates as 'Wits Treasury') , which attempts to match contemporary poets, writers and painters with their classical counterparts. Meres was a young clergyman who left London soon afterwards for a living in Rutland but achieved lasting fame as the first person to name Shakespeare in print as a playwright.

Meres published examples rather than complete lists for the poets, playwrights and painters featured in his book, grouped in that order. Some seventy contemporary writers are featured, mostly with full names and titles. Meres was quick to claim acquaintance with his subjects, as in 'my friend Master Richard Barnfield' (a poet), less so with the nine entries for Shakespeare which all lack 'William' and give no indication that Meres knew anything about him other than his surname. (Michael Drayton has the most with twelve mentions). At the time of publication in 1598 the Stratford man would have been thirty-four so it was certainly possible for him to have been the author of the twelve plays listed in the review. One of the comedies ascribed to him was *Love's Labour's Won*, a play of which there is no trace.

More enigmatically, included in the entry for Shakespeare, Meres refers to '... his sugared sonnets [circulated] among his private friends'. Who were these friends? And how reliable was Meres who must have known something many others didn't. The sonnets were not published for another eleven years, no other earlier references to them have been found, so Meres was obviously well informed and close to the scene.

The sonnets were first published on 20th May 1609 by Thomas Thorpe but how he acquired them and from whom is unknown, with the implication that he may have done so unscrupulously. His quarto edition ended with the long poem *A Lover's Complaint*, now accepted as also written by Shakespeare. The title page dedication to a 'Mr. W. H.' has defied centuries of speculation about this person's identity and is no nearer to being resolved. Thorpe also refers to the writer as 'our ever-living poet', the publishing convention used for the work of a writer who had recently died. This has always presented a problem for those defending the attribution to the man from Stratford-upon-Avon as he did not die until 1616.

The sonnets in their accepted ordering were next published in 1640, although Sonnets 138 and 144 had previously appeared in a 1599 anthology *The Passionate Pilgrim*. The sonnet form is also used in the plays, most notably in *Romeo and Juliet* and *Love's Labour's Lost*. The sonnets are mostly constructed from three quatrains with a final couplet, all in iambic pentameter, the meter used most extensively in the Shakespeare plays. The rhyming scheme for these is *abab cdcd efef gg*. Wordsworth criticised Shakespeare for not adhering closely enough to this classical form. Sonnet 145 would serve as an example. Apart from being not quite up to the literary standard of the other sonnets it is written in tetramaters, four iambic feet.

In common with the plays of Shakespeare the sonnets were not fully appreciated until the late nineteenth century. The plays are written indirectly in the third person tense and contain few topical allusions that might help to identify the author. The sonnets are more directly spoken as a first person narrative and so might be considered as autobiographical but whether deliberately or by mischance they too contain no conclusive identity clues. Nor are the sonnets uniformly sequential or chronological, there is much juxtaposition of theme and content in the numbering. Intensive literary analysis of the sonnets by generations of scholars has gleaned little beyond what is evident from the page.

The largest group are the 'Fair Youth' Sonnets 1-126, in which the writer addresses affectionate remarks to a much younger man. A scholarly consensus identifies Henry Wriothesley as the 'Fair Youth' addressed in the sonnets. He was the third earl of Southampton and sixteen years before the publication of the sonnets had been the dedicatee of Shakespeare's two long poems *Venus and Adonis* and *The Rape of Lucrece*, hence the connection. Some scholars favour William Herbert as the fair youth. As the third earl of Pembroke he was one of the dedicatees of the First Folio, his brother Philip Herbert being the other.

The 'Rival Poet' sonnets 76-86 come within the longer sequence. In these the writer is aware that he has competition for the affections of the young man and seems reconciled to losing out to his rival. The 'Dark Lady' features in sonnets 127-152, and unveils violent conflicting emotions in the writer. Fascination, disgust and rejection make these poems uncomfortable reading. Sonnet 147 is particularly anguished and strongly written. As the nation's principal seaport London was home to many expatriate merchant families from the eastern Mediterranean and so could have provided a woman of dark complexion. No such woman has ever been identified and so must remain yet another unsolved part of the Shakespeare authorship mystery. The last two sonnets 153 and 154 refer to the therapeutic benefit of hot tubs, services provided in most big cities including London.

The ostensibly homoerotic content of the 'Fair Young Man' sonnets is hard to reconcile with the generally heterosexual orientation in the plays, and prompts the need for an explanation. The low numbered sonnets 1-17 are couched in loving but reproachful terms and have become known as the 'Procreation Sonnets'. In them the writer appears to be acutely and painfully aware of the fragility of human life, the transience of beauty and the ravages of time. He urges the young man to immortalise himself by marrying and having children. 'Make thee another self for love of me' (Sonnet 10).

Could this suggest that they were father and son rather than gay lovers? Awkward phrases such as 'my lovely boy' (126) would fall into place, if so. Who else but an ageing man would yearn for a grandson? And even more so if the writer as well as the recipient was a nobleman with much to gain or lose in the inheritance stakes. The second earl of Southampton had been suspected of Catholic sympathies, which included complicity in the Ridolfi plot to murder Queen Elizabeth, and was imprisoned in the Tower of London at a time when his heir Henry the third earl would have needed to be conceived. He was also estranged from his wife, Mary Brown, so the circumstances existed which could have made her adultery possible. There is no evidence that the countess had a love affair with another member of the court but such a liaison could provide an explanation for the otherwise impenetrable nature of some of the lower numbered sonnets.

The orthodox Stratfordian approach which favours the prosperous Warwickshire grain trader as the author of Shakespeare's plays is less assertive about the sonnets which tend to be discreetly side-lined in most biographical accounts of Shakespeare's life, almost as if they were an embarrassment. Understandably so. These self-revelatory poems conjure up an older, reclusive and deeply troubled man. They cannot be matched in any meaningful way to Shakspere from Stratford-upon-Avon. They speak in the most personal terms of sex, secrets, unrequited love, lust and betrayal, scandal and disgrace.

Sonnet 29 opens with the line, 'When, in disgrace with fortune and men's eyes'. Sonnet 37 contains the line, 'So then I am not lame, poor, nor despised'. Sonnet 112 contains the line, 'Which vulgar scandal stamped upon my brow'. Sonnet 121 opens with the line, ''Tis better to be vile than vile esteemed'. This low self-worth which permeates so many of the sonnets is specifically directed at the author's wish for anonymity. He neither wanted nor expected his name to be remembered. He was profoundly aware of his genius as a writer but was reconciled to an inevitable outcome, that his works would immortalise others but not himself. 'My name be buried where my body is', from Sonnet 72 perpetuates this sense of nihilistic resignation to a predetermined fate, that he was doomed to obscurity after death. Since this is exactly how it worked out in practice Sonnet 81 on the same theme deserves to be quoted in full

Sonnet 81

Or I shall live your epitaph to make,
Or you survive while I in earth am rotten.
From hence your memory death cannot take,
Although in me each part shall be forgotten.
Your name from hence immortal life shall have,
Though I, once gone, to all the world must die.
The earth can yield me but a common grave
When you entombèd in men's eyes shall die.
Your monument shall be my gentle verse,
Which eyes not yet created shall o'er-read,
And tongues to be your being shall rehearse
When all the breathers of this world are dead.
    You still shall live – such virtue hath my pen –
    Where breath most breathes, even in the mouths of men.

No comparable writer has bared his soul so comprehensively in print or shared his struggle with the dark complexity of human relationships. The level of metropolitan sophistication evident in these exquisitely crafted poems point to a highly cultured and melancholic aristocrat with the time and means to write these deeply psychological cries from the heart.

7　The Plays

Influences on Shakespeare
Montaigne's Essays
The Case for Shakespeare as Collaborator
Notes on the plays – in First Folio Order

Influences on Shakespeare

Tracing the back stories of plays to find a literary source has always been hindered by the Stratford man's lack of a formal education. Classical texts providing the sources were written in either Latin or Greek, many of them only available in the country of origin. Few of them had been translated into English at the period when the plays would have been written, the last decades of the sixteenth century and the early years of the seventeenth century.

Contemporary texts in European languages, mostly French and Italian, have provided many of the plots, settings, characters and general inspireation for the more cosmopolitan of the Shakespeare plays, and much of the verse. Stratfordians insist that their man must somehow have acquired the polyglot level of education needed to read and comprehend these texts but it is difficult to see how. Only the universities or the courts, and the libraries that went with them, could have provided it, or failing these, receiving some form of expensive private tuition. No such evidence exists.

No date of first writing can be confirmed for any of the plays. Dates of first performance exist for some of the plays but few can be quoted with certainty, particularly those staged in the royal palaces or at the Inns of Court where few records have survived. The London publishing industry was still some distance away in time so the registration and publication dates of individual plays cannot be completely relied on. To dodge licence fees, or the censor, cheap quarto editions could be slipped through with a note on the title page to the effect that they had already been performed at court and so did not need further scrutiny. In the years following the First Folio of 1623 many Shakespeare plays were adapted, abridged or pirated, making life difficult for literary researchers.

Stratfordian dating structure remains grounded on an author born in 1564. When considering which writers influenced which, this year of birth puts Shakespeare on the receiving end. It suggests that he routinely sought help and advice from established writers, John Lyly and Christopher Marlowe as examples, and was influenced by them. This remains the default position in literary orthodoxy as set out at length in *Shakespeare Beyond Doubt*, a collection of essays published in 2013 and edited by Paul Edmondson and Stanley Wells.

It should not be necessary to labour this point but it is an important point. Students of English literature for very many years have been taught that Shakespeare's plots, settings and characters were seldom his own original work but sourced from the writings of others, either from literature in foreign languages or from his university-educated fellow writers. Independent scholars who openly doubt that the Warwickshire man wrote the plays (Baconians, Derbyites, Marlovians, Nevillites, Oxfordians et al) maintain that Shakespeare was mostly the originator and not the borrower. Which would make more sense, given his stature as the one true genius of English Renaissance literature.

The tenacity displayed by researchers over many years is remarkable, their diligence and application in reading through obscure texts in search of clues can only be admired. Yet their trawls for classical allusions, or for parallel word clusters by other writers, have become ever more tenuous and remote. Their value to our understanding of Shakespeare is rarely demonstrated. Even when sources are identified and quoted there is no proof that the person who wrote Shakespeare had access to the books in question, or that he actually used them in his plays and poetry.

Montaigne's *Essays*

The French aristocrat Michel de Montaigne (1533-1592) was a contemporary writer with a discernible influence on Shakespeare. Muir refers to him as Shakespeare's 'kindred spirit'. As a natural psychologist of great insight and learning he was able to encapsulate his own highly personalised view on the world around him into a series of discursive essays across a broad range of interests. Although considered principally as a writer Montaigne's stature as a humanist and moral philosopher with an interest in the natural sciences elevates him to the level of an original thinker of the first magnitude in Renaissance Europe. The comparison with Shakespeare is well made.

The four Shakespeare plays which contain quotable references from the essays occur in *Hamlet*, *King Lear*, *Timon of Athens* and *The Tempest*. The crossover references and word clusters lifted from Montaigne are not contested, the issue when considering them in relationship to the authorship mystery is calendrical. *Hamlet* was registered with the Stationers Company on 26th July 1602 but the translation from French into English by John Florio (1553-1625) was not published until 1603. Montaigne's *Essays* in their original language had been available in London since 1580 which raises the question as to whether or not, or how well, the author of Shakespeare could read and understand philosophical essays written in French. Wells and Taylor in their Textual Companion get round this awkward problem by maintaining that 'Florio clearly existed in manuscript years before it was published'.

Shakespeare's primacy as an original poet, dramatist, historian, libertarian, moralist and philosopher is seldom contested but the extent to which he was influenced by Montaigne, by the Frenchman's astringent scepticism in particular, is less often mentioned. Much of Hamlet's philosophising seems to have been inspired by reading Montaigne and the combination of his ideas expressed in Shakespeare's words make for great literature. For both a preoccupation with the brevity of life and the certainty of death is a feature of their writing. Hamlet expresses it thus, immediately before the fatal duel with Laertes.   (5.2.165-67)

We defy augury. There's a special providence in the fall of a sparrow. If it be now, tis not to come. If it be not to come, it will be now. If it be not now, yet it will come. The readiness is all.

Shakespeare as Collaborator

Edmond Malone's attempts to establish a chronology for the plays has been replicated by all the main Shakespearean scholars, with equal lack of success. E.K. Chambers in 1930 produced metrical league tables for the plays based on the proportion of prose, rhyme, blank verse, weak and feminine endings but came no nearer a reliable dating sequence. Wells & Taylor in 1987 produced similar tables based on the incidence of colloquialisms in verse, 't i'th' o'th' th' 'em 'll as examples, but again without positive results. Sophisticated modern computing power has been used to trawl the Shakespeare texts for rare word use, contractions, first words, word length, syllables per word, use of rhyme, proportion of verse to prose, lines with an eleventh syllable or Latinised grammatical constructions but have still failed to do any better in plotting a sequence for the plays.

Computer expertise is claimed to have had more success in identifying lines of texts included in the Shakespeare canon but which were possibly written by others. Attribution Studies (collaboration writ large) has an agenda with relevance to the authorship debate, seemingly to demystify the cult status long enjoyed by William Shakespeare. The perceived intention is to reduce him to more human dimensions, repositioning him as a competent working dramatist writing to order, collaborating with others as and when required by the theatre owners.

Sir Brian Vickers has long been the most forceful advocate for the co-authorship of some of the lesser-known and less frequently performed Shakespeare plays. (Vickers, Brian, *Shakespeare, Co-Author*, OUP 2002). He is scornful of those who are '… determined to cling at all costs to the post-Romantic image of Shakespeare as a solitary genius having no need of aid from lesser mortals'. To those many who still hold to this view it seems a strange reversal of opinion to come from the Stratfordian corner. Until recent times unstinted admiration for Shakespeare was the order of the day. Now we are asked to believe that he was just one among many jobbing London wordsmiths paid by the hour to cobble together play-scripts for theatre bosses such as Francis Langley and Philip Henslowe.

Interpolations are discernible in several of the plays but these could have been added at any stage and cannot be considered as having been intentionally written as a partnership exercise. Plays can be started by one writer and completed by another with no need for the revising or secondary author to have known the original author personally. What appears to be interpolation is often the author revising his own work. Wells and Taylor in their *Textual Companion* write 'Editors and critics have long resisted the obvious conclusion, that Shakespeare occasionally, perhaps habitually, revised his work'.

Those who support the notion that co-authorship was common practice in the early theatre cite Henslowe whose accounts contain examples of plays with more than one author. The scholar Peter Kirwan quoted in *Shakespeare Beyond Doubt* writes on page 184, 'The idea of a single artistic mind presiding over a whole body of work is at odds with the very nature of professional theatre'. This remark would be equally contentious if applied to any art form where the single prepared mind so often flourishes. It prompts the question to ask what, exactly, is meant by 'collaboration'? Are we to imagine Marlowe and Jonson et al sitting round a table and having a script conference? One contributing the plot, another the jokes, someone else to sparkle up the dialogue? It is hard to believe and seems unlikely.

Professor Gary Taylor, a Shakespeare editor with the Oxford University Press, mentioned above, argues strongly in support of the case for Shakespeare as an author who routinely collaborated with others. In *Shakespeare Beyond Doubt* he writes, 'Shakespeare was a star, but he was also a team player. He formed temporary partnerships with other professional playwrights to work on specific projects. For instance he teamed up with George Peele to write *Titus Andronicus*. At least three different writers got together to produce *Henry VI Part 1*: Thomas Nashe, Christopher Marlowe and Shakespeare. He paired with Thomas Middleton on *Timon of Athens*, with George Wilkins on *Pericles*, with John Fletcher on *Cardenio*, *All is True* and *The Two Noble Kinsmen*'. Professor Taylor adds a surprising statement: 'None of Shakespeare's plays is the product of an isolated genius'.

The examples he puts forward are based on a wide spectrum of stylistic analyses which must be considered seriously because of the detailed knowledge of the texts needed to reach these conclusions. Yet stylometric evidence similarly applied by other experts in the field has reached contradictory conclusions, which brings into doubt the reliability of this method of research. Computers are good at what they do, data can be endlessly sorted and listed, but it is doubtful if computational stylistics has added anything of value to our comprehension and intellectual appreciation of the Shakespeare plays and poetry. There is no reliable documentary or bibliographic evidence that Shakespeare 'teamed up' with any of the writers named by Professor Taylor, either willingly or otherwise.

Professor John Jowett, another Shakespeare editor, has his own list of possible collaborators. 'The dramatists with whom Shakespeare almost certainly or probably worked [with] who can be named include Christopher Marlowe, George Peele, Henry Chettle, Thomas Dekker, Thomas Heywood, Thomas Middleton, George Wilkins and John Fletcher. If Shakespeare revised *The Spanish Tragedy* [by Thomas Kyd] he worked on a play that was also revised by Ben Jonson'. Jowett continues, 'Careful scrutiny of the Shakespeare collaborations shows him as both writing a draft for someone else to complete (as is clearly seen only in *Timon of Athens*) and (as is more common with Shakespeare) completing a play begun by another dramatist. Elsewhere, he interacts closely with fellow-dramatists in such a way as to suggest unsequenced co-writing'. In his notes to *Sir Thomas More* in the 2005 Oxford Complete Works, Jowett writes, 'Shakespeare's authorship of the majority of Sc. 6 has been accepted by most scholars ... His contribution shows him as a thoroughgoing professional sharing with colleagues whose work he respected in an essentially collaborative enterprise'.

This is the point of departure for dissenting scholars (Baconians, Marlovians and Oxfordians among them) who continue to doubt that the Warwickshire businessman William Shakspere wrote the plays of Shakespeare, even in the baffling form of 'unsequenced co-writing' as suggested by Professor Jowett. These opposing scholars maintain there is no evidence that the author of the plays collaborated with anyone. Not one item of correspondence passing between Shakespeare and any of the collegiate authors listed above has ever been found, nor one word from any of the printers, publishers and booksellers in literary London that would show how collaboration worked in practice.

Professor Lukas Erne in his 2003 monograph *Shakespeare as Literary Dramatist* argues that Shakespeare first prepared his plays for the stage and then later revised and adapted them for the printing press. If so it would render futile computer analysis based on changes of style alone.

Notes on the individual plays with relevance to the authorship come next, in First Folio order. References are to Geoffrey Bullough's *Narrative and Dramatic Sources of Shakespeare* and Kenneth Muir's *The Sources of Shakespeare's Plays*.

The Tempest

This is one of the eighteen plays in the First Folio of 1623 which had not been previously registered with the Stationers' Company, although there is record of a performance at court in 1611. Another play *The Spanish Maze*, possibly an earlier version of *The Tempest*, was performed in 1604. The plays in the First Folio were arranged into three separately numbered sections, named as Comedies, Histories and Tragedies. These were roughly chronological. *The Tempest* was the first play in the Comedies section and consequently the opening play of the entire First Folio compilation, which would suggest that the editors considered it to be an early play. Prospero's family-history lecture to his teenage daughter Miranda could have been infiltrated more skilfully, which might point to an early date of composition, perhaps with later revision.

The Tempest observes the unity of space and time, as does *The Comedy of Errors*, in both the stage action is played through in a single sequence. The other plays have dynamic staging where locations interchange or go backwards and forwards in time. Long running enmity between the rival noble families of Milan and Naples led to the exile of the Duke of Milan to an island. Richard Roe in *Shakespeare in Italy* makes the case for Vulcano, a volcanic island off the north coast of Sicily.

The duke, named Prospero in the play, has spent twelve years plotting revenge against his treacherous brother Antonio, and his enemy Alonso the King of Naples. As Prospero he has reinvented himself as a wizard and with his supernatural powers arranges for his erstwhile enemies to be shipwrecked on his island where he subjects them to a series of indignities. Stories about wizards are always popular, then as now, so *The Tempest* is regularly performed and admired for its eccentric mix of strange characters. Prospero himself remains one of the least likeable of Shakespeare's main protagonists, an embittered and self-pitying man whose deep depression fails to lift even after his revenge is worked through at the end of the play.

Who could have written *The Tempest*? Traces of the popular Italian theatrical form known as *commedia dell'arte* based around stock characters can be found in this play. This would incline towards a writer who had seen performances in the main squares and palaces of Italian cities, and who had some understanding of the Italian language. Literary sources would include scenes from Virgil's *Aeneid*, Ovid's *Metamorphoses* and Montaigne's *Essays*. For an author competent in Latin and French all these were available by 1580. This would support the case for an author born earlier than 1564.

The Two Gentlemen of Verona

This is another of the eighteen plays in the First Folio of 1623 which had not been previously registered with the Stationers' Company. *Two Gentlemen* has the smallest cast list of all Shakespeare's plays. It is generally agreed to be an early work, lacking the certainty of technique and the felicity of language found in the later plays. This presents difficulties for traditionalists supporting an author born in 1564. How early is early? The most commonly cited date is 1590 but the sure touch in *Venus and Adonis* published in 1593, if used as a benchmark, would put the composition of *Two Gentlemen* before this by many years. The Wells and Taylor 2005 edition of *The Complete Works* avoids the difficulty by offering no date of composition for this play.

A parallel difficulty arises when assigning an author to a play set in Italy, with Italian characters. These include Speed and Launce, two servants in the Zany tradition of *commedia dell'arte*. The play also contains geographical details that could only originate from someone with first-hand knowledge of northern Italy. This would include the network of canals on the Lombardy plain which made possible the journey between Verona and Milan, two inland cities, entirely by boat. The plotting tradition of a woman coming between two close male friends is well worked out with a go-between maid and a young lady aristocrat cross-dressed in disguise as a man. This play also contains the much admired song 'Who is Silvia?' She is the daughter of the Duke of Milan so everything comes out right in the end.

Bullough cites the 1559 Spanish prose romance *Diana Enamorada* by Jorge de Montemayor as the closest source, also Boccaccio's novella *Tito and Gisippo*. This narrows the authorship search to someone with access to books in foreign languages, and who had acquired some historical and topographical knowledge of the area by visiting northern Italy.

The Merry Wives of Windsor

The Merry Wives of Windsor has the highest proportion of prose writing in any Shakespeare play. It is the only play in the Comedies section which does not have a foreign setting, and is the only play in the canon devoid of ennobled characters. Instead we have a prosperous bourgeoisie. George Page and Frank Ford, the two husbands of the 'merry' wives, are owners of property, their friends include Doctor Caius a physician, Robert Shallow a Justice and Sir Hugh Evans a clergyman and schoolmaster. Sir John Falstaff is also a knight and Fenton the successful suitor for the spirited Anne Page has the swagger of an aristocrat, even if an impecunious one in search of a well-endowed wife.

The presence of Falstaff in this play is problematical. He bears little resemblance to the rumbustious character in the two *Henry IV* plays and the question of whether *Merry Wives* was written before, during or after them is still hotly debated by Shakespeare scholars. As a play it succeeds, with plenty of energetic stage business to entertain an audience. Falstaff is seeking sexual relief but his clumsy approaches to the two wives, Mistress Page and Mistress Ford, are firmly rebuffed. Although not before Master Ford has been alerted to the danger and goes in search of Falstaff intending to do him harm. Falstaff escapes but ends up tipped into the Thames in a laundry basket, and then escapes a second time disguised as a washerwoman.

With Shakespeare there is always a darker subtext, in this case Frank Ford's hysterical over-reaction to the idea that he might have an adulterous wife. He ransacks his own house in search of her lover becoming ever more distraught as he does so. Male insane jealousy on the slightest of evidence features in other Shakespeare plays, for example Claudio suspecting Hero in *Much Ado About Nothing*, and most disastrously of all, the fate that befell Desdemona at the hands of Othello. Whoever wrote Shakespeare may not have had any formal medical training but his observations of people under stress are forcefully written.

Does Falstaff deserve his humiliation by the two wives and their horde of malicious children recruited for the purpose? Humour also carries a sharp edge of cruelty and it is hard not to be sympathetic with the much put-upon fat knight. The children attack him from the safety of a bunker. Mistress Page organises the ambush with the instruction, 'Let them from forth a saw-pit rush at once' (4.4.53). Windsor Castle Great Park contained a timber yard and saw-mill, this is marked on a map of the Windsor Estate made by Johannes Norden in 1607.

The speech by Mistress Quickly (disguised as the Fairy Queen) on the preparations for the annual Garter ceremony (5.3.55-75) strengthens the association. The Garter ceremony is held at St George's Chapel, on or near the Saint's Day of 23rd April every year. Whoever wrote *The Merry Wives of Windsor* would appear to have had some topographical knowledge of the area, and also an understanding of its purpose and traditions.

Measure for Measure

A strongly written play in which matters of a sexual nature are central to the plot and outcome. What would interest an Elizabethan playgoer and bring in the ticket money? *Measure for Measure* has them all: wronged women, duplicitous lovers, a severed head, a brothel madam, a corrupt magistrate who propositions a beautiful young novitiate nun, and a mysterious absentee nobleman. This is the duke of Vienna, who disguises himself as a wandering friar and spies on the other characters in the play. Why he should be motivated to do this is not clear. It would seem risky as well as eccentric, given the volatile nature of European society arising from the Protestant Reformation.

The main story-line is climaxed by a bed-trick, substituting one woman for another, in this case to spare the nun and deceive the lustful principal. The juggling of two women in a midnight assignation is arranged and forced through by the disguised nobleman who then reveals himself as the rightful Duke. Rewards and punishments follow but the action is resolved and order restored.

Relating this play to the authorship mystery revolves around the identity of the incognito nobleman. Although supposedly set in Vienna the mechanics of the plot mirror events in Paris in the 1580s. King Henri III of France was noted for his eccentric behaviour, which included dressing as a monk and retreating to a cell. He was a transvestite and a homosexual given to extremes of behaviour at a time when the rival tension between Catholics and Protestants in France made life difficult for everyone. King James in London possessed some of the same character traits but attempts to link him to the Duke in *Measure for Measure* have received little support.

Measure for Measure was one of the eighteen plays appearing in the First Folio of 1623 which had not been previously registered with the Stationers' Company. It is the only Shakespeare play with a Biblical title. It comes in St Matthew's gospel in response to Christ's sermon on the mount: 'With what measure ye mete, it shall be measured to you again'. Objection to the distasteful sexual content in this play led to it being labelled as a 'problem' play by critics in previous centuries, and was under-performed for this reason. This would not apply in the more forgiving social mores of western society today. The author would most likely have received credit for courageously tackling the darker side of human nature in this gritty play.

The Comedy of Errors

This is another of the eighteen plays in the First Folio of 1623 which had not been previously registered with the Stationers' Company. It is the shortest play in the Shakespeare canon with some 1,700 lines. There are no cues for music but *The Comedy of Errors* contains a high proportion of legal terminology over the law of contract. A performance of the play is recorded as having taken place at Gray's Inn during the Christmas festivities of 1594. Those present, presumably members of the legal profession and law students, would have been able to appreciate and understand the legal allusions. Supporters of the Stratfordian version of the authorship have suggested that this legal knowledge could have been acquired by Shakespeare working as a lawyer's clerk during his so-called 'lost years' as a young man.

Bullough provides two literary sources for this intricately plotted play about twins. These are two comedies written by the Roman dramatist known as Plautus, his *Menaechmi* and *Amphitruo*, both about twins being mistaken for one another. Shakespeare's adroitly written play steers a sure course through the hilarious misunderstandings which arise naturally from a storyline based on twins, on two sets of twins in this case, never allowing it to degenerate into farce. The play is also about money, or in the case of the Syracusan merchant Egeon stranded in Ephesus, his lack of it. Egeon's failure to raise the ransom that would rescind his evening execution darkens this otherwise entertaining play. Syracuse in Sicily and Ephesus in Turkey are in a trade war at opposite ends of the Mediterranean so the authorities are not inclined to be merciful to Egeon, even though moved by his sad tale of a lost family.

As in other plays set in and around Italy and the Adriatic this play features commedia dell'arte stock characters. The two Dromio twins are recognisable as wily servants, there is a courtesan, a quack doctor and the Duke, an overbearing town official. Doctor Pinch the quack doctor deserves a closer look. He is called in by the relatives of Antipholus of Ephesus who fear that he may have become deranged and ask for help in restoring his sanity. His wife Adriana pleads, 'Good Doctor Pinch, you are a conjuror. Establish him in his true sense again'. For 'conjuror' read 'therapist' and Pinch offers sensible and modern sounding advice that he 'be laid in some dark room'.

This play also contains a spirited if somewhat sharp-tongued woman in Adriana, similar to Katherine in *The Shrew*, and like Katherine she has a more docile younger sister. The high proportion of rhyme would suggest this as an early play written by a young man with some knowledge of the region and its customs.

Much Ado About Nothing

This play is set in Messina the capital of Sicily. Victorious soldiers led by Don Pedro the Prince of Aragon accept the hospitality of Leonato the Governor of Messina and switch their attention from war to love. Claudio is one of Don Pedro's young officers, he takes a fancy to Leonato's beautiful young daughter named as Hero, and a marriage between them is quickly arranged. The leader of the defeated army is also present. This is Don John, the bastard half-brother of Don Pedro. Although reconciled to the defeat he is resentful, and jealous of Claudio. He instructs his servant Borachio to fabricate evidence to demonstrate that Hero had taken a lover on the eve of her wedding.

Claudio is convinced by the evidence and rejects Hero at the moment of marriage, and does so in intemperate language. Hero collapses with shock and is believed dead in this enactment of what might be termed an 'honour killing'. When the deception is later revealed, and Hero recovers, the marriage ceremony is completed. This harsh rejection of a young woman, most likely little more than a child, and the lack of contrition from her easily-duped cad of a husband, expose the dark side of a patriarchal society.

Comedy comes in the form of an incompetent night-watch squad led by a speech-mangling constable named Dogberry. Members of the watch are vital to the plot as they overhear Don John's henchmen plotting against Hero and eventually manage to convince Leonato that his daughter has been the victim of a miscarriage of justice. There is an interesting comparison in a play by John Lyly. This comes in *Endimion*, one of his six Court Comedies. It contains a similar bungling night-watch band, much inclined to debates of impenetrable logic. The date of composition for neither play is known, so, as in many other instances of Shakespeare's literary linkage to parallel texts, it cannot be certain which preceded which or who copied from whom.

Much Ado About Nothing is justly admired for its main female character, Beatrice. She is an unmarried adult woman with a sharp tongue and a fiercely independent nature. Shakespeare as always was years ahead of the pack in creating such a spirited and amusing heroine, a modern woman in every way, and one well able to take care of herself in a male dominated environment. What does this reveal about the author? Shakespeare as a dramatist is credited with creating several strong female characters, Beatrice among them, which adds to the authorship mystery as there is no obvious candidate by this definition.

Love's Labour's Lost

This is the first play published under the Shakespeare name. It appeared in 1598 as 'A Pleasant Conceited Comedie called Love's Labour's Lost' and that it was 'Newly corrected and augmented by W. Shakespere'. The play is set in Navarre, a small kingdom on the border between France and Spain. There is no record of a public performance before 1839 when it was staged at the Theatre Royal, Covent Garden, London.

Bullough offers no classical source but sees the play as influenced by the writings of John Lyly. Although mainly remembered for his two 'Euphues' novels Lyly had also written six comedies for performance in the royal courts, *Endimion* the best known. These were characterised by an exuberant, overblown style of writing which soon ceased to be fashionable but which Shakespeare's superior talent was able to transmute into witty and sparkling dialogue. Modern scholarship identifies *Love's Labour's Lost* as one of a small group of plays in which Shakespeare's brilliance as a writer reached its pinnacle of perfection. The other plays so considered would include *Richard II, A Midsummer Night's Dream* and *Romeo and Juliet.*

Bullough also observes many similarities with Italian *commedia dell'arte* whose stock characters would include Pedant (Holofernes), Clown (Costard), Braggart (Armado) , and Curate (Nathanial). These form a 'below stairs' company to stage a play, *The Nine Worthies*, with which to entertain the lords and ladies but their efforts are mocked. This constitutes a 'play within a play', of which there are several in Shakespeare, the best known being *The Murder of Gonzago* in *Hamlet.*

Ferdinand the King of Navarre persuades three young lords to share with him an austere life of study and prayer. This high-minded plan is promptly scuppered by the arrival of a fairy-tale princess accompanied by three lovely young ladies. Fairy-tale because the ensuing action has an other-worldly quality of magical make-believe as the four young couples chastely fall in love, mislay love-letters, woo the wrong partners in a masked dance and pledge undying devotion on very short acquaintance.

But a Shakespeare play always has a sting in the tail, as in this case where the lyrical nature of the language is abruptly shattered by a messenger bringing news of the French king's death. The princess and her ladies have to leave immediately and return to France so they all fall back to earth with a bump, returned in an instant to the real world of loss and separation. That the identity of the person capable of writing this beautifully crafted play remains unknown must qualify as a matter of universal regret.

A Midsummer Night's Dream

Another intricately plotted play, this one about two pairs of lovers lost in a wood at night. Unhappily for them a bickering couple are in the same wood at the same time. These are Oberon and Titania, the king and queen of the fairies. Oberon orders his sprite, known as Puck, to humiliate his estranged queen with a magic potion that results in her becoming 'enamoured of an ass'. Oberon likewise sends Puck to anoint the eyes of an Athenian lover lost in the wood but the potion is administered to the wrong lover and the misunderstandings multiply. A high society wedding, mixed-up young lovers, a Fairy King and Queen plus magic love potions, all add up to box office success and *The Dream* remains one of the most widely admired and regularly performed plays in the Shakespeare canon.

The offsetting artisan storyline is also strongly plotted with some well differentiated characters. These form an amateur dramatic group of players led by Peter Quince a carpenter, and which includes Nick Bottom a weaver. Theseus the duke of Athens is about to marry Hippolyta the queen of the Amazons and the am-dram troupe plan to perform the play of *Pyramus and Thisbe* in the revels that follow the wedding. This is taken from book IV of Ovid's *Metamorphoses* in the 1567 translation by Arthur Golding. They rehearse in the same wood as the young lovers and Titania the fairy queen. Bottom morphs into a humanoid donkey, Oberon's potion takes effect and the queen invites him into her bed.

Were the audiences of the day expected to see Titania as a double for Queen Elizabeth having enjoyable sex with a donkey? It would be risky. Would a knowledgeable London audience see Bottom as a parody for the queen's French suitor the duke of Alençon? The word 'Monsieur' is repeated eleven times to force the link. 'Monsieur' is the title given to the heirs of French kings, which Alençon was, on the occasion of his visit to London in 1581. As a 'play within a play' performed before Duke Theseus and his bride, the rendering of *Pyramus and Thisbe* was sympathetically received.

But as always in Shakespeare there is more than meets the eye. Beneath the glittering poetry of *The Dream* lies the awkward fact that Hippolyta was a captive in Athens and her marriage to Theseus was coerced. Egeus the father of Hermia had sought the weight of the law to punish his daughter severely for refusing a forced marriage to Demetrius, a man she did not love. Oberon had used his magical powers to punish and humiliate his wife Titania, who had offended him. Whoever wrote this play would seem to be sympathetic to the plight of women in a patriarchal society. They were expected to know their place, and they mostly did, so Shakespeare's spirited women are greatly to be admired.

The Merchant of Venice

This famous play exposes some of the many difficulties which arise when the Shakespeare authorship mystery is debated. Bullough quotes numerous sources from Italian literature, none of them translated into English at the time when the plays would have been written. In addition to an understanding of the Italian language the author shows familiarity with the customs, laws, civic buildings and watery surroundings of Venice, the most cosmopolitan of Renaissance cities. To maintain that this breadth of knowledge about a foreign country could have been acquired by proxy as hearsay is untenable. The practical explanation would be for the author to have visited Italy and stayed in Venice long enough to be able to write a masterwork of world literature based on Venetian financial and legal procedures.

Dr Noemi Magri of Mantua in her *The Italian Renaissance in Shakespeare's Plays and Poems* deals specifically with the trial scene in this play, in particular the significance of the 'single bond' arrangement insisted on by Shylock when making the loan of three thousand ducats to the bankrupt merchant Antonio. Shylock seizes the opportunity to avenge the insults he has suffered from Antonio by ensuring that the contractual obligation of the 'pound of flesh' forfeiture refers to Antonio and only to Antonio. To ratify this arrangement he insists on the matter being referred to a notary so that he can obtain a written acknowledgement of his rights. Venetian law was derived from Roman law but there was no parallel office of notary in English law of the period.

The sensitive issue of anti-semitism is endemic in *The Merchant of Venice* but once again Shakespeare demonstrates his skill as a dramatist by giving Shylock enough good lines to establish him as a strong theatrical character. He is portrayed as a vulnerable, suffering and misjudged man, even as showing signs of dementia when the verdict goes against him. He is understandably distraught when his daughter Jessica (dressed as a boy) decamps with the family wealth to marry a Christian. Conversion under duress is another sensitive issue and no blame attaches in communities where there is little other option.

Shakespeare was also aware of the privileges accorded to strangers (foreigners) under Venetian law. Antonio demonstrates this when speaking to his friend and fellow merchant Solanio '... the trade and profit of the city consisteth of all nations'. (3.3.30-31) Shylock as a Jew counted as a stranger and the Duke (Doge) of Venice would not have allowed any wrong to be done to him for fear of alienating the many other foreign merchants on whom the prosperity of the city relied.

The unbridled joy of the various pairs of lovers after the trial, and the safe return of Antonio's lost ships, when contrasted with Shylock's misery, could be seen as an inappropriate finale to this sombre play.

As You Like It

This was one of the eighteen Shakespeare plays which did not appear in print until its inclusion in the First Folio of 1623. The first known performance was at the New Theatre Royal in 1669. The first performance using the full Shakespeare text was at the Drury Lane Theatre in 1740. This resulted in it becoming popular and it has been regularly performed ever since. The spacious pastoral setting in a forest offers the aristocratic main players a welcome respite from the oppressive nature of the court. Set in the Ardenne area of northern France they revel in the opportunity for self-expression, and the freedom of restraint that allows them to form romantic liaisons.

All works of fiction are allegorical to some extent and the exiled court of Duke Senior now exists in a time warp of its own, similar to Prospero's island, where nothing is quite what it seems. There is magic in the air but it is the magic of Shakespeare's imagination, inventiveness, stagecraft and writing skill which makes an implausible plot believable and richly entertaining. There are four pairs of lovers, nicely differentiated by social class, but all live happily together in their sylvan paradise. There is plenty of sexual innuendo but it is all in the best possible taste.

Another of Shakespeare's strong women dominates the proceedings. This is Rosalind who spends most of the play dressed as a young man known as Ganymede. She instructs the man she loves, Orlando, in the art of courtship. Surprisingly he does not recognise her but becomes aroused, prompting the question as to whether he loves her as the cross-dressed Ganymede in a same-sex male relationship. Her cousin Celia, also disguised, is attracted to Rosalind in a same-sex female relationship. Bearing in mind that boys played female roles at the time when the plays would have been written adds a further level of complication.

Bullough gives only two sources for *As You Like It*. The first source is from Chaucer, *The Tale of Gamelyn* published c1483. This features the ill-treatment of a younger son by an older son, as in Oliver and Orlando in the Shakespeare play. The second source is a mainly prose work by the writer Thomas Lodge (1558-1625), one of the so-called 'University Wits'. This was published in 1590 with the title *Rosalynde*. An ongoing problem with dating any Shakespeare play is that they all show evidence of having been thoroughly revised and levelled up. Whether the revision was carried out by the author or others remains a matter of scholarly debate but the possibility exists that the first drafts of *As You Like It* were written well before 1590 and that Lodge's *Rosalynde* was taken from Shakespeare's play rather than the other way round.

The Taming of the Shrew

This was one of the eighteen plays appearing in the First Folio of 1623 which had not been previously registered with the Stationers' Company. Shakespeare's skill as a dramatist allows him to weave two disparate plots together and from them conjure an entertaining play from unpromising material. In *The Taming of the Shrew* ardent young men are queueing up to woo the young and pretty Bianca but her father will not allow this, insisting that Katherine, his older daughter, must be married first. Easier said than done because Katherine comes in a less attractive package and the reasons why she remains unmarried soon become clear. She is the 'Shrew' of the title, an irritable, quarrelsome woman by definition, and even with the lure of a substantial dowry no man can be found who wants her for his wife.

The impecunious Veronese nobleman Petruccio is fortune-hunting in Padua and sees his chance, 'I come to wive it wealthily in Padua'. (1.2.74). Shakespeare thus has a problem and solves it cleverly. If the ageing bad-tempered Katherine is made to seem too unattractive then Petruccio's bid for her hand in marriage is exposed as unpleasantly cynical. So Shakespeare makes her spirited and sexually desirable, a woman who would despise a weakling suitor but would respect a man strong enough to subdue her. Their preliminary psycho-sexual banter explores the ways in which this can be achieved. The skill of successful falconry is deployed as imagery, on the premise that the wildest of hawks can be tamed if the trainer is sufficiently ruthless and controlling in the early stages.

Audience attitudes to misogyny have changed as western society continues to evolve. The abuse and oppression of women is a perennial source of concern, in the home as well as in the workplace. Performances of *The Taming of the Shrew* can still be uncomfortable viewing for some, men as well as women. What are the chances that Petruccio and Katherine will live happily ever after? Not high, one might suspect. Either way it compels admiration for Shakespeare's consummate skill as a dramatist. The play is as relevant today as it was when first written and performed.

All's Well That Ends Well

This is one of the so-called 'problem' plays, not only difficult to classify but containing distasteful material. The main character is a woman, Helen, and she is another of Shakespeare's spirited women. Helen knows what she wants, she knows how to get it, and is persistent and resourceful in overcoming the difficulties strewn in her way. What Helen wants is Bertram, the young Count of Roussillon, where she lives. He goes to Paris to attend on the ailing King of France. Helen is the daughter of a physician, before his death he disclosed some of his special cures to her. Confident that with this knowledge she can heal the King she too goes to Paris and duly works the miracle. The King, restored to full virility, offers Helen the choice of his young courtiers, from whom she selects Bertram.

Bertram declines, ostensibly because of the difference in their social standing, perhaps also from indignation at being used to settle the King's medical bill. The King insists, so Bertram and Helen are married within the hour. It could have been 'happy ending' but Bertram remains implacably opposed to his new young wife. He refuses to consummate the marriage, imposes impossible conditions for a reconciliation and evades his responsibilities as a married man by decamping for Florence to fight in a local war currently taking place.

It is not obvious why Bertram has taken such a virulent dislike to his wife. Young men usually listen to their mothers and Bertram's mother, the dowager countess, had befriended Helen when they all lived under the same roof, and approved of Helen's sincerely felt love for her son. On the campaign trail Bertram seeks sexual relief with Diana his landlady's daughter, who is available. Helen meanwhile has travelled to Italy in disguise, infiltrated the ranks and pays Diana to allow herself to be substituted in a 'bed-trick' arrangement. Thus impregnated by her cad of a husband Helen returns to the court in Paris for arbitration by the king. Having fulfilled her husband's conditions, even if by subterfuge, Bertram capitulates and promises the king that from now on he will 'love her dearly, ever ever dearly'.

How distasteful for an Elizabethan or Jacobean audience would have been the deployment of the 'bed trick'? In a city where bull and bear-baiting was a popular form of entertainment, probably not much. The American writer Marliss C. Desens cites over two-hundred and fifty examples in her book *The Bed-Trick in Elizabethan Renaissance Drama* published by the University of Delaware in 1994. The ethics of this method of deception have been much debated by moralists when configured against the standards of the present day. It could be viewed as a form of stalking which is a criminal offence if proved, or as entrapment, or in an extreme case as constituting female rape of a male as there was no consent.

All's Well That Ends Well was one of the eighteen plays appearing in the First Folio but which had not been previously registered with the Stationers' Company or mentioned elsewhere before 1623. There is no recorded performance of this play before 1741.

Twelfth Night

The play opens with Duke Orsino in a deep depression. He is the duke of a fictionalised Illyria and is suffering the misery of unreciprocated love. The woman who does not love him, the countess Olivia, dotes instead on a young man named Cesario. Nothing in Shakespeare is ever quite what it seems because Cesario is the disguised female half of a pair of cross-gendered twins. She has been separated from her twin brother Sebastian and believes him drowned and dead. Not so because Sebastian is alive and well and in an apparently same-sex loving relationship with the sailor Antonio.

This provides opportunities for the comic stage business associated with identical twins being mistaken for one another, as in *The Comedy of Errors*. The psycho-sexual subtext also has echoes of *As You Like It* where characters behave amorously toward disguised persons of the same sex. In *Twelfth Night* this arises through the countess and her fondness for the masculine dressed Cesario who is really a girl named Viola, a girl who would have been played by a young male actor at the time when the play would have been written and first performed. *Twelfth Night* was one of the eighteen plays not registered with the Stationers' Company until the publication of the First Folio in 1623. It is a multi-faceted play full of songs, poetry, pathos and joy, still regularly performed and admired.

As so often in Shakespeare there is a dark underside, in this play it is the cruel humiliation of Malvolio. (Other Shakespeare characters are similarly mocked and abused, Paroles in *All's Well* and Falstaff in *Merry Wives* as examples). Malvolio is Olivia's punctilious steward, an upright puritan not much inclined to indulge in the bibulous below-stairs merriment of her poor relations. They punish him with a forged letter, apparently from the countess, inviting him to win her favour by dressing and behaving foolishly. The letter is addressed to *The Fortunate-Unhappy* which could imply that Malvolio was identified as Queen Elizabeth's unbending Lord Chancellor, Sir Christopher Hatton, who wrote verse under the pen name *Felix Infortunatus*. Which could point to an author close enough to the court to be aware of the connection but also one careful not to put his real name on the title page.

The Winter's Tale

The play opens with Leontes the king of Sicilia in a depressive and anguished state of mind. On minimal evidence he accuses his wife Hermione of adultery with his friend Polixenes the king of Bohemia, who is on an extended visit. He believes that Polixenes and not himself is the father of her newly born daughter, Perdita. Needing to extricate himself from a dangerous situation Polixenes returns home, leaving Hermione to be condemned and her baby daughter Perdita taken to some desolate place 'quite out of our dominions' and left there to die.

The irrational and cruel treatment of his wife by Leontes has been compared with the brutal way in which King Henry VIII disposed of his second wife Anne Boleyn, the mother of Queen Elizabeth. Hermione's speeches in her own defence (Act 3 Scene 2) are similar to Anne Boleyn's protestations of innocence in the transcripts of her trial. If Anne Boleyn was Hermione then her banished daughter Perdita (the lost one) could be viewed as based on the experiences of Queen Elizabeth herself, since she suffered similar childhood rejection and endured a precarious survival in adolescence.

At this point *The Winter's Tale* as a play would seem to be heading into the grim depths of tragedy but instead it alters course and becomes a more audience-friendly love story. The Oracle of Apollo has declared Hermione to be chaste, Leonte is overcome with remorse and their baby daughter abandoned on the coast of Bohemia is rescued by two shepherds and brought up as their own daughter. Sixteen years elapse, Perdita and the king of Bohemia's son Florizel have fallen in love and speak some of the most beautiful poetry in all Shakespeare. The author's theatrical mastery overcomes the plot difficulties to contrive a happy if not altogether convincing ending. *The Winter's Tale* was one of the eighteen plays appearing in the First Folio of 1623 which had not been previously registered with the Stationers' Company.

Of authorship interest is the mention of the sculptor Romano when describing the lifelike statue of Hermione (Act 5 Scene 2). The speaker declares it to be worthy of Romano 'that rare Italian master'. Giulio Romano (1499-1546) spent his life at the court of the Gonzago family in Mantua where he was the dominant architect, painter, sculptor and interior designer. Any traveller who had visited Mantua could hardly fail to be aware of Romano's work, reputation, and influence. It would have made a lasting impression. Whoever wrote Shakespeare remembered it enough to prompt this one and only named mention of a Renaissance artist in any of the forty plays.

Shakespeare's English History Plays

Of the ten English history plays attributed to Shakespeare only *King John* and *Henry VIII* are separate stand-alone plays. The other eight, which chronologically come between them, may be grouped into two sets of four (tetralogies) rather than as a continuous sequence of eight, an octology. The second group which appears to have been written first begins with the funeral of Henry V in 1422 and ends with the accession of Henry VII in 1485. These are the three parts of *Henry VI* and *Richard III*. The second group of four prequels the others, *Richard II*, and the two parts of *Henry IV* and *Henry V*.

The first tetralogy	1 Henry VI	The second tetralogy	Richard II
	2 Henry VI		1 Henry IV
	3 Henry VI		2 Henry IV
	Richard III		Henry V

These plays were mostly performed by the Lord Chamberlain's Men to entertain the Queen, her courtiers and visiting foreign dignitaries at the palaces of Whitehall and Greenwich. Only two of the History plays were publicly performed at the Globe, *Richard II* in 1601 and *Henry VIII* in 1613. In the First Folio the plays are historically sequenced but the precise order in which they were written is still debated. The lapse of time between composition and performance, or composition and publication, cannot be stated with certainty, nor which versions of some of the plays, *King John* as an example, were performed.

Bullough gives Hall and Holinshed as the primary sources for this sequence of Shakespeare's English history plays. Edward Hall (1498-1547) was a Cambridge man (Eton and Kings), who went on to study at Gray's Inn in London. The full title of his great work is *The Union of the Two Noble and Illustre Famelies of Lancastre and Yorke*, ending with the marriage of Henry Tudor and Elizabeth of York. Hall is the historian most closely associated with successfully promoting a sympathetic image of the Tudor regime. He is also credited as the main inspiration for Shakespeare's double tetralogy, eight history plays in sequence from *Richard II* (succeeded to the throne 1377) through to *Richard III* (died 1485). Hall's work was prohibited under Queen Mary Tudor and his books were publicly burned.

Raphael Holinshed (died c1582) was responsible for compiling and editing *The Chronicles of England, Scotland, and Ireland*. The first edition appeared in 1577, in two volumes, with an expanded second edition in three volumes following in 1587. The lengthy second edition has the closest links to passages in the plays. Holinshed was attached to William Cecil's household staff in London and had access to his large collection of books, many of which were subsequently found to contain references from elsewhere in the Shakespeare canon.

Other sources for the history plays were Samuel Daniel's epic poem *The First Fowre Bookes of the Civile Wars* which covered the reign of Richard II, and unpublished manuscripts such as the *Wakeford Chronicle* which was drawn on for *King John*. The 1559 anthology *A Mirrour for Magistrates* chronicled the downfall of numerous grandees during the period of civil strife covered by the Shakespeare English history plays and commonly referred to as the Wars of the Roses. (White for York, red for Lancaster).

No other dramatist has attempted such a grand conception of a country's national history. Shakespeare's broad sweep covers the hundred years between the downfall of Richard II and the defeat of Richard III. Bringing history before our eyes through actors on a stage was a genre he created and perfected. For centuries after his death it influenced how history was taught, and to some extent how it is still taught. King John is still entrenched in the national sub-conscience mind as evil, Richard II as effete and Henry V as heroic. Modern scholarship is less convinced but it is Shakespeare's verdict on them that is likely to outlast the others.

The Life and Death of King John

The Life and Death of King John is one of the eighteen previously unregistered plays which appeared in The First Folio of 1623. It is one of only four Shakespeare plays to be written entirely in verse, the others being *Richard II*, *1 Henry VI* and *3 Henry VI*, nor does it contain any songs or references to music. There is no recorded performance of *King John* before 1737.

King John inherited the throne from his brother Richard in 1199 and died poisoned by a monk in 1216. During his ten-year reign Richard I had lived in England for a total of five months, leaving his younger brother to govern with limited resources. John encountered resistance from his recalcitrant nobles, many of them questioning the legitimacy of his accession when his young nephew Arthur had what many of them considered to be a superior claim. The play deals mainly with John's efforts to combat insurrection at home and contain dynastic strife in France. The most prominent character in the play is not King John but King Richard's natural son Philip the Bastard, later knighted as Sir Richard Plantagenet.

Of authorship interest is the existence of another similar and slightly longer play *The Troublesome Reign of King John*. This was published anonymously in 1591, in two parts. There is a scholarly consensus that this is an inferior play but whether it was an early work by Shakespeare later revised, or was written by someone else, remains a subject of debate. The least contentious explanation would be for *Troublesome Reign* to be the early version, possibly first composed in the 1580s, which was then extensively rewritten by the same author in the 1590s.

Although the two plays have similar wording *Troublesome Reign* is more belligerently anti-Papist. The source material was available well before 1591. The first edition of Holinshed's *Chronicles* came out in 1577 and John Foxe's *Martyrs* in 1583. Earlier still John Bale wrote *Kynge Johan* in 1540, with a known performance in 1561. Bale was associated with the playing company known as Lord Oxford's Men and wrote anti-Catholic morality plays. Intriguingly Francis Meres in his *Palladis Tamia* of 1598 mentions a play by Shakespeare named *King John* but there is no knowing which was the version he had in mind.

Also from an authorship point of view is the question of Shakespeare's medical knowledge, in particular his capacity for creating characters in possession of an abnormal state of mind. In this play it is Constance, the mother of Arthur, a rival claimant to the English throne. Arthur is the sixteen year old duke of Brittany, the son of King John's elder brother Geoffrey. His mother has obsessively devoted her life to urging his cause and has enlisted King Philip II of France as their main supporter. When it becomes obvious that John cannot easily be overthrown, and she suspects that he plots Arthur's death, her highly charged emotional state triggers an astonishing level of invective as she rails in despair and rage. King John himself breaks under the unending burden of constant bad news and ends the play as a senile and embittered invalid. Shakespeare's writing is powerful throughout in this masterly play.

The Life and Death of King Richard II

This is the first and pivotal play in the two tetralogies. It sets in motion a sequence of events which had a lasting effect on English history and still resonates centuries later. The concept of divine right, that an anointed sovereign was an agent of God and should not be disobeyed, still less deposed, was deeply embedded in the medieval mind. Richard engineers his own downfall by arbitrarily exiling his cousin Henry Bolingbroke after a quarrel with Thomas Mowbray the duke of Norfolk. Bolingbroke returns with an army and a grievance. Capable and ambitious he flouts convention by toppling Richard and claiming the throne for himself, reigning as King Henry IV.

Written in verse throughout, *Richard II* is rated highly as a master-work of dramatic art and exalted language. The deposed king, no longer 'the deputy elected by the Lord' muses in an elegiac, melancholy manner on his downfall. In prison, as he waits for his murderer, he reflects sadly on the penalty for his weakness and indecision. 'I wasted time and now doth time waste me'. (5.5.49). But the consequences stemming from the double crime of regicide and treason soon reverberate throughout the land. The savage and acrimonious strife between the rival factions of York and Lancaster was the bloody sequel to Richard's murder. Bolingbroke's usurped kingdom brought him little pleasure.

Considered from the authorship viewpoint the play was at its most relevant in the 1590s as the childless Queen Elizabeth's reign was nearing an end but with the issue of the succession unresolved. Holinshed's Chronicles of 1587 provided source material for Shakespeare's play as did Samuel Daniel's *The Civile Wars* written at about the same time. Marlowe's *Edward II* published in 1594 has another weak king as its subject and has been proposed as the model for Shakespeare's *Richard II*. The direction of influence is uncertain, in the absence of firm dating it is entirely possible that Shakespeare's was the earlier play and Marlowe the borrower. An anonymous play *Thomas of Woodstock* could precede *Richard II* which opens as if it was a sequel. It is sometimes tentatively referred to as *I Richard II*.

King Henry IV Part 1

This play was registered and published in 1598, the year after *Richard II* was published. It follows on from *Richard II* with Bolingbroke now king lamenting the wayward conduct of his son known as Prince Hal, and comparing him unfavourably with the earl of Northumberland's equally obstreperous son known as Hotspur.

Henry IV Part One also features Sir John Falstaff, a larger-than-life hard-drinking, high-spirited rogue who has always been a favourite with playgoers. An earlier play named *The Famous Victories of Henry the Fifth* was registered anonymously in 1594. This short and somewhat amateurish play was expanded and written up into three full length plays, known as *1 and 2 Henry IV* and *Henry V*. It is assumed and seems likely that *Famous Victories* was an early work by the author known as William Shakespeare who also wrote the three resulting plays. The short early play contained a dissolute character named Sir John Oldcastle who is seen as the prototype for Falstaff. The Oldcastle family and their descendants the Cobhams complained and the name was changed. William Brooke, 7th Lord Cobham served briefly as Queen Elizbeth's Lord Chamberlain.

King Henry was never free from the taint of usurpation, with the inference that he too was vulnerable and could be similarly toppled. His woes are compounded by financial problems and rumblings of discontent in Wales and the north of England. Henry Percy known as Hotspur, and his father the earl of Northumberland, mount a full-scale challenge with the intention of deposing the king in favour of Edmund, Lord Mortimer, Hotspur's brother-in-law. Negotiations fail and the battle of Shrewsbury takes place, during which the king's son Prince Hal kills Hotspur in a one-on-one encounter. Thus vindicated he is temporarily reconciled with the king, his father.

King Henry IV Part 2

This play follows on from the previous play which would tend to confirm the theory that the author had planned the sequence of events covering the civil wars as a single grand concept. This broad march and panorama of events which took eight plays to work through must by any standards qualify as a literary *tour de force*, the product of a powerful intellect written with an unrivalled mastery of the English language. These are great plays in their own right, cumulatively they served to underpin and reinforce love of country, to instil national pride and make a virtue of patriotism.

Sick and guilt-ridden King Henry presides over a bitterly divided and unhappy country. His sorrows spring directly from the murder of King Richard and he knows this act of regicide will haunt him until his death, which is fast approaching. Exacerbated by the relapse of his eldest son, whose fondness for louche company still distresses him, the king's sad decline overshadows this play of troubled times.

Nor is Falstaff his usual cheery self as the weight of years bear down. His poignant exchange of reminiscences with his old friend Justice Shallow are beautifully written. Falstaff boasts, 'We have heard the chimes at midnight, Master Shallow'. To which Shallow replies, 'That we have, that we have; in faith we have, Sir John, we have. Jesus, the days we have seen!' (3.2.211-216).

Whoever wrote Shakespeare was well aware that even after a hundred years of strong Tudor rule the absence of a clear successor to Queen Elizabeth posed a danger of violent overthrow from within financed by foreign powers from abroad. Through the medium of public performance these chronicles of a parallel period of English history made starkly clear the dire consequences of disunity and dissention. The power of the Shakespeare pen was never more forcefully or successfully deployed.

King Henry V

On his deathbed the old king gave his son some good advice on how to avoid troubles at home

> Be it thy course to busy giddy minds
> With foreign quarrels

Advice that the twenty-six year old king duly put into action by setting sail for France and winning the Battle of Agincourt against a superior French force. This bold act was chronicled by Shakespeare writing at the top of his form. It enshrined for all time the image of Harry the chivalrous warrior king, able to return home in a blaze of glory to lead a nation now unified under a strong leader. As propaganda it still works, and is a prized part for actors to play.

The soldier poet Philip Sidney who also wrote prose was critical of dramatists. In his *The Defence of Poesy* he described at some length how he saw the limitations of the stage.

> A ship is wrecked and the audience has to imagine the rock on which it foundered. Two armies fly in, represented with four swords and bucklers, and then what hard heart will not receive it for a pitched field?

Perhaps in response to these illustrations of staging difficulties, which could be applied to any play performance, Shakespeare begins all five acts of *Henry V* with a Chorus. These lengthy introductions are spoken by an actor who sets the scene and describes the coming action. Chorus has some memorable lines to speak. In Act 2, for example: 'Now thrive the armourers'. (Shakespeare is never out of date).

Henry VI Part One

Scholars have long debated whether this play was entirely written by Shakespeare, with Thomas Nashe and Christopher Marlowe considered as the most likely co-authors. There is no record in the Stationers' Register of a play about Henry VI until its inclusion in the First Folio of 1623 so this is the earliest text. It is written in verse throughout with no prose lines. It covers the first twenty years of Henry's reign and is the only Shakespeare play in which Joan of Arc appears.

Henry VI inherited the crown as a nine-month old baby, following the untimely death of his father Henry V in 1422. Humphrey Duke of Gloucester was appointed as Protector of the infant king but the gap opening at the top encouraged rival factions to compete for influence, with the crown of England as the ultimate prize. This is the play (2.4) in which the quarrelling rival leaders confront one another in the Temple Gardens in London and pick roses. Richard Plantagenet, later the duke of York chooses a white rose, John Beaufort the earl of Somerset for the Lancastrian side plucks a red rose. The setting may have been a pleasant day in summer but the outcome was a viciously contested private war between rival noble families that disfigured the nation's history for half a century. The only consolation in the years to come was the great literature conjured out of so much savagery by the pen of William Shakespeare.

The dominant character in *1 Henry VI* is the battle-hardened general Sir John Talbot who fights bravely against the forces led by Joan La Pucelle, known as Joan of Arc, but he and his son are both killed in the conflict. The duke of York captures Joan, she is summarily tried and then executed, burned at the stake. Henry is advised to sue for peace and to marry a French princess. Acting on his behalf the duke of Suffolk negotiates a marriage with Margaret, daughter of the duke of Anjou.

As head of state King Henry's limitations are cruelly exposed and sensing weakness the rival factions of Lancaster and York begin forging alliances that would provide them with a base from which to launch a bid for Henry's throne. He is more of a saint than a soldier. At the age of twenty he founded Eton College and King's College, Cambridge but is exposed as politically impotent against the malevolent forces ranged against him.

Henry VI Part Two

The First Part of the Contention

This play was published anonymously as a quarto edition in 1594 under the title '*The First Part of the Contention of the two Famous Houses of York and Lancaster*'.

At the age of twenty-four King Henry is married to the fifteen year old Margaret of Anjou. As part of her marriage settlement large areas of territory were ceded to the French and soon the last of the possessions gained by Henry V, Normandy and Gascony, were lost. Staged performances of the Shakespeare history plays may have served the patriotic purpose of demonstrating the need for the country to be united against a common enemy (in this case Spain), as opposed to the crippling effects of dissention. Queen Elizabeth was flirting with the idea of marrying the duke of Anjou so a play retailing the terrible consequences that flowed from King Henry's disastrous marriage with Margaret of Anjou a century earlier may have seemed ideally topical.

Margaret's strong character and determination to become a significant player in the family feuding between her nobles soon became evident. This is complicated by her love for the married duke of Suffolk, their first joint enterprise being to bring down and then have murdered the king's uncle and Protector, Humphrey duke of Gloucester. Of all Shakespeare's spirited women Queen Margaret must rate as the bloodiest, fiercest and most ruthless operator in the man's world of feudal warfare, with its rapidly shifting alliances and trail of noble corpses.

A popular uprising led by Jack Cade was sponsored by the duke of York to inconvenience the king and prepare a bid for the throne. The Lancastrians were able to put the insurrection down and have Cade killed but the Yorkist fortunes were on the rise. Supported by the earl of Warwick a brutal purge of top Lancastrians resulted in Suffolk's banishment and subsequent murder, deeply mourned by the queen. Suffolk's severed head is returned to her and she cradles it in her arms on stage. The duke of York triumphs at the first pitched battle between the two sides at St Albans. The hapless king and Margaret his queen are forced to flee the field.

King Henry VI Part 3

The True Tragedy of Richard Duke of York

This play covers the period 1455-1471 and follows on from The First Part of the Contention. Richard duke of York has engineered a period of Yorkist supremacy and the play revolves around his steady progress towards the English throne. His two sons Edward and Richard begin to feature prominently in aiding his bid, between them they force King Henry to recognise them as his rightful successors, bypassing his own son Prince Edward. This infuriates Margaret who attacks York with an army and when he is captured taunts him and stabs him to death. He has just accused her as 'O tiger's heart wrapped in a woman's hide' to which she responds (2.1.138)

> Off with his head and set it on York gates
> So York may oversee the town of York

The cost of maintaining the French possessions has drained the Exchequer and made good governance difficult. Soldiers from the disbanded army returned from France and became willing mercenaries for the rival factions. With their numbers thus augmented the battles between the feuding warlords escalated in violence with heavy casualties on both sides. There were fifteen pitched battles during the Wars of the Roses, eleven won by the Yorkists, only four by the Lancastrians.

When the earl of Warwick intervenes on the Yorkist side Margaret is defeated and captured at the Battle of Tewkesbury in 1471. Edward and his younger brother Richard are revenged for their father's murder by killing Margaret's son Prince Edward in front of her. Edward is crowned as King Edward IV and the former king, Henry VI, is consigned to the Tower where he is stabbed to death by Edward's crook-back brother Richard.

King Richard III

This long play, the second longest in the canon, covers the years from 1471 to 1485. It ends with the Battle of Bosworth, the death of King Richard and the victory of Henry Tudor. He is crowned on the spot to become King Henry VII. It is one of Shakespeare's most popular plays, regularly performed and admired.

This is largely because Richard's villainy is redeemed by his sardonic humour, and his ability to engage with the audience, making them almost co-conspirators as he genially murders his way to the throne. Shakespeare's mastery of stagecraft is to steer a clever route through a complex series of events, never allowing Richard to degenerate into a pantomime villain while making clear his preference for the Lancastrian cause. In contrast to the preceding history plays where the kings have minor roles, Richard is the main protagonist and commands the stage throughout.

The meeting of the three royal widows (4.4) is another example of the author's sensitivities to the feelings of women. In this poignant chorus they count up their dead, mostly inflicted on one another, 'Plantagenet doth quit Plantagenet, Edward for Edward pays a dying debt' as Queen Margaret grieves. She is the widow of the murdered King Henry and the mother of Prince Edward slain on the battlefield. She in turn murdered Richard duke of York whose widow joins her in grief, having lost her eldest son Edward IV, her second son killed in battle, and her third son the duke of Clarence murdered on the instructions of her youngest son Richard, now the king. Edward IV's widow Queen Elizabeth mourns her two young sons, Edward V and Richard duke of York, the so-called 'Princes in the Tower' the latest victims of King Richard. The duchess of York apologises to her, 'My damnèd son, that thy two sweet sons smothered'.

On the eve of the Battle of Bosworth the sleepless King Richard is visited by the ghosts of his dead relatives and others of his many victims. He dies bravely but his course is run, and as the last of the Plantagenets the old way of life dies with him. Portrayed by Shakespeare in the glowing light of a halo the earl of Richmond as the newly crowned King Henry VII astutely marries Elizabeth the daughter of the Yorkist Edward IV, thus uniting the two rival families.

This ended the sequence of eight plays which brought a troubled century before our eyes and ears in a masterwork of poetic drama. As the supreme practitioner of the English language and the chronicler of its history, William Shakespeare at the turn of the century was deservedly voted in as our Man of the Millennium. A writer of genius who enriched us all.

(King Henry VII)

Shakespeare did not write a play about King Henry VII, the first Tudor monarch, creating a gap in the sequence between Richard III and Henry VIII. Why he did so can only be a matter for speculation, the most obvious reason for a dramatist would be the lack of exciting incidents to write about. The turbulence and mayhem of the Wars of the Roses was followed by a comparatively peaceful period in English history, for which the new king receives the credit.

The discovery of the Americas, with the opportunities for exploration and trade that they offered, jerked the country out of the middle ages and into the bracing new world of science and international commerce. King Henry VII was not a feudalistic warrior king, he was an efficient administrator and tax-gatherer who rescued his country from being a failing state with a shattered economy and returned it to peace and profit. He was a low-profile monarch, pragmatic and managerial, but not sufficiently attractive to be the central character of a play.

This could not be said of his flamboyant and charismatic younger son who inherited as King Henry VIII.

King Henry VIII

This play opens with a description of the Cloth of Gold extravaganza in 1520 and covers the period up to the christening of Princess Elizabeth in 1533. In a large cast there are parts for most of King Henry's entourage at court, among them Thomas Cranmer, Thomas Cromwell, the duke of Buckingham and Cardinal Wolsey. At court there is plenty of drama to drive the action forward, namely the king's infatuation for Anne Boleyn, their precipitate marriage and the unedifying divorce proceedings with Queen Katherine.

The first stirrings of Protestantism create divisions among the courtiers, with the downfall of those unfortunate to be in the right place at the wrong time. Queen Katherine behaves as well as any woman can on being discarded and Buckingham loses his head. Wolsey is disgraced and impoverished by the sovereign he had served so loyally, but still manages to die with dignity (3.2.356-58)

> Had I but served my God with half the zeal
> I served my king, he would not in mine age
> Have left me naked to mine enemies.

The play ends with the birth and christening of Princess Elizabeth. The date of composition is unknown but it would have been during her lifetime in the later years of her reign and before her death in 1603. At Elizabeth's baptismal ceremony the author took care to slip in a glowing tribute to King James, with words spoken by Thomas Cranmer the archbishop of Canterbury. He foretells the coming of a golden age of Peace, Plenty, Love and Truth. He also prophecies that she will die a virgin and that her greatness will be continued by her successor (5.4.41-44).

The play which unfolds in a series of disconnected theatrical episodes is believed by some scholars to be co-authored by John Fletcher, although there is no direct evidence to support this claim. Co-authorship is not the same as collaboration. It is possible that Fletcher, a competent dramatist, revised an original play by Shakespeare. Bullough gives Holinshed's *Chronicles* as the main source of detail for the play. The trial of Thomas Cranmer is taken from John Foxe's 1583 edition of *Actes and Monuments of Martyrs*. The alternative title *All is True* does not appear in the First Folio.

Henry VIII is a play that lends itself to patriotic pageantry. It was performed in 1727 for the coronation of King George II and in 1953 for the coronation of Queen Elizabeth II.

Troilus and Cressida

Bullough cites Chaucer's medieval version of the Troilus and Cressida story as the main influence. It is not found in ancient sources. With the exception of Cressida all the main characters are taken from Homer's *Iliad*. The earliest English translation of the *Iliad* was made by Arthur Hall and published in 1581. George Chapman's translation came in 1598. Although this Shakespeare play was included in the First Folio of 1623 it was omitted from the Catalogue of contents and inserted between *Henry VIII* the last of the Histories and *Coriolanus* the first of the Tragedies.

Troilus and Cressida, the third longest play in the Shakespeare canon, is a deeply cynical and pessimistic drama deploring the futility of armed conflict and the inconstancy of women. The character of Pandarus although venal and devious is observed with clinical detail, an example of the author's fascination with troubled minds. Pandarus (the pander) facilitates a liaison between his niece Cressida and King Priam's son Troilus. They pledge undying love and spend a night together but the next day Cressida is traded by her father Calchas in exchange for a prisoner. Far from being heartbroken Cressida, a Trojan girl, promptly enters into a loving relationship with Diomedes a Greek commander.

What sort of person could have written a play of such cynicism, suffering and bitterness? Its somewhat awkward structure could indicate that it was an early rather than a late work, nor have scholars found it easy to assign a genre to such a complex and profoundly philosophical play. Ulysses has two revealing speeches in the play, one on degree and one on time, both examining human standards of conduct, their values and ethical principles, and finds them wanting. These are very modern concerns.

Coriolanus

This follows on from Shakespeare's long poem *The Rape of Lucrece*. In the post-Tarquin Rome of 490BC the Roman republic hardly exists. Surrounded by hostile states Rome struggles to survive but does so mainly through the exploits of their most successful general, known as Coriolanus. His latest victory over the Volscians in southern Italy strengthens his hero status and the first moves are made to elevate him to the rank of Consul.

A saviour in war can be a liability in peace. Civil restlessness in a time of famine provokes the plebeians into rebellion. They become disenchanted with Coriolanus whose haughty indifference to their plight forces him to leave Rome, change sides and ally himself with their old enemy the Volscians. In revenge for the Roman's rejection of him Coriolanus leads an army with the intention of attacking Rome and overthrowing the republic. This does not happen because he is beseeched by his wife, mother and young son on their knees to spare the city. He does so knowing that he has signed his death warrant and is soon afterwards murdered by the Volscian leaders who are furious at his betrayal.

Coriolanus is one of the eighteen unregistered plays appearing in the Folio of 1623, and there is no record of its existence before that date. Bullough considers that all the source material came from Plutarch's *Lives.* There was a translation by Thomas North published in 1579, and it is assumed that this provided the information in the play. North retitled the book as *Lives of the Noble Greeks and Romans Compared Together.* North's translation was not from the original but from the translation into French by Jacques Amyot. This was available in London from 1569 and this version may also have been consulted. Either way the lapse in time before the play's appearance in 1623 is part of the overall mystery. The manuscript may have remained unrevised in the possession of the playwright, and after his death by his executors, and then included unchanged in the First Folio.

Conventional dating is for composition in 1608 although there is no direct evidence to support this theory. Other scholars have argued that analysis of style and versification in *Coriolanus* could have made a much earlier date of composition possible. There is no record of a performance before 1669 when it was shown at Drury Lane Theatre in London.

Titus Andronicus

Set in the later days of the Roman empire this play is a fictional revenge tragedy between the families of Titus an army general and Tamora queen of the Goths. It is a bloodbath of murder and mutilation. Because it is so unlike the other canonical plays many scholars have doubted whether it was written by Shakespeare. Many would go farther and wish that it had not been written by Shakespeare, rating it as unworthy of such a widely admired dramatist.

Bullough can find no single source and concludes that the play is mainly fictional. There are some classical allusions, for example the parallel story of Philomel as told in Ovid's *Metamorphoses*. Philomel was raped and mutilated so that she could not identify who had assaulted her. Lavinia in *Titus Andronicus* suffers the same fate but is able with the help of Titus to use her mouth and feet to trace the names of her rapists in the sand, these being Demetrius and Chiron, the sons of Tamora. For those unable to read the original Latin there was the translation by Arthur Golding issued in 1567. This book is actually referred to in the text (4.1.41-43)

| TITUS | Lucius, what book is that she tosseth so? |
| YOUNG LUCIUS | Grandsire, 'tis Ovid's *Metamorphoses*. |

Although the body count in *Richard III* is even higher, and the death of Cordelia in *King Lear* is equally brutal and revolting, there is something demeaning about *Titus* that modern audiences find offensive and distasteful. Popular at the time, and frequently performed, it was seen as no more violent that the plays of Thomas Kyd and John Webster. It was acted by several companies which testifies to its popularity but has complicated the research. Professor Sir Brian Vickers has demonstrated that a substantial portion of the text was written by George Peele and this seems to be the currently held position.

Romeo and Juliet

Romeo and Juliet by Shakespeare is the world's ultimate love story. It has everything. Love at first sight, dazzling poetry, magic death-defying potions, a hard-hearted father forcing his daughter to marry a man she does not love, three sword-fighting deaths and a masked ball where Romeo and Juliet meet in glamorous circumstances. Juliet's servant, known as Nurse, facilitates the rapturous night in bed the two lovers spend together.

The play has a compelling narrative pace from start to finish, with a headlong sequence of events crammed into a few days. But there would be no happy ending. This is understood by the audience who know a pair of doomed lovers when they see one. That it will not end well is implicit in the plot structure of irreconcilable family feuding, Romeo being a Montague and Juliet a Capulet.

Whoever wrote Shakespeare had an absorbing interest in medical matters, particularly so when portraying characters in a disturbed state of mind. Romeo, an adult man, is in a deep depression when the play opens and has further depressive episodes in the play. He also has a violent nature, killing two men and finally taking his own life. The author also appears to have possessed some measure of familiarity with apothecaries and their distillations, as personified by Friar Laurence in the play. The plot turns on a house quarantined by the plague, thus preventing the explanatory letter reaching Romeo to inform him of Juliet's induced death-like state.

Romeo and Juliet was printed in several quarto editions from 1597 but did not name Shakespeare as the author until Q4 in 1622. There was no recorded performance until after the Restoration, when Thomas Betterton played Mercutio in a production of 1662. Bullough gives as the main source a long narrative poem *The Tragical History of Romeus and Juliet* which appeared in 1562, and in which Juliet's age is given as fifteen. In Shakespeare's famous play she is thirteen.

Not much is known about the author of this earlier poem, itself derived from Matteo Bandello's prose work *Novelle* published in 1554. He is named as Arthur Brooke, a law student who died by drowning at sea when only twenty years of age. Nor is there is a satisfactory explanation for the number of lines and word clusters from his Romeus poem which found their way into Shakespeare's *Romeo and Juliet*. It does however demonstrate the older man's skill as a dramatist in working up unpromising material. Brooke's meandering account covers nine months. Shakespeare wraps it up in five days.

Timon of Athens

Bullough cites Plutarch's *Lives* as the main source for this play. Details of Timon's life are included in the entries for Mark Antony and Alcibiades. It was one of the eighteen unregistered plays appearing for the first time in the Folio of 1623. A version of this play was performed in 1674 by Thomas Shadwell. The first known performance of the full text was given in Dublin in 1761.

Timon of Athens is another of Shakespeare's plays difficult to categorise. It is included in the First Folio as a tragedy but as Timon's troubles are self-inflicted and concerned with money it might have been more accurately placed with *The Merchant of Venice*. There seems to be a consensus that *Timon* was co-authored, with Thomas Middleton the most likely collaborator. As with all the other plays believed to be co-written there is no direct evidence, only stylometric comparisons between texts. Whether or not there was a revising author the play remains disjointed and unfinished.

Once again the question of Shakespeare's medical insight is relevant to this extraordinary play. Timon's reckless dissipation of his fortune suggests a mental problem, similar to the inability of some gamblers to stop until all their money is gone. The brain mechanism for calculating risk seems to be lacking in Timon, as is his naivety in seeking to borrow his way out of trouble. Some alcoholics present with the same symptoms of excessive prodigality, either as ostentation or in the expectation of gratitude.

What comes next is equally predictable as one form of extremist behaviour is followed by another. Timon takes himself off to a cave in the desert where he lives in degradation, gnawing on roots he has dug up with a spade in order to survive, cursing the while in a frenzy of self-loathing rhetoric that is remarkable, even by Shakespeare's highly imaginative standards of colourful invective. Timon is a long part with many words to speak but if spoken well can have great theatrical force.

Shakespeare's knowledge of syphilis and its progressive symptoms is another medical condition under scrutiny in this difficult play. How and when he acquired such detailed knowledge of this gruesome affliction, untreatable at the time, is unknown.

Julius Caesar

Elizabeth Tudor spent the whole of her life in danger of murder or assassination. When she was two and a half years old her mother Ann Boleyn was executed. She was imprisoned for almost six years by her half-sister Mary Tudor, and as Queen from the age of twenty-five survived a succession of well-planned and determined attempts to kill her. Denounced by successive popes as a heretic, a dispensation was offered in advance to any successful assassin who would be sanctioned as committing a dutiful act. The armed might of Spain and Portugal was deployed against her but foundered with the defeat of the Spanish Armada. At the age of sixty-eight she faced down an abortive palace coup by the earl of Essex and his men.

So a play set in ancient Rome and depicting on stage the treachery of high ranking nobles as they plot to murder their top general Julius Caesar would have been a familiar situation for Elizabeth and her closest friends and ministers. Brutus is one of several Shakespeare main characters who are easily duped and persuaded by sinister advisers to commit misdeeds. These would be Othello by Iago, Hamlet by the Ghost of his father, Claudio by Don John, to whom may be added the sincere but misguided Brutus deceived by Cassius.

The Lord Chamberlain's Men mostly performed the Shakespeare plays to the upper echelons of society, to the lawyers and government administrators at the Inns of Court, to the dons and scholars at Oxford and Cambridge, and of course to the Queen and her most reliable courtiers and their wives and families in the royal palaces. These men and women were the opinion formers, the influential office holders who needed to be rallied and convinced. More than any other single play *Julius Caesar* warned of the catastrophic consequences of civil unrest that immediately follow an assassination, most of all for the prime movers. This was certainly true of Brutus and Cassius who both suffer an ignominious death. The law of unintended consequence also applies. The rise of Mark Antony was an eventuality not foreseen by the conspirators.

Bullough gives North's 1579 translation of Plutarch's *Lives* as the main source of *Julius Caesar*, taken from the entries for Julius Caesar, Marcus Brutus and Mark Antony. North's translation was from Jacques Amyot's rendering into French, not from the original Greek. This French translation was available in London in 1559. Casca's list of portents was drawn from Ovid's *Metamorhposes*, the translation into English by Arthur Golding being available from 1567. *Julius Caesar* first appeared in print in the Folio of 1623, one of the eighteen plays previously unregistered. The first authentically recorded performance was at the palace of Whitehall in 1612.

Macbeth

Macbeth is Shakespeare's second shortest play (after *Comedy of Errors*). It is one of the eighteen plays in the First Folio which had not been previously published. The earliest recorded performance was in 1611 at the Globe Theatre in London, with the possibility that the text was subject to revision before appearing in the Folio. In 1603, following the accession of King James VI of Scotland as King James I of England, those responsible for staging plays had to be wary of the new king's sensibilities where any disparagement of Scotland or things Scottish was likely to provoke the royal displeasure. James was obsessed with the practice of witchcraft, attended the trials of women accused of being witches and in 1597 had published a tract on the subject with the title *Daemonologie*.

Bullough indicates the 1587 edition of Holinshed's *Chronicles* as the main source for the play. This contains a chapter covering the years 1034-1057 and includes the murder of King Duff and the exploits of Macbeth, tracing his rise to power and subsequent decline and fall. The date of composition for the play is unknown but many see as compelling evidence the Porter's use of the word 'equivocator' and Macbeth's use of 'equivocation' which relate to the trial of the Gunpowder plotters in 1606.

The 'Gowrie conspiracy' of 1600 involving King James VI of Scotland is also seen as a possible source of inspiration for the playwright and would support a date of 1601 for composition. John Ruthven the 3rd earl of Gowrie was a wealthy landowner with large estates in Perthshire. The Ruthven and Stuart families were closely linked, with James owing the earl a huge sum of money. The king was out hunting near Perth when he was lured by the earl's youngest brother to divert to Gowrie House on the pretext that they had detained a man carrying a large sum of gold. What happened next has never been satisfactorily explained but it appears to have been a plot to capture and murder the king at Gowrie House. The king was saved by the prompt actions of his followers, swords were drawn and the earl and his brother were slain. This sequence of events could be seen as parallel to the murder of Duncan in the play. The Gowrie brothers had intended to murder a Scottish king in their own home, in private, having invited him inside under trust.

In this famous play the author's medical knowledge is deployed with telling effect. Macbeth's fatal ambition and cruelty, his hallucinations, his epilepsy, his wife's disintegrating mental descent into madness, and the nightmare apparitions of the 'foul and midnight hags' make this one of Shakespeare's most gripping plays. It is a favourite with audiences and provides great parts for actors. The gothic horrors of a bleak Scottish castle provide an appropriate setting for Shakespeare's vivid language and superb stagecraft.

Hamlet

Hamlet in *Hamlet* is referred to as a student at the German speaking university of Wittenberg so in the normal course of events he would have been youthful, most likely under the age of twenty. This is not reflected in the play where his world-weary philosophising would be more appropriate for a much older man. From the outset Hamlet behaves erratically and the play is seen from his distorted viewpoint. He returns from university to find his father the king of Denmark dead, his uncle preferred for the succession and in a newly married relationship with his widowed mother. Hamlet is deeply disturbed by these events. This manifests in his rapid changes of mood, by his simulated derangement, and by communicating with his dead father from beyond the grave. Thus motivated to wreak revenge he sets in motion a series of events which result in multiple deaths, including his own.

Whoever wrote Shakespeare was sensitive to the workings of the troubled mind. In their enclosed castle community Hamlet's unpredictable behaviour creates a highly-charged air of excitability which unsettles the other characters. The Oedipus theory which supposes that all men at some time in their lives have incestuously desired their mothers is no longer fashionable but modern productions of *Hamlet* now include a bed in the closet scene featuring Hamlet and his mother, Queen Gertrude. (3.4) Hamlet cannot bear the thought of his recently widowed but still attractive mother having enjoyable sex with his uncle King Claudius and expresses his disgust in a passionate exchange of reproach and recrimination. The closet scene (which includes the murder of Polonius), is dramatic writing at its very best in this most famous of all plays.

King Lear

King Lear is a study in dementia. Shakespeare's ability to create great literature from characters with deeply troubled minds reaches its *ne plus ultra* in *King Lear*. The king was obviously not in his right mind in thinking it was a good idea to parcel out his kingdom while still alive, and his irrational reaction when it goes wrong should have been seen as further symptoms of his rapidly deteriorating mental condition. His irresponsible demands to reward his rowdy entourage with hospitality would understandably have exasperated Goneril and Regan and their husbands beyond endurance.

That does not excuse their un-daughterly cruelty towards him as the downward spiral to insanity gathers momentum. The storm scene and the blinding of Gloucester are dramatic writing with terrible force. The words Lear and Gloucester speak in consolation to one another, one mad and the other blinded, are heart-breaking. Lear carrying the dead body of his youngest daughter Cordelia seen for the first time on stage would be a vividly imprinted image for any playgoer. *King Lear* is a masterwork of the human capacity to endure, matched only by Beethoven's most sublime and powerful music.

Othello

Othello has similarities with *Hamlet* in that the action is worked out among a small group of people in the privacy of an enclosed space. Much of the play takes place in the hours of darkness and is compressed into a few days, which builds momentum, so that the course of events once set in motion work remorselessly through to their tragic resolution. Just as Hamlet is easily persuaded of his uncle's guilt by the Ghost, and acts accordingly, so is Othello easily convinced by Iago of Desdemona's adultery on the thinnest of evidence. Although jealousy is often cited as the raison d'etre of this sad play it is more of a revenge tragedy in which Iago finds a cruel way to punish Othello for the perceived slight of being passed over for promotion.

Scholars agree that the main source of Othello is taken closely from an Italian novella, the *Hecatommithi* by Geraldo Cinthio published in 1565. There was no translation into English until 1753 but the linguistic parallels strongly suggest that the author was able to read the original in Italian. The first recorded performance was in November 1604 at the banqueting hall in Whitehall palace before King James and his wife Queen Anne.

A feature of Shakespeare's writing is his originality and readiness to explore new themes and situations, mostly without examples to copy from, or kindred spirits to provide inspiration. Even if not working entirely in isolation he seems to have been sufficiently insulated from other writers to develop along different lines and produce his own style of writing and construction. To write a play in which the main character was a Moor, a black man, and to portray him sympathetically as a nobleman and highly regarded top commander, inspires respect for a prodigious and original literary talent.

Antony and Cleopatra

Antony and Cleopatra is Shakespeare's other great love story, and as in *Romeo and Juliet* it ends tragically with both pairs of doomed lovers killing themselves. Romeo and Juliet are young lovers but Antony and Cleopatra are high-status adults with everything to lose, and do, literally dying for their destructive passion for one another. Antony is one of the three Triumvirs who rule the Roman empire, Cleopatra is the queen of Egypt, they should have known better but once having met cannot keep apart. The exalted language in which they conduct their over-heated love affair is some of Shakespeare's finest. It is a magnificent play about two of the ancient world's most famous people.

Antony and Cleopatra was entered in the Stationers' Register in May 1608. The play begins in 40 BC, two years after the end of *Julius Caesar*, a much more austere play. A performance by David Garrick's company is recorded for 1759. Because Antony was married (to Octavia, Caesar's sister) the play was seen as immoral and their lovemaking as adulterous. The first full performance of the Folio text had to wait until 1849 but was still not well received.

Bullough gives Plutarch's *Lives* as the main source of the play, taken from the entry for Marcus Antonius. The translation into English by Thomas North was available in 1579. This was not from the original Greek but from the earlier translation into French by Jacques Amyot and available in 1559. Samuel Daniel's *The Tragedy of Cleopatra* was published in 1594 and has been proposed as influencing Shakespeare's play appearing in 1608. This is possible but as the source material was available many years previously the direction of travel is not conclusive.

Cymbeline

Cymbeline (Cunobelinus) was a puppet king of Rome, reigning in pre-Christian Britain from 33BC. He is a passive character in the play but his second wife, known only as 'Queen', has big plans, namely to marry her son Cloten to Cymbeline's daughter Innogen, and then to dispose of her husband, leaving her son Cloten as the new king. This plan fails because Innogen has secretly contracted a marriage to Posthumus, described as poor but worthy. This displeases everyone and Posthumus is banished, travelling to Rome where he feels more at home than in Britain.

Posthumus is portrayed as a weak and indecisive character. Also gullible, easily tricked by a rascal named Giacomo into believing that his wife had been unfaithful in his absence. He arranges for his wife Innogen to be murdered as punishment but she is alerted in time and is able to escape. Disguised as a boy she makes her way into the safety of the Welsh mountains. This is a breeches part with great possibilities for a young actress.

By contrast with the undeveloped main male characters *Cymbeline* features two more of Shakespeare's strong-willed women. The Queen may be unlovable but she makes a convincing villain. Her step-daughter Innogen is loyal, spirited and resourceful. She has many adventures before she is reunited with her husband in an all-round happy ending. This need not detract from the lively nature of the play. Because it is not anchored to a specific historical time it lends itself to the idea of a woodland romance, which is how it is mostly produced for the stage.

Cymbeline is one of the eighteen plays in the First Folio of 1623 which had not previously been published. Because of this it is assumed to be a late play and it is certainly the last play in the book and classed as a Tragedy. Structurally it would appear to be an early play even if revised later. The first record of a performance was in 1610, at the Globe Theatre in London. Bullough once again gives Raphael Holinshed's *The Chronicles of England, Scotland, and Ireland*, as the main source, in this case from the earlier 1577 version which has a pseudo-historical account of Cymbeline's reign and his defeat of a Roman tax-gathering raiding party.

Pericles

Pericles, Prince of Tyre was published in quarto form in 1609. The author's name on the title page was given as William Shakespeare. It was not included in the First Folio of 1623, the most probable reason that it was a corrupted and incomplete text assembled from memorial reconstruction. It was also possibly co-authored. Although there were other subsequent quarto editions it was again omitted from the Second Folio of 1632 but finally included in the Third Folio of 1664.

Some editors at various times have maintained that Shakespeare was the sole author of *Pericles* but most accept George Wilkins (1576-1618) as the most likely co-author. In 1608 Wilkins published a novel with the title *The Painful Adventures of Pericles, Prince of Tyre*. Bullough cites an earlier version of the same story by Laurence Twine, *The Pattern of Painful Adventures* which appeared it 1576. It was a translation of the story of Apollonius of Tyre from John Gower's *Confessio Amantis* pubished in 1483.

Many scholars from Malone forward have seen *Pericles* as associated with a cluster of Shakespeare plays that pay homage to a literary tradition of writing stories as fables. These plays are *Cymbeline*, *The Tempest* and *The Winter's Tale*. Although now several hundred years old, audiences still find them pleasurable. There is an equally long tradition, still applicable, that readers of escapist literature or viewers of such plays or films have learned from childhood to understand that complex or difficult ideas and emotions are most conveniently expressed as allegory. Belief is suspended as gods and goddesses appear and disappear, beautiful maidens are raised from the dead, ships are wrecked but all are saved, with an understanding between audience and players that love will triumph and all will come right in the end.

Prince Pericles sets out on a long journey and it is mainly a spiritual journey of attachment and loss, good versus evil, truth over deceit, sorrow followed by joy. And like all fairy tales his journey ends happily.

The Two Noble Kinsmen

Shakespeare's fascination with disturbed states of mind has a sympathetic manifestation in *The Two Noble Kinsmen* with the character of the Jailer's Daughter. Her age in the play is given as eighteen. Although she is allotted a big part in the play she does not figure in any of the source literature and would thus seem to be an authorship creation. The play was entered into the Stationers' Register in 1634 with two authors named, the first being John Fletcher the second William Shakespeare. Which of these introduced the Jailer's Daughter into the story, and wrote the scenes in which she occurs, is not known, but as mental illness features in so many of the plays attributed to Shakespeare he would be the more likely of the two.

The play opens with a prologue acknowledging the debt to one of Geoffrey Chaucer's *Canterbury Tales*, in this case *The Knight's Tale*, itself derived from Boccaccio. This tells the story of two knights, Palamon and Arcite, who start out as close friends but who come to blows over a woman. A version of the story with the title *Palamon and Arcite* was performed before the Queen at Christ Church, Oxford in 1566. Another version with the title *The Rivals* by William Davenant appeared in 1664. Wells and Taylor say there were no other recorded performances of *The Two Noble Kinsmen* until 1928, at the Old Vic Theatre in London.

Palamon and Arcite are two soldiers on the losing side in a battle against Theseus the duke of Athens who has them imprisoned in his castle. While there they see Emilia, sister of Hyppolita and both fall in love with her. Arcite is ransomed but Palamon remains in prison. The Jailer's Daughter is moved by the sight of such a lovely young man under restraint and forms a deep attachment to him. This is not reciprocated even when she facilitates his escape into the forest and follows him there. Her sexual frustration aggravated by his rejection is more than she can bear and as depression sets in she becomes increasingly out of touch with reality. She wanders and sings, 'Willow, Willow, Willow', an echo of Desdemona's desperate last hours in *Othello*. Her father's friend, known only as the Wooer, rescues her from the forest, preventing her attempt to drown herself. (4.1.94-95).

> She saw me and straight sought the flood. I saved her and set her safely to land.

This chimes with the adolescent Ophelia in *Hamlet* who succeeded in drowning herself. Neither of the girls seemed to have had a mother to hand, they both loved men who didn't love them, both employed imagery of the natural world and in their distress both spoke in a busy-brain tumbling of disconnected words and fantasies. Her father the jailer and his friends are concerned at what they see as her descent into madness. They act compassionately towards her saying, 'Poor soul' and ''tis pity'.

They consult a Doctor who marvels, 'How her brain coins!'. (4.3.37). He muses further, ''Tis not an engrafted madness, but a most thick and profound melancholy'. This would appear to be an accurate diagnosis of acute clinical depression and although no calming medication was available the doctor offers a workable solution which meets with the approval of her father and her father's friend, the Wooer. This is to gently infiltrate the Wooer into her dimly lit room as Palamon, and to maintain the pretence long enough for her to accept him as such and agree to a marriage. Not quite a happy ending, but almost.

The Life of King Edward III

King Edward reigned from 1327-1377. The play *King Edward III* was entered in the Stationers' Register of 1595 and published anonymously the following year, with a note that it had been at 'sundry times played about the City of London'. It is written entirely in verse.

Bullough did not include *Edward III* in his sources of Shakespeare's plays but other researchers have put forward Holinshed's *Chronicles* as the most likely source. Because it would seem to be an early play this was most probably from the first 1577 edition. An additional source in view of its French content could have been Froissart's *Chronicles* in the English translation by Lord Berners of 1525.

The play covers King Edward's exploits against the Scots as allies of the French, including raiding Roxburgh Castle and rescuing (then attempting to seduce) the countess of Salisbury who was held prisoner there. These and disparaging comments about the Scots which may have offended King James could be one explanation why the play was not included in the First Folio of 1623. Nor was it included as a Shakespeare play by Francis Meres in his *Palladis Tamia* anthology of 1598.

Performances of *Edward III* have been few and far between. The most recent, at its Summer Festival in 2016, was staged by the Hudson Shakespeare Company. This is based in Jersey City, Hudson County, New Jersey. It is a touring company and specialises in performing the less well known Shakespeare plays such as *Timon of Athens* and *The Two Noble Kinsmen*.

Famous Victories

The Shakespeare trilogy of British history plays comprising the two parts of *Henry IV* plus *Henry V* appear to have been derived from a much earlier play *The Famous Victories of King Henry Fifth* registered anonymously in 1594. *Famous Victories* is a short elementary work lacking literary merit. Since no known juvenilia by Shakespeare has ever been found this play has always been of interest to authorship researchers for this reason. If by the same hand the inference drawn is that it was written by the same author at a much younger age, perhaps as a student. The sourced material for the early play is considered to come from Edward Hall's history of the Tudors known as *The Union of the Two Noble and Illustre Famelies of Lancastere and Yorke* published in 1550. The first edition of Holinshed's *Chronicles* which appeared in 1577 is also cited as a likely literary source.

8 The Contenders

Shakespeare Authorship Profile
Notes on Authorship Nominees

John Lyly	1553-1606
Fulke Greville	1554-1628
Anthony Munday	1560-1633
Mary Sidney Herbert	1561-1621
Francis Bacon	1561-1626
William Stanley	1561-1642
Christopher Marlowe	1564-1593
Sir Henry Neville	1564-1615
William Shakspere	1564-1616
Roger Manners	1576-1612
Thomas Sackville	1536-1608
Ben Jonson	1572-1637

Shakespeare Authorship Profile

What sort of person could have written the plays and poetry attributed to William Shakespeare? It is a valid question. If not the Warwickshire grain trader then who? Although some fifty or more contenders have been suggested as the true Shakespeare these can be whittled down to a dozen worthy of serious consideration. The basic requirement would be for someone who had received a wide-ranging classical and humanist education, the kind of education available only from private tuition and attendance at a university. This narrows the field.

Schools attached to cathedrals and monasteries existed to teach Latin to future priests and monks, not to educate poets and playwrights. Secular grammar schools were few and far between and still mostly taught Latin to prepare boys for a desk-bound career in the civil service. Of all the many putative alternative authors not one has been proposed as coming from a mainly illiterate if hardworking family such as that in which William Shakspere was born and raised. The serious contenders have all been either aristocrats or members of the *haute bourgeoisie*.

Queen Elizabeth and her principal advisers were alert to the propaganda value of dramatic art harnessed as an expression of national pride and identity. Throughout Europe crowned heads and their nobility sought to employ the most prestigious artists, sculptors, musicians and writers. As a patron of the arts the queen created the circumstances where such talent could flourish. The primacy of Shakespeare in helping to create and sustain the cultural revolution that has come to be associated with the reign of Queen Elizabeth has never been disputed. Only his identity.

The vexed question of the patrician viewpoint cannot be evaded. The high-minded seriousness found in so many of the formal speeches contained in the Histories and Tragedies express the thoughts of a superior person. Superior not only in social rank but in concern for the human values of morality and conduct. The most famous plays, those assumed to be among the last written, display a redemptive sympathy and tolerance towards those who err. This is not a commonly held or popular view, then as now, but it merits comparison with those men and women of similar intellectual stature in science and philosophy who shared Shakespeare's lofty humanitarian values.

Anyone who has acted in a Shakespeare play or studied one for an examination soon becomes aware of the trademark word clusters and sound patterns, most of all in the steady heart-beat rhythm of iambic pentameter. This unique style and originality lies at the core of the authorship mystery. Those who challenge the Stratfordian chronology maintain that a birth year of 1564 would relegate the author to a subordinate level where he is much influenced by other writers. Some dissenting groups such as those which support the earl of Oxford believe that Shakespeare developed his own distinctive style of writing English because he had few models to work from and was forced to be original. This would require him to have been born earlier than 1564. It is the fundamental point at issue between Stratfordian orthodoxy and those who doubt.

The following writers all had an association with the plays of Shakespeare. Some as revisers and editors, others in a secretarial capacity, as possible co-authors or as alternative authors. In their own way they all had a contribution to make to the authorship mystery.

Brief notes follow on John Lyly, Fulke Greville, Anthony Munday, Mary Sidney, Francis Bacon, William Stanley, Christopher Marlowe, Henry Neville, William Shakspere, Roger Manners, Thomas Sackville and Ben Jonson.

John Lyly

John Lyly (c1553-1606)

John Lyly was educated at Magdalen College, Oxford, and went to London in 1576. There he gained fame with the publication of two prose romances, *Euphues: The Anatomy of Wit* (1578) dedicated to Lord De La Warr, and *Euphues and His England* (1580) dedicated to his patron and later his employer, the earl of Oxford. With these two books Lyly was admired not so much for what he wrote as in the way that he wrote it. He was the first prose stylist, and although by later standards it was excessively mannered, the many young university-educated writers coming to London in increasing numbers were quick to see the potential for fine writing that he had pioneered.

After 1580 Lyly devoted himself to writing plays with dialogue in prose, notably his six court comedies. For some ten years in the 1570s and 1580s Lyly was employed by Edward de Vere the earl of Oxford and acted as his stage manager during the period when he held the lease of the Blackfriars Theatre. Some scholars suspect that these plays may have been joint ventures by de Vere and Lyly. From surviving correspondence they appear to have had a close working relationship. The six plays were *Campaspe, Sapho and Phao, Endimion, Gallathea, Midas* and *Mother Bombie*. The literary critic J Dover Wilson in his biography of John Lyly cited his comedy *Endimion, The Man in the Moon* as strongly influencing Shakespeare, most obviously in the sharp-witted dialogue in *Love's Labour's Lost* and in the elegance of the speeches in *A Midsummer Night's Dream*. Another Shakespeare play, *Much Ado About Nothing*, has a sub-plot featuring a squad of bungling watchmen which could have been derived from a similarly hopeless crew in Lyly's *Endimion*.

Lyly's successful early career was not sustained, overtaken as a dramatist by younger men, by Christopher Marlowe most of all. At court he failed to find preferment with Queen Elizabeth and from the biographical accounts of his life he died a poor and unhappy man,

Fulke Greville

Fulke Greville (1554-1628) Baron Brooke

Fulke Greville was a Warwickshire man born into a wealthy family, the only son of Sir Fulke Greville. After leaving Jesus College, Cambridge he came to London and entered the royal service at the court of Queen Elizabeth. He was the exact contemporary of Philip Sidney and the two men became close friends. Greville shared Sidney's love of poetry and both also wrote in a formal prose style. They numbered some well-known writers among their friends, among them Edmund Spenser, Samuel Daniel, Francis Bacon, Gabriel Harvey and Edward Dyer. (Sir Edward Dyer, 1543-1607, has been touted as an outside possibility for the Shakespeare authorship).

Greville represented Warwickshire in Parliament four times between 1592 and 1621. He was a competent government administrator, appointed by Queen Elizabeth as Welsh Secretary in 1583. He rose to become Treasurer of the Navy in 1598 and was Chancellor of the Exchequer from 1614 until 1621. He was knighted by Queen Elizabeth in 1597 and in 1621 was raised to the peerage by King James as Baron Brooke. As a further sign of favour he was granted Warwick Castle by King James and restored it at his own expense.

Greville's most famous work, *The Life of the Renowned Sir Philip Sidney*, was written between 1610 and 1614 but not published until 1652. He had earlier contributed an elegy on the death of Sidney to *The Phoenix Nest*, an anthology of some eighty poems which appeared in 1593. Most of Greville's works were published posthumously, and all were of a serious nature. As a dramatist he wrote two tragedies *Alaham* and *Mustapha*. In 1633 he published *A Treatie of Humane Learning*, a philosophical verse treatise on knowledge. Also in 1633 appeared *Certain Learned and Elegant Works* which included the sonnet cycle, *Cælica*, consisting of verses on religious and philosophical themes.

In 1609 he purchased the large property of King's Place in Hackney from the countess of Oxford, the widow of Edward de Vere the earl of Oxford. When he received his barony in 1621 he renamed the property as Brooke House. Greville never married but the house remained in his family for the next two hundred years. It suffered bomb damage in the 1939-45 war and was demolished in 1946.

As an authorship contender Greville's busy life spent in the public service would be enough to cast doubt on how he could have simultaneously written forty plays and numerous sonnets. Logistically it would have been impossible. Similarly with the serious content and subject matter of Greville's surviving literary output. No one can deny

190

that Shakespeare's early plays, and even some of the later plays, were plentifully supplied with puns and jokes and humorous situations. Greville was a stern Calvinist and a writer of opaque humourless verse. Frivolous he wasn't. But Shakespeare could be, and often was, so Fulke Greville does not fit the profile.

Anthony Munday

Anthony Munday (1560-1633)

Anthony Mundy was a prolific and versatile writer whose career was coterminous with that of Shakespeare. Including translations from romances in French and Spanish he wrote over eighty works, seventeen of them plays, although only two of these have survived, both loosely based historically on the life of the famous outlaw known as Robin Hood. He edited some late editions of John Stow's *Survey of London* and wrote several of the annual pageants staged at the installation of the Lord Mayor of the city of London. Francis Meres in his 1598 literary review *Palladis Tamia* awarded him the accolade of being 'our best plotter'. He was the main author of the collaborative play *Sir Thomas More* which some scholars believe was revised by Shakespeare.

He worked as an actor in the earl of Oxford's acting company before becoming a full-time writer. He dedicated his poetry anthology *The Mirror of Mutability* to the earl and also worked for him in a secretarial capacity in the late 1570s and early 1580s. He became involved in the Martin Marprelate exchange of pamphlets which complained that the Protestant state religion had become as oppressive and authoritarian as the Roman Catholic regime they had broken away from at great anguish and expense. Although never acclaimed as a great writer or thinker Munday had broken new ground as a competent reporter of his times, one of the first to prove that it was possible to make a living from full-time writing.

Mary Sidney

Mary Sidney Herbert (1561-1621) Countess of Pembroke

Mary Sidney, the younger sister of Sir Philip Sidney, was the first English woman to achieve a substantial literary reputation. Granddaughter of the duke of Northumberland she was also the niece of Robert Dudley the earl of Leicester who arranged her marriage at the age of fifteen to the wealthy William Herbert, earl of Pembroke. Formidably well-educated, in languages most notably, she found herself at this early age the chatelaine of Baynard's Castle in London and the huge Wilton House estate near Salisbury in Wiltshire.

She was the mother of four children, two of whom were boys, William the eldest and Philip the youngest. William inherited as the third earl of Pembroke and was permanently at court in senior positions, for many years as the Lord Chamberlain and then as Lord Steward. In his capacity as Chamberlain he was the arbiter of what could or could not be written and printed, or performed, on the London stage. Mary's younger son Philip (married to Edward de Vere's daughter Susan) was a favourite of King James who raised him to the peerage as first earl of Montgomery. Mary's two sons were thus the 'Incomparable Pair of Brethren', immortalised as such in the First Folio dedication.

The countess will always be associated with her brother Philip's best known prose work *Arcadia*, originally written to entertain her. Unfinished at his death at the battle of Zutphen in 1586 she revised and enlarged it in 1593. Since then it has always been known at *The Countess of Pembroke's Arcadia* and there are some references from it in Shakespeare. Bullough cites it as a minor source for both *Hamlet* and *The Winter's Tale*. More significantly it provides the tragic Gloucester sub-plot in *King Lear*. Bernard Shaw in his *Dramatic Opinions and Essays* expresses his belief that Mary Sidney was Shakespeare's role model for the dowager countess of Roussillon

> … the most charming of all Shakespeare's old women, indeed the most charming of all his women, the Countess of Roussillon in *All's Well That Ends Well*.

Mary Sidney founded and led for twenty years a literary salon with regular gatherings at Wilton House near Salisbury. Now referred to as The Wilton Circle they formed an influential group of writers and poets. The circle included Edmund Spenser, Michael Drayton, Samuel Daniel (the tutor of her children) and the politician-poet Sir John Davies (1569-1626). Daniel's epic poem *The First Fowre Bookes of the Civile Wars* provided source material for Shakespeare's *Richard II*.

Mary Sidney has had some limited support as the main author of Shakespeare's plays, mostly in the USA where there is a Mary Sidney Society which intermittently publishes a journal, *The Cygnet*. There is an extant biography of her by Robin P Williams with the title *Sweet Swan of Avon*. (This refers to the Wiltshire Avon rather than the Warwickshire Avon). As with other contestants for the Shakespeare authorship she is disqualified by her busy lifestyle, numerous activities and gregarious nature. Apart from the lack of evidence in support of this possible tie-in there is little or no correlation of source material, style or structure with the plays of Shakespeare.

The belief that she was involved in some way with the Shakespeare authorship still persists however, and may have an element of truth. If the Herbert family sponsored and underwrote the cost of compiling and publishing the First Folio of 1623 her literary expertise may have provided valuable help in editing and processing the various Shakespeare manuscripts through to publication. The link between the Herbert family and Shakespeare was further strengthened in 1743 when Henry Herbert the 9th earl of Pembroke commissioned the sculptor Peter Scheemakers to make a replica of his Westminster Abbey statue of Shakespeare to stand in the entrance hall of Wilton House. It still stands there today.

Francis Bacon

Francis Bacon (1561-1626) Viscount St Alban

Francis Bacon made a lasting impression as a philosopher and proto-scientist. His skill as a writer provided him with the ability to express his ideas with style and clarity. His *Novum Organum* (New Method) of how to conduct and present the findings of scientific research earned him an international and enduring reputation as a Renaissance scholar and polymath. His main preoccupations were in philosophy, science, theology and jurisprudence. These formed the subject of his *Essays*. His most famous book was *The Advancement of Learning*. These heavyweight works gained him a literary reputation as a writer of great intellectual stature so it is understandable that when seeking a credible author for Shakespeare his should be the one of the first names put forward for consideration.

Francis Bacon was the nephew by marriage of William Cecil, Lord Burghley. Educated at Cambridge and enrolled at Gray's Inn he had a good early career as a lawyer and parliamentarian. He sat as a Member for several constituencies from 1581 until 1614 when he represented Cambridge University. He received little preferment from Queen Elizabeth but was knighted and then ennobled by King James as Viscount St Alban. He rose to be Lord Chancellor in 1618 but was then forced out of office after allegations that he had accepted bribes. If all political careers end in failure this was indeed the case for Francis Bacon who died in debt eight years later.

Bacon has been described as the most poetic of philosophers and Shakespeare as the most philosophical of poets but putting the two together exposes the differences between them rather than the similarities. Apart from a few die-hard cryptologists it is hard to find supporters for Bacon as Shakespeare. The disparity of subject matter rules it out, and in common with other rivals Bacon's was a life of public service with every day accounted for, leaving little spare time for writing forty plays.

William Stanley

William Stanley (1561-1642) 6th earl of Derby

With the initials 'W S' and his own company of actors it is understandable that the earl of Derby should be considered as a strong possibility for the Shakespeare authorship. He had inherited the playing company in 1593 along with his title from his brother Ferdinando, the 5th earl of Derby, for most of life known as Lord Strange. Lord Strange's Men had been an active company from the late 1580s but were split up when Ferdinando died, some staying on as Lord Derby's Men, others joining a troupe led by Lord Hunsdon the Lord Chamberlain. These became famous as the Lord Chamberlain's men with Richard Burbage as their leading actor and by tradition were associated with the dramatist known as William Shakespeare.

On 26th January 1595 at Greenwich Palace, in the presence of the Queen, Stanley married the earl of Oxford's eldest daughter Lady Elizabeth Vere. He was thirty-four, his bride twenty, and although not authenticated, the play *A Midsummer Night's Dream* may have been performed as part of the feasting and revelry. When registered with the Stationers' Company in 1600 the title page stated that it had been 'sundry times publicly acted'. Such plays were often performed at aristocratic weddings and the Stanley-Vere wedding would have fitted into the time frame.

William Stanley was immensely wealthy with estates and property in Cheshire, Cumberland, Lancashire, Yorkshire, and Wales as well as London. The Stanley family also owned the Isle of Man, and he held the title as Lord of Mann. The earl was also well connected, his mother Mary Clifford being the daughter of Mary Tudor, the sister of King Henry VIII. Under the Third Succession Act his mother was heir to Queen Elizabeth but predeceased her by dying in 1596. Stanley was closely associated with William Herbert, 3rd earl of Pembroke, and his brother Philip Herbert, earl of Montgomery. They served as his trustees in 1628 when handing over his estates to his son James, later the 7th earl Derby. The two brothers enjoyed lasting fame as the joint dedicatees of the Shakespeare 1623 First Folio, the 'incomparable pair of brethren'.

William Stanley's credentials for the authorship are impressive. He was educated at St John's College, Cambridge and attended other universities during his widespread travels in the early 1580s. He served as a diplomat in Paris and in 1603 was appointed to the Privy Council by King James. As an aristocrat, as a patron of the arts, as the employer of a company of actors and generally being in the right place at the right time he deserves to be considered. As he lived for another nineteen years after publication of the First Folio but published no more plays in all that time the case is weakened. The association with Shakespeare still lingers on however and the literary earl may have helped in revising or editing the plays and in bearing or sharing the cost of the First Folio printing and distribution.

Christopher Marlowe

Christopher Marlowe (1564-1593)

Precocious would be the word to describe the literary talent of Christopher Marlowe. He differs from the other alternative authors of Shakespeare by having produced drama and poetry of the highest quality in his twenties. He was already an established poet and playwright when his exact contemporary William Shakspere of Stratford-upon-Avon was making his first visit to London.

Marlowe's plays included *Tamburlaine, The Jew of Malta, Edward II, Dr Faustus* and his first work *Dido, Queen of Carthage*. If Marlowe could write great plays as a young man, why not Shakspere? The difference lay in Marlowe's formal education which provided him with the literacy required of an author. He was educated at The King's School in Canterbury and received a Bachelor of Arts degree from Corpus Christi College, Cambridge in 1584.

Marlowe's literary accomplishments ceased on 30th May 1593 when he was stabbed to death at a tavern in Deptford, by tradition over the 'reckoning', the bill for food and drink. Only a small number of people have seriously believed that the death was in some way faked so that he could avoid jurisdiction by fleeing the country and then write the plays of Shakespeare. The untimely death of any talented young man is a source of sorrow, a lament for unfulfilled potential and shattered dreams, but death is always final and has to be accepted, however reluctantly.

The case for Christopher Marlowe although never strong has never completely gone away either. Scholars have always suspected that Marlowe (and perhaps Thomas Nashe also) had a hand in writing *1 Henry VI*. More recently this has been extended to 2 and 3 *Henry VI* as well.

Henry Neville

Sir Henry Neville (1564-1615)

The case for Henry Neville as Shakespeare is of recent origin, proposed in 2005 by William Rubinstein and Brenda James in their jointly written biography of Neville, *The Truth Will Out.* They seek to demonstrate that Neville's life parallels closely the 'accepted chronology' of Shakespeare's works. The 'chronology' referred to is that arrived at by Edward Dowden in 1881 and accepted by most later scholars, notably E.K. Chambers in 1930 and Wells and Taylor in 1987. One of the main reasons there is an authorship problem is because dissenting scholars maintain that the publishing data of the period, although sparse, is not compatible with a birth year of 1564, when the author would have been too young. The dating and sequencing of Shakespeare's plays has been contentious ever since. Malone abandoned his attempts at the end of the eighteenth century and the chronology remains 'disputed' rather than 'accepted'.

Henry Neville matriculated from Merton College, Oxford in 1577. The following year he accompanied his tutor Henry Saville on a continental tour. For almost all of his adult life he served as a Member of Parliament and was active in the public service as a politician and administrator. He was appointed High Sheriff of Berkshire in 1595 and Deputy Lord Lieutenant in 1596. He was knighted in 1597. He was Ambassador to France 1599-1601 and attended the Court of Henri IV.

The Nevilles were an old military family. As the earls of Westmorland they contributed to the nation's history, being prominent in the Wars of the Roses on the Lancastrian side. A century later the Nevilles and their northern neighbours the Percies launched a rebellion against the Protestant regime in London, their intention to overthrow Queen Elizabeth and replace her with Mary, Queen of Scots who was a Catholic. Known as The Rising of the North the rebellion was led by Thomas Percy the 7th Earl of Northumberland and Charles Neville the 6th Earl of Westmorland. On this occasion they were on the losing side as the rebellion was swiftly crushed. Thomas Percy was captured and executed. Charles Neville fled to the continent where he died in exile.

Sir Henry Neville followed the recalcitrant family tradition by backing the losing side in the Essex Rebellion of 1601. This failed ignominiously and the two leaders Robert Devereux the earl of Essex and Henry Wriothesley the earl of Southampton were both sentenced to death. The earl of Essex was beheaded but Southampton's sentence was commuted to imprisonment in the Tower of London. Neville, a close friend of Southampton, was also imprisoned in the Tower but both were released on the orders of King James when he ascended to the throne in 1603. Neville was also fined £5,000 pounds by the Queen, an enormous sum in those days, but was allowed to pay it off in instalments.

Of the main contenders for the Shakespeare authorship only Neville has no evidence of being a writer, or of engaging in writerly activities such as attending salon gatherings to discuss work in progress. He was not involved in the theatre, staged no plays and did not offer patronage to young writers. He has no published works either anonymously or under his own name, in prose, poetry or drama.

William Shakspere

William Shakspere (1564-1616)

It is not possible to produce biographical notes for the Stratford-upon-Avon businessman, however brief, because no primary sources exist. Intensive research over hundreds of years has retrieved some eighty references to Shakspere, mostly mentions of his name on legal documents or in business transactions, but none on literary matters. Nor do they provide information from which a conventional biography could be constructed. All the books ever written purporting to tell Shakespeare's life story, or to account for specific episodes in his life, are fictional. That there has been a considerable number of such books does not make them any more authentic.

Consider these facts. No record exists of Shakspere's childhood, youth or education. Nothing at all is known about him until the registration of his marriage at the age of eighteen in 1582. In adult life there is a long gap between the years 1585-1592 when there is no documentation, nor again until 1595. In London there is a gap from 1605 until 1612 when he was named as a witness in law suit. No image of Shakspere made during his lifetime has ever been found, nor any recorded sightings of him either in Stratford or London.

Nothing he ever said or did has come down to posterity which means there are no descriptions of his appearance such as his size and shape, his tone of voice, his mode of dress, his good or bad habits, his domestic life, his sense of humour, whether or not he was bald, clean-shaven or bearded, short-tempered or amiable. Nothing that would bring him to life as an ordinary person, or how he might have been perceived by his friends and fellow dramatists. No dates can be determined for the writing of any of his plays or poems, few performance dates can be stated with certainty, and no account exists of his daily routine as a practising actor and writer, either on his own or collaborating with others.

If the author of Shakespeare's works sought anonymity he did so with complete success, including in his home town of Stratford-upon-Avon. No one there apparently suspected that the grain merchant resident in the house known as New Place doubled up as a literary genius who would one day become world famous. His death in 1616 passed without a single recorded comment either in Stratford or London, and no valedictory verse was penned to mourn his passing.

Roger Manners

Roger Manners (1576-1612) 5th earl of Rutland

Roger Manners was awarded Master of Arts degrees at Oxford and Cambridge universities. He also attended at Padua university in Italy and studied law at Gray's Inn. He travelled extensively, visiting many European countries. Manners was married to Philip Sidney's daughter Elizabeth. She was also the step-daughter of Robert Devereux the earl of Essex. Although of fragile health Manners took part in foreign military campaigns led by the Earl of Essex. He participated in the Essex rebellion against Queen Elizabeth in 1601, for which he was heavily fined. In 1603 King James sent him on a diplomatic mission to the King of Denmark.

His education, travels and aristocratic family connections would qualify him as a contender for the Shakespeare authorship by those who believe that only such a high-ranking courtier would be capable of writing authentically about life in the upper echelons of society. A factor that could have worked to his advantage was that the last ten years of his life were spent as a reclusive invalid and so provided him with time to write and revise. Even so his death at the age of thirty-five left him short of time for the full Shakespeare oeuvre of plays and poetry. That he wrote some or all of the Sonnets has been suggested as a compromise, given the mysterious nature of the complex relationships they contain, and which continue to baffle students of Elizabethan literature.

Thomas Sackville

Thomas Sackville (1536-1608) Earl of Dorset

Thomas Sackville was a second cousin to Queen Elizabeth. He was educated at Hart Hall, Oxford (Hertford College) and St John's College, Cambridge, going on to become a barrister of the Inner Temple. He entered parliament at the age of twenty-two and rose steadily to become the Lord Treasurer. He held several high official positions, including Chancellor of Oxford University. He travelled extensively in France and Italy and was employed as a diplomat in France and the Low Countries. A Garter knight, he was for his entire life a high-ranking palace insider close to the Queen and the ruling elite.

With his interests in poetry, music and drama he meets most of the requirements for the Shakespeare authorship and has a strong case, particularly as a possible writer of the sonnets. Born in 1536 he fits the publication time frame more comfortably than any of the other candidates, both for the plays and the sonnets. Famously reticent in not wishing to be associated with his works in print, Sackville could be the 'concealed poet' hinted at by scholars and critics of the period.

Sackville collaborated with Thomas Norton in writing the play *Gorboduc*. This was written in blank verse and took the form of a Senecan tragedy with long formal speeches but no stage action. It was performed before Queen Elizabeth on 18th January 1562 by the Gentlemen of the Inner Temple. It was a play with a political message at a time when her grasp on power was under constant threat from dissident groups. It spelled out the dire consequences of disloyalty, and warned rival factions at court to behave themselves. The characters in the play were drawn from the chronicles of Geoffrey of Monmouth. Gorboduc as a character also features in Spenser's *The Faerie Queen*.

At court Sackville aligned himself with the faction that included William Cecil and the earls of Sussex and Oxford. Edward de Vere the earl of Oxford has broad support as Shakespeare but those who favour Sackville in the authorship stakes point to the disparate quality evident in their early works. The modest amount of poetry de Vere published under his own name is mostly dismissed with faint praise as mediocre at best. Sackville's early poetry on the other hand was warmly praised by his contemporary writers, most notably by Edmund Spenser. This high opinion was shared by many subsequent scholars and critics.

A popular anthology of stories from English history, *A Mirror for Magistrates* appearing in 1563, contained two long narrative poems by Thomas Sackville. The first of these with the title *Induction* is considered as influencing Edmund Spenser's *The Faerie Queen* and also Shakespeare's similar poem *The Rape of Lucrece*. Sackville's other narrative poem *The Complaint of Henry Duke of Buckingham* foreshadows the downfall and death of so many illustrious men in Shakespeare's Histories and Tragedies.

Many of the Shakespeare plays have complex revision histories and the extent to which this was authorial, or undertaken by others, is central to the authorship mystery. Sackville's death in 1608 would allow for the substantial revision of *Macbeth* and *King Lear* which included topical allusions to the Gunpowder Plot of 1605. Whether the author of the canonical plays was also responsible for the apocryphal plays and the bad quartos is still a subject of scholarly debate.

Did the author of the plays also write the Sonnets? Doubts have been expressed that they were by the same hand and the overlap between them is not easy to disentangle. The constant refrain of old age and infirmity in the sonnets would be more appropriate if coming from Sackville than for any of the other contenders. A man who could describe himself as 'beated and chapped with tanned antiquity' (Sonnet 62) would surely be more than middle-aged. Sackville lived on into his early seventies, dying the year before the sonnets were published by Thomas Thorpe in 1609.

Thomas Sackville, earl of Dorset, was the complete grandee, a Renaissance Man in every way, gracing the Tudor regime with his many years of public service at the highest level. He was loyal, upright, good at everything he did. Above all he was successful, generously rewarded at every stage of his career by Queen Elizabeth and then by King James. He died a wealthy and respected man after fifty years of marriage and this must cast doubt on his suitability to be considered as the author of Shakespeare's plays.

Where is the anguish? The suffering? The failure and bitterness? Apart from the mundane objection that his busy professional life allowed him little time for writing plays he does not fit the profile of the troubled but gifted genius which emerges from a study of the plays.

Ben Jonson

Ben Jonson 1572-1637

Ben Jonson was the most prominent writer in English during the reign of King James, 1603-1625. He was a satirist with a somewhat jaundiced view of society. His enduring literary reputation is for a writer of comedies, the most famous being *Volpone* (The Fox) which was first performed in 1606 and published 1607. Many of his characters are given demeaning names, as examples Sir Epicure Mammon and Sir Pertinax Surly, both in *The Alchemist*. Other comedies include *The Silent Woman* and *Bartholomew Fair*. The lecherous fop Sir Diaphanous Silkworm is a character in *The Magnetic Lady*.

From contemporary accounts Jonson was possessed of a combative nature, twice imprisoned after clashing with the authorities. He was admired by his fellow writers, younger writers in particular, for his lack of deference. Even so his talent for stagecraft earned him an attachment to the Jacobean court as a writer of Masques. This form of entertainment allowed members of the court to dress up, sing and dance and generally enjoy themselves away from the public gaze. These lavish productions with sumptuous costumes and scenery were commissioned for special occasions such as a wedding between members of the court, or to entertain visiting foreign dignitaries, or for feast days and holidays.

Jonson wrote over thirty of these masques, all of them subject to approval by the Lord Chamberlain. From 1615 until 1625 this post was filled by William Herbert the 3rd earl of Pembroke. In 1616 he facilitated the publication of Jonson's collected works, *The Workes of Benjamin Jonson*, the first such collection for a living writer. This contained plays as well as masques and uniquely was in the larger folio size, preceding the Shakespeare Folio by seven years.

William Herbert and his younger brother Philip Herbert the earl of Montgomery were named in the dedication of Shakespeare's collected plays known as the First Folio. This was published in 1623 and as they were the dedicatees, 'the incomparable pair of brethren', it is assumed that they commissioned and financed its production. This would have required a considerable outlay of time and money which focuses attention on the identity of the author they were commemorating. The Herberts were a literary family related to many similar wealthy and ennobled families attached to the court, so the inference could be drawn that they were doing it for one of their own.

William Herbert appears to have sought Ben Jonson's help in putting the Shakespeare folio together, based on their close association in producing theatrical works for the court. With the experience Jonson gained from compiling and publishing his own collected works into a folio edition this would seem a logical move for William Herbert to make.

At this late stage the level of association between the two men can only be conjectured but Jonson must surely have known the identity of the author that the Herbert family wished to conceal. He wrote most if not all of the prefatory words and verse for the First Folio, pinning the authorship firmly on the Warwickshire man, the 'Sweet swan of Avon', at the same time diverting attention away from the actual writer of the plays.

After the restoration of 1660 Shakespeare from Stratford-upon-Avon with his known lack of a formal education was considered an inferior writer to Jonson, a man much respected for his classical learning. There is a paradox here because Jonson was the step-son of a bricklayer and never went to university while all of the listed contenders for the authorship received first-rate privileged educations. The lesson being that it pays to be cautious when assessing an author's work based on the opinions of others.

9 The Case for Edward de Vere

Linking Edward de Vere to the plays
Dangerous Liaisons
A Reclusive Invalid
Objections to Edward de Vere as Shakespeare

Edward de Vere

Edward de Vere (1550-1604) 17th earl of Oxford

For almost a century Edward de Vere has been the most widely supported alternative Shakespeare author. There are many societies around the world dedicated to promoting his cause and engaged in ongoing research. The De Vere Society in the United Kingdom and the Shakespeare Oxford Fellowship in the United States of America would be two such organisations. For this reason the case for Edward de Vere is examined more closely and at greater length.

Thomas Looney's book *Shakespeare Identified in Edward De Vere the Seventeenth Earl of Oxford* appeared in 1920 and had an immediate, profound and lasting impact on the authorship debate. No one had seriously considered the earl of Oxford as an authorship contender until then but once over the shock many were persuaded that Looney had succeeded where others had failed.

Edward de Vere the earl of Oxford was not a famous Elizabethan and little was known about him until brought to prominence by Looney's biography. He was overshadowed by some of the more flamboyant writers, adventurers and politicians associated with Queen Elizabeth's court: Walter Raleigh, Philip Sidney, Martin Frobisher, Francis Drake, John Dee, Edmund Spenser, John Lyly, Christopher Marlowe, Christopher Hatton, Robert Dudley and William Cecil among them. These all had more coverage than the literary earl who was known as a minor poet but not as a writer of plays.

Edward de Vere's high social status as the Lord Great Chamberlain, his long association with Queen Elizabeth and her chief ministers, with his father-in-law Lord Burghley in particular, would provide an explanation for the specialist knowledge of the inside workings of a royal court evident in many plays. This familiarity with the highest echelons of society distinguishes the plays of Shakespeare from those of his contemporaries, indeed from most other plays in the English language before or since. The patrician manner of speaking in which the high-born main characters address one another, and the subtle adjustments they make when dealing with subordinates, reflect the rigid hierarchical social structure of the times. It could be deduced that this was how the author thought and spoke himself.

De Vere had the reputation of being a difficult man, haughty and quarrelsome. He was unkind to his first wife and neglected his children. He was recklessly extravagant and dissipated his inherited fortune on foreign travel and on business ventures that failed, also by supporting a salon of writers and underwriting theatrical productions. He spent time in prison after fathering a child with his mistress, one of the Queen's gentlewomen, and was wounded in street brawls with her indignant relatives. He never regained the Queen's favour and spent the last years of his life as an embittered house-bound invalid pleading for loans and favours.

His poor health provided him with a genuine excuse to ensure that he had no burdensome civic or charitable duties to perform. He held no paid office and never took time away from London to lord it over his Essex estates. He was no better as a father than he was as a husband, and after the early death of his first wife Anne Cecil, his three daughters were brought up by his mother-in-law Mildred Cecil. In his last home of King's Place in Hackney with his second wife Elizabeth Trentham he could have had sufficient years of seclusion in which to write and revise the plays, many of them issued in quarto form until his death in 1604.

Those sympathetic to Oxford as Shakespeare view his many faults as intrinsic to the nature of genius, a form of mental abnormality which can manifest in many ways but is always driven by a single-minded lifetime commitment. It is in the nature of genius to be self-absorbed and indifferent to the suffering this causes to others, to family members most of all. Such people seem to have a perceived intention of how they need to construct their lives in order to maximise their talent. Writers need time to write. Large-scale writing projects, such as a five-act play, would have needed many months of concentrated effort to bring to completion.

Anyone coming new to the Shakespeare authorship mystery should first acquaint themselves with the subject matter of these extraordinary plays, and the idiosyncrasies of the main characters, so that they may more accurately assess who could have written them.

It is in the stressful nature of his own life that Edward de Vere the earl of Oxford most closely matches the downfall of so many great men in the plays. The ever-present dread of treachery, the corrosive nature of ambition and the bitterness of failure run as constant themes through the Shakespeare Histories and Tragedies. Madness and suicidal despair haunt the world-famous plays of *Hamlet*, *King Lear*, *Macbeth* and *Othello*. Whoever wrote these plays possessed a powerful intellect. They could also be viewed as the products of a deeply troubled mind.

Linking Edward de Vere to the plays of Shakespeare

Edward de Vere was born in 1550 at Hedingham Castle in Essex, the ancestral home of the Vere family. It was a life of wealth and privilege. His father John de Vere the Sixteenth earl of Oxford was the Lord Lieutenant of Essex and the owner of vast estates and property. In addition to being the principal magnate of the eastern counties he also held the title of Lord Great Chamberlain of the Realm of England. More to the point the earls of Oxford had maintained a company of touring players since 1492, known as Lord Oxford's Men. On 9th August 1561, when Edward de Vere was eleven years old, they welcomed Queen Elizabeth and her entourage to Hedingham Castle as part of her Summer Progress in East Anglia, staying for six days. The banqueting hall with its huge Norman arch would have been able to provide the lavish spectacle that was expected of any noble family entertaining the Queen.

One year later, when he was twelve years old, Edward de Vere's life changed dramatically. His father John de Vere died unexpectedly at the age of forty-six and Edward inherited the earldom and the office of Lord Great Chamberlain. Queen Elizabeth immediately summoned him to London to be entered into the Court of Wards. This was set up to protect underage noblemen and administer their estates until they came of age at twenty-one. Master of the Court of Wards was the Queen's most trusted adviser William Cecil who took Lord Edward into his London home, Cecil House in the Strand, and was appointed as his guardian. The greater part of the Vere estates were assigned to Robert Dudley the earl of Leicester, a soldier and courtier who enjoyed the Queen's friendship and patronage.

If the case for Edward de Vere has merit then 'Shakespeare' as his alter ego started here, at twelve years old, in Cecil House in London. Every aspect of the authorship mystery has its origin in this magic-wand transition from a hilltop castle in rural Essex straight into the political heart and centre of Tudor power as exercised by Queen Elizabeth and her eminence grise William Cecil, later ennobled as Baron Burghley.

Cecil House was a huge brick-built palace with four corner turrets, sufficiently grand for entertaining the Queen and foreign dignitaries. Edward's nine years as a royal ward brought him into close contact with those responsible for the governance of the country. His ears could not have helped becoming attuned to the formal manner of speech in which they addressed one another, and to observe how they conducted themselves in their public and private lives. William Cecil and his wife Mildred as speakers of classical Greek were impressively well educated, as was the Queen, with the emphasis on languages, in particular Latin the language of scholarship and French the language of diplomacy. Edward

211

de Vere's several hours of strictly enforced daily tuition was based on obtaining proficiency in these two languages.

Shakespeare scholars do not agree on much but there has always existed a consensus that somehow or other in his youth the author must have read many books on a wide range of subjects. For Edward de Vere this is easily explained. In the home of his childhood tutor Sir Thomas Smith, during his attendance at Cambridge University 1558-59 (Queens' College and St John's College), as a law student at Gray's Inn, and in Cecil House throughout his wardship, he had access to some of the largest collections of books in the country. When William Cecil's library of some two thousand books was dispersed in 1678 the catalogue entries show that it contained many of the works cited by research scholars as providing source material for the Shakespeare plays and poetry.

How much contact Edward had with his family's company of actors as a child, or with John Bale his father's writer in residence, is not recorded but as his main pursuits in adult life were connected with the theatre it could have provided him with an early interest in the performing arts. In 1566 at the age of sixteen he accompanied Queen Elizabeth on a visit to Oxford University for an awards ceremony, which included an MA degree for the young earl himself. This was not entirely honorary as he had been well educated in the classics. As part of the ceremonies Richard Green, Master of the Children of the Chapel, staged a two-act play *Palamon and Arcite* based on Chaucer's *The Knight's Tale*. Whether or not Lord Edward was involved in the production is not known but it surfaced later in 1634 as *The Two Noble Kinsmen* with Palamon and Arcite as the main characters. This is now an accepted play in the Shakespeare canon, usually shown as co-authored with John Fletcher.

A fellow resident at Cecil House was Edward de Vere's uncle Arthur Golding, a member of Sir William Cecil's administrative staff. A classical scholar educated at Cambridge, his lasting achievement was a translation from Latin into English of Ovid's *Metamorphoses*. This was published in 1567 when Golding was thirty-one and his nephew seventeen. Whether this was a master-and-pupil collaboration (as some scholars believe) can never be proved but whoever wrote Shakespeare knew it line by line. Almost all of the many hundreds of classical allusions across the canon can be traced back to this translation of the *Metamorphoses*.

In 1568 the play *Horestes* was performed at Gray's Inn where Edward was a law student. This was based on Caxton's translation from the French of part of the *Oresteia* trilogy. It was the first play to make use of the soliloquy to convey an actor's thoughts to the audience, something which became a feature of Shakespeare's stagecraft writing. The author of *Horestes* was given as John Pickering, of whom nothing is known and so could have been a pseudonym to conceal the writer's identity, whether de Vere or another. A play by George Gascoigne a former student at Gray's Inn, *The Supposes*, provided the Luciento-Bianca sub-plot in *The Taming of the Shrew*.

212

Also resident at Cecil House was Raphael Holinshed, compiler and editor of the famous *Chronicles* that will always bear his name. This appeared in 1577 with an expanded version coming in 1587. Shakespeare scholars do not agree on much but again there is a consensus, namely that the main source material for the British history plays was drawn from Holinshed's *Chronicles*. As with Arthur Golding there is no direct evidence that Edward de Vere collaborated with Raphael Holinshed but as they both had access to the well-stocked Cecil library it could explain the close connection. In 1567 Holinshed was on the jury which obligingly acquitted the earl from murdering a servant with a sword thrust, reducing the charge to self-defence. In 1573 Holinshed came to de Vere's rescue once again, issuing a statement that exonerated him from involvement in a domestic-dispute murder on Shooters Hill, near Greenwich.

At the age of nineteen Edward had a long period of illness spent in rented rooms at nearby Windsor. The nature of the ailment is unknown but because his surviving letters suggest that in later life he suffered from melancholia (depression) this may have been an earlier episode following the death of his mother the previous year. The following year he joined the army of Thomas Radcliffe the earl of Sussex who had been tasked by the Queen to suppress an insurrection by Catholic nobles in the north of England and Scotland. This became known as the 'Rising of the North'. Urged on by William Cecil the rebellion was put down by Radcliffe with appalling severity. The Vatican responded angrily to this harsh treatment of Catholics and excommunicated Queen Elizabeth as of illegitimate birth and a heretic. The steadily escalating conflict with Catholicism, led by the Spanish Habsburg dynasty, was the backdrop against which Edward de Vere the earl of Oxford lived out his life,

Before completing his nine years of wardship he began buying books for himself. (Nelson, p.53). From the London bookseller William Seres he purchased several books with a direct bearing on the Shakespeare authorship. These included a Chaucer, a translation of Plutarch into French by Jacques Amyot, and a Geneva Bible. This Bible with revealing marginalia in de Vere's distinctive italic handwriting is now housed in the Folger Library in Washington DC. Of over a thousand annotations and under-linings Dr Roger Strittmatter demonstrated in his 2001 PhD dissertation to the University of Massachusetts that 246 of these could be matched with words and passages in the plays. This was one of the few authorship links to come to light since Looney's original discoveries were published in 1920.

The heavy-weight reading material mentioned above could suggest that for such a young man de Vere had a humanitarian and literary cast of mind. He commissioned Thomas Bedingfield, one of his former tutors in Cecil House, to make an English translation from the Italian of *Cardanus Comforte*. Published in 1573 this is the book of philosophical essays that Hamlet carries about with him and quotes from in his 'to be or not to be' speech.

If viewed as preparation for creating the works of Shakespeare then Edward de Vere's nine years as a royal ward were of inestimable benefit, providing him with a privileged education and enough high-level contacts and experiences to launch and sustain an early writing career. All human activity is a trade-off in one way or another, and in the case of the young earl of Oxford his good fortune in becoming part of Queen Elizabeth's extended family in metropolitan London was offset by the money troubles which plagued him for the rest of his life.

The main source of contention was the difficulty in reclaiming his estates when he came of age at twenty-one. The Queen, Lord Burghley and Robert Dudley the earl of Leicester had looted them first and effectively deprived him of much of his lawful inheritance. To make matters worse he had to borrow to pay for the huge livery fees he had accumulated as a royal ward. This was compounded by his guardian's promotion to the post of Lord High Treasurer which allowed him to continue exercising control over the earl's financial affairs. In the same year de Vere married Cecil's fifteen year old daughter Anne. Whether or not the marriage was coerced it extended still further William Cecil's leverage over the earl who may have hoped that this family alliance would ease his money problems instead of making them worse. At court the young earl aligned himself with the Cecils in an anti-Leicester faction. Nor was he on friendly terms with Leicester's nephew Philip Sidney, a fellow scholar at Cecil House, with whom he later quarrelled over the right to use a tennis court. This required the intervention of the Queen to prevent them from fighting a duel with rapiers.

Oxford's marriage to the young Anne Cecil was desperately unhappy, not helped when a year later William Cecil, now ennobled as Baron Burghley, forced through the trial and execution of Oxford's cousin Thomas Howard the duke of Norfolk, the son of his aunt Frances Vere the countess of Surrey. Burghley as leader of the Protestant administration had feared for the consequences if the Catholic duke of Norfolk was allowed to marry the imprisoned Mary Stuart and between them produce a Catholic heir to the throne. This brutal act may have served the country well by removing a potential threat to the security of the realm but at a personal level it alienated the twenty-two year old earl of Oxford who had tried and failed to obtain clemency for his Catholic cousin.

For the rest of his life Oxford was suspected of Catholic sympathies, even as being a closet Catholic himself. Although these suspicions were unfounded he was never again trusted by the Queen or her Protestant enforcers, Lord Burghley and Sir Francis Walsingham prominent among them. Whether he regretted it or not this ensured that the option of a career at court had been effectively closed off to him, forcing him to seek fulfilment elsewhere. Although born into a military family he never became a full-time soldier, nor did he leave London and return to Hedingham Castle so that he could engage in the sporting pursuits available to a landowner.

In other circumstances he might have considered a career in law or politics but this was not the direction his life was taking. He had a liking for louche company, actors and writers among them, which would have been inappropriate for anyone permanently at court. Even before the end of his nine years as a royal ward the first murmurs of concern over his conduct can be inferred from contemporary documents. Criticism of a highly placed aristocrat was risky so they chose their words carefully. Among those who wrote disparagingly about the young earl were the writer and noted scholar Gabriel Harvey, Charles Arundel a member of the Howard family, and the courtier George Talbot, later the 7th earl of Shrewsbury.

Oxford wanted to travel, preferably at the government's expense, but all his submissions to the Queen and his father-in-law Lord Burghley for service abroad were firmly rejected. After much lobbying he was eventually granted a licence to visit Italy, paying his own way, and in 1575 finally arrived in Venice. Although not supported by documentary evidence it is likely that during his several months spent in and around Venice he would have visited the studio of the great painter Titian who was still alive at the time, although in his late eighties.

In his poem *Venus and Adonis* the writer Shakespeare accurately describes Titian's fifth autograph replica of the famous painting, the one which shows Adonis wearing a red cap. He was equipped with dogs and spear to go hunting for a wild boar and would not be diverted from this purpose, rejecting the outstretched imploring arms of the naked Venus. This version differs from the others by showing Adonis in a red cap, the only one of the five to do so. The only explanation that serves is for the writer of the poem to have seen this version of the painting for himself when visiting Venice.

In September 1575 Oxford became ill while in Venice. He wrote home to Lord Burghley that he had 'been grieved with a fever but with the help of God I have recovered the same and am past the danger thereof although brought very weak thereby'. Although the plague was rife in Italy, peaking in 1576 with the death toll in thousands, it is more likely that the earl had succumbed to a bout of malaria, also widespread in Italy at the time. Malaria, known in England as the 'ague', is a recurring condition and so could have been one of the causes of Oxford's poor health from his late thirties until his death in 1604. Historically Italy had suffered greatly from the ravages of the mosquito, also known as 'Roman fever'. A deadly strain of malaria almost wiped out the Roman army in the fifth century and this may have contributed to the fall of the poorly defended city of Rome that followed.

Edward de Vere's sixteen months on the continent of Europe provided the inspiration for many plays. These plays, now world famous, or earlier versions of them, began to appear in the 1580s and accelerated the surge in literary excellence which has become associated with Queen Elizabeth's reign. In a remarkably short space of time the English language had evolved into a powerful and infinitely flexible medium of expression, for which much of the credit can be directly attributed to the author of Shakespeare. It would not be exaggerating to claim that Edward de Vere's continental travels represent one of the most influential journeys ever made by any writer. Thirty Shakespeare plays (listed on page 79) are set partly or wholly outside the British Isles, many of them in Italy and other countries bordering the Mediterranean and the Adriatic.

Using Venice as his base de Vere made four tours and there is sufficient evidence to believe that he visited or passed through Florence, Genoa, Mantua, Milan, Naples, Padua, Rome, Siena, Venice and Verona. Palermo in Sicily may be added to the list (and also possibly Messina, the setting for *Much Ado About Nothing*) but the other island states of Corsica and Sardinia were not visited and are not mentioned. Nor are the Italian towns of Bologna, Livorno, Parma, Ravenna, Rimini or Turin. These towns and cities were not included in de Vere's itinerary and no plays are set in them, nor are they mentioned in any of the other plays.

While at sea on his return journey in April 1576 the ship in which he was travelling was attacked and ransacked by pirates. These were believed to be Dutch, operating from the port of Vlissingen, anglicised as Flushing. Oxford was lucky to escape with his life but had to suffer the loss of all his possessions and purchases, including the clothes he was wearing which were stripped off. The Queen and Lord Burghley were outraged and complained to the Dutch ambassador. The Prince of Orange sent a written apology and assured them that the culprits were being rounded up and punished. The French ambassador in London from 1575-84 was Michel de Mauvissière. He recorded the incident about the pirates in his *Memoires* published c.1590.

Later, in 1606, one of Edward de Vere's continental travelling companions, Nathaniel Baxter, wrote a poem to honour the marriage of the earl's daughter, Lady Susan Vere, to Philip Herbert, soon afterwards ennobled as the earl of Montgomery. This contains some interesting information, for example that the Queen had ordered de Vere to return to England because of the mounting disease risk. She most likely had the plague in mind but Baxter refers instead to the deadly bite of the mosquito, 'Hopping Helena with her warbling sting... Like as they poisoned all Italy'. This poem also mentions the party's interception by sea pirates on the return journey.

> Naked we landed out of Italy
> Inthralled by pirates, men of no regard:
> Horror and death assailed nobility

There is a parallel reference to this incident in *Hamlet*. King Claudius banishes the prince to England but the ship he is sailing in is attacked by pirates. Hamlet writes to Horatio (Act 4, Scene 6) explaining that he had been robbed, roughly treated and returned naked back to Denmark. The incident with the pirates is not part of the story of the play, nor essential to the plot, so the reason for its inclusion adds to the authorship mystery. Although not a conclusive topical allusion it could be seen as an item of supporting evidence for the earl of Oxford as the principal writer of the Shakespeare plays.

The earl's first child, a daughter named Elizabeth, was born on 2nd of July 1575 while he was on his continental tour. When this came to an end in April 1576 there was an unwelcome development with far-reaching consequences. Oxford had been persuaded that the child was not his and on returning to London refused to meet his twenty-year old wife and rejected the paternity of his daughter, to the great distress of the Cecil family and others, including the Queen. All attempts at reconciliation were rejected by Oxford and no amount of persuasion or pressure by Burghley and the Queen could soften his resistance.

This harsh treatment of his wife on the weakest of malicious hearsay evidence has had an adverse effect on Oxford's suitability as the Shakespeare author. It fits uneasily with some of the high-minded moralising in the plays. His inexcusable behaviour to his wife and her family is hard to understand, explain or condone. It remains a serious objection to him as the true author of Shakespeare.

Not having a wife Oxford took a mistress, one of the Queen's attendant gentlewomen, Anne Vavasour. On the 21st March 1581 she gave birth to their son, baptised as Edward. The Queen was infuriated and had them imprisoned separately in the Tower. The Queen tried to make a reconciliation with his wife, and the acceptance of his infant daughter, a precondition of his release but still he refused. He was released from the Tower after fourteen weeks but was exiled from court for another two years. Eventually he capitulated and resumed his marriage by which time his daughter Elizabeth was six years and five months old.

Family honour was offended by the earl's liaison with Anne Vavasour and the resulting illegitimate baby. Her uncle Thomas Knyvet (later 1st Baron Knyvet), was a successful career courtier with the rank of Master at Arms and he took it personally, with a steady escalation in the level of angry recrimination. The smouldering enmity between the rival court factions of Oxford and Knyvet escalated into vicious street fighting, culminating in a pitched battle on 3rd March 1582. Both men were wounded, the earl more seriously, and one of his men was killed. This family feuding in public is replicated in the opening scenes of *Romeo and Juliet*. It is also of significance to the authorship mystery. Although the nature of the wound suffered by de Vere is unknown it severely impaired his mobility in later life, condemning him to a more sedentary existence. One conducive to writing, perhaps.

An attempt to keep the quarrelling families apart was made by Sir Roger Townshend (1544-90), the member of parliament for Raynham in Essex. Following the execution of Thomas Howard the duke of Norfolk he had become the business manager for his estate which included looking after the interests of the duke's three sons and two daughters. Townsend feared that the earl of Oxford and his brother-in-law Peregrine Bertie were planning an ambush for Thomas Knyvet. This never happened but it offers another authorship link. Peregrine Bertie, Baron Willoughby d' Eresby, was married to Lady Mary Vere, Edward's sister. In his capacity as the British Ambassador to the Danish royal family Bertie shuttled back and forth to the castle at Elsinore. On behalf of the Queen he had invested the Danish king, Frederick II, with the Order of the Garter, making in all five visits on official government business between 1582 and 1585.

In 1578 Edward de Vere the earl of Oxford employed the author John Lyly as his private secretary, also as his stage manager when he took over the lease of the Blackfriars theatre in 1583. In return Lyly dedicated his prose romance *Euphues and his England* to his employer and patron. This was the sequel to *Euphues: The Anatomy of Wit*, two books which made Lyly famous and founded a style of affected and pretentious writing, much parodied once it ceased to be fashionable.

In 1580 the earl purchased a large house and garden in Bishopsgate known as Fisher's Folly, setting it up as a literary salon and writers' workshop. Anthony Munday, Robert Greene, Thomas Watson and Edmund Spenser were among the authors mentored by de Vere, and all gratefully dedicated books or verses to their generous patron. Munday and the clergyman Abraham Fleming at various times also assisted Lyly in his secretarial capacity to the earl.

In the same year de Vere took over the company of actors known as The Earl of Warwick's Men and renamed them as Lord Oxford's Men, reviving his father's acting company after an interval of sixteen years. In the summer months the newly renamed company toured the provinces throughout the 1580s. De Vere also maintained a smaller troupe of young actors and singers in London known as Lord Oxford's Boys, drawn from The Children of the Chapel Royal and Paul's Boys, (from St Paul's Cathedral). These young men were in demand to play female roles and many graduated to employment in the adult companies. They staged some of Lyly's plays at the Blackfriars, among them *Campaspe* and *Sapho and Phao*.

The first twenty years of Queen Elizabeth's reign, 1558-1578, did not yield much in the way of literary excellence, a situation which then changed for the better so rapidly that to refer to it as a cultural revolution would not be an exaggeration. Edmund Spenser, John Lyly, Philip Sidney and his sister Mary Sidney, and later Christopher Marlowe, were a flowering of talent that quickly established the English language as capable of adaptation to any literary requirement.

Edward de Vere the earl of Oxford had just turned thirty when a succession of plays, later known to have Shakespeare connections, began to appear anonymously in the early 1580s, coinciding with the period during which he presided over his literary commune based at Fisher's Folly. Having exchanged the restrictions of the court for these more congenial surroundings he had created the circumstances in which he could strengthen and develop his own literary and musical talents.

Edward de Vere's involvement with professional musicians began at an early age and demonstrates an interest in all aspects of music, including composition. References to music occur throughout the Shakespeare canon, including in the stage directions. Songs (over a hundred) are a feature of the plays, as are dances and dancing, tavern and domestic music, the appreciation and instruction of music, and descriptions of musical instruments. The madrigalist John Farmer dedicated two books of compositions to him. In the second of these, *First Book of English Madrigals* (1599), he thanks the earl for his generous patronage in a surprisingly candid tribute.

> … without flattery be it spoken, those that know your Lordship know this, that using this science (music) as a recreation your Lordship have overgone most of them that make it a profession.

Oxford was a patron to the composer William Byrd, seven years his senior. Among Byrd's 470 listed compositions appears the keyboard work *My Lord of Oxford's March*, also known as *The March before the Battle*. In addition to Byrd and Farmer his music protégés included the composers Robert Hales and Henry Lichfield. Early poems published in anthologies under Edward de Vere's own formal name (Earl of Oxenford), were mostly song lyrics. Some lute, keyboard and ensemble pieces bear his name, for instance *My Lord of Oxenforde's Maske* from Thomas Morley's *First Book of Consort Lessons* (1599). Thomas Morley (1557-1602), another composer of madrigals, lived close to Fisher's Folly in Bishopsgate. Morley's setting of the song 'It was a lover and his lass' from *As You Like It* (Act 5, Scene 2) has remained in print to the present day.

By this time the earl of Oxford had sold off so many of his estates that he was barely solvent. Having squandered his patrimony he tried to recoup by investing heavily in a voyage to search for gold. This was funded by the London merchant Michael Lock (1532-1620) and led by the experienced navigator Martin Frobisher (1535-1594). Two exploratory north-west voyages had returned with promising samples from the rocky coast of what is now Canada, the southern extremity of Baffin Island. In 1578 a small fleet of ships capable of bringing back many tons of ore set sail from Plymouth. The expedition was sponsored by Queen Elizabeth with a grant of £1,000. Frobisher was appointed admiral of all the lands and seas he discovered and authorised to take possession of them in the Queen's name.

A generous return on the ore was predicted so the investment money was soon raised. Edward de Vere's initial share was for £1,000 but wishing to invest more and lacking properties to sell for ready cash he took out a bond for £2,000 with the organiser Michael Lock, raising his stake to £3,000. The ships returned in October with a thousand tons of ore but by now the efforts to smelt gold from the earlier shipments had failed, confirming them to be worthless iron-pyrites, unkindly called 'fool's gold', with more of the same just landed. Everyone lost their money, the Queen, Edward de Vere and most of all the money-lender Michael Lock who was speedily removed to the Fleet Prison accused of fraud.

Edward de Vere's loss of three thousand pounds calls to mind *The Merchant of Venice* in which the money-lender Shylock is owed a corresponding amount in ducats. In this play the spendthrift Bassanio, having run through his own money, asks his close friend Antonio (the merchant of the title) for a loan so that he can woo and marry the heiress Portia and begin spending hers. Antonio is financially overstretched at the time but being in love with Bassanio takes out a three thousand ducat loan with Shylock. His treasure ships are believed lost in a storm and he has to default on the repayment, thus invoking the famous 'pound of flesh' penalty clause.

Is Shylock a literary incarnation of Michael Lock? Are de Vere's three thousand pounds and Antonio's three thousand ducats more than just coincidence? The disastrous Canadian voyage has another possible reference in a Shakespeare play. This occurs in Act 2 Scene 2 (line 380) of *Hamlet* when the prince ruefully admits, 'I am but mad north-north-west'. So he was, lured like many others before and since into parting with money for a get-rich-quick scheme that failed to deliver.

Since attaining his majority in 1571 at the age of twenty-one Edward de Vere inherited his father's debts which were not finally paid off for another ten years. He was also racking up debts of his own. One third of a titled ward's estate reverted to the crown and he had to sign an obligation to pay double the amount if he defaulted on the payments. As fast as he sold off lands and property to pay his creditors the law of diminishing returns ensured that the gap between arrears and solvency was never closed. To finance his travels, to live in style, to flourish as a patron of the arts, and to write and produce for the theatre, he sold off his inherited estates until none were left.

Add in his losses with the Michael Lock north-west expedition and by his mid-thirties he was reduced to pleading for financial assistance from his father-in law Lord Burghley. Incredible though it must have seemed at the time, the extensive Vere estates accumulated over five hundred years had disappeared in less than twenty. Although he had contributed to his own downfall by his high maintenance lifestyle de Vere was so closely bound in to the governing establishment by ties of kinship and marriage that his complete financial ruin would have caused undue embarrassment and had to be prevented.

His rescue came on 26th June 1586 when the Queen granted him an annuity of £1,000, a substantial amount of money at the time. His annuity was later renewed by King James, although he only lived to receive it for one more year. What he had to provide in return for this princely allowance has never been made clear, although there are vague references to 'mine office' in his later correspondence. Whether it was to act as entertainments officer to the court, or to write propaganda in support of the Tudors and the Church of England, or simply to maintain his status and dignity as Lord Great Chamberlain will never be known.

Throughout this period the country was on a war footing, fearing the militarised wrath of Catholic Spain, with the entire coastline braced to repel an invading army. In 1585 the Prince of Orange appealed to Queen Elizabeth for help in the Dutch resistance to the occupying Spanish forces. In response she sent a small army led by Robert Dudley the earl of Leicester. Edward de Vere was one of several members of Queen Elizabeth's court who volunteered to serve. This was his second experience of armed conflict, the first being helping to suppress the Rising of the North in 1570.

Worse was to follow. The earl was one of the commissioners who investigated Mary Stuart's complicity in a plot against Queen Elizabeth and recommended the death penalty for treason. The Scots queen's execution in 1587 guaranteed that Spain would retaliate and the so-called 'Armada' set sail for England in1588, ferrying an occupying force of many thousands of soldiers. This venture ended in defeat for the Spanish but it gave the earl of Oxford one last chance of military action. He sailed in the armed sloop 'Edward Bonaventure' captained by James Lancaster as part of the flotilla of thirteen ships commanded by Sir Francis Drake. In the horseback victory parade to the service of thanksgiving at St Paul's Cathedral later in the year, de Vere in his capacity as Lord High Chamberlain rode immediately in front of Queen Elizabeth. It was his last public engagement before disappearing from sight in the official records of the period, it is assumed from poor health.

The earl of Oxford's first wife the former Anne Cecil died in June 1588. There is no record that he attended her funeral (as Hamlet was absent from Ophelia's funeral), the most likely explanation being that he was at sea serving with the naval fleet trying to intercept the Spanish invasion force. In December 1591 or early in 1592 (the exact date is not known) he married his second wife Elizabeth Trentham, another of the Queen's attendant gentlewomen, and an heiress. Countess Elizabeth proved to be a capable woman who restored her husband's domestic circumstances to order. Better still, in 1593, the new countess produced the long-awaited heir, Henry de Vere, later the 18th earl of Oxford. She also purchased a large property in the suburb of Hackney for them to live in, known as King's Place. This was sufficiently far from the court to provide the settled way of life conducive to study and full-time writing needed by an author.

Dangerous Liaisons

There exists an uneasy consensus among authorship doubters and others that the lives of Queen Elizabeth I, Edward de Vere the 17th earl of Oxford, and Henry Wriothesley the 3rd earl of Southampton were somehow inextricably linked. Although a generation apart the two earls had both been royal wards at Burghley House in the Strand, London, formerly Cecil House. In 1594 Lord Burghley tried and failed to persuade Southampton to marry his granddaughter Elizabeth Vere, the eldest daughter of Edward de Vere. The year before, 1593, Southampton had received the dedication of a narrative poem *Venus and Adonis* with the author shown as William Shakespeare, the first recorded use of the famous name. Southampton has also featured in Shakespeare studies as a prime candidate for the so-called 'Fair Youth' addressed in the Sonnets.

One of the more tenacious stories about Queen Elizabeth is that as a flirtatious teenage princess she was made pregnant by her guardian Sir Thomas Seymour, and gave birth to a son. This has become known as the 'Prince Tudor' theory. Seymour was the brother of Jane Seymour the third wife of Henry VIII and so was uncle to the boy king Edward VI. (As was his elder brother the Duke of Somerset, appointed as Lord Protector). Thomas Seymour was married to Catherine Parr, the widow of King Henry, with the teenage Princess Elizabeth sharing their house in Chelsea. Seymour was obsessed by the girl, causing his wife Catherine to send her to the royal residence at Hatfield for her own protection. Catherine died in childbirth not long afterwards and so could not prevent her infatuated husband from pursuing the princess to Hatfield.

By tradition the resulting baby, a boy, was smuggled into a family of suitable rank and brought up as one of their own. The birth of Edward de Vere fitted the time frame and the thick walls of Hedingham Castle would have provided the necessary concealment and discretion appropriate for a royal bastard. It should be noted that children conceived out of wedlock were excluded from the succession so even if de Vere was the so-called 'Prince Tudor' he would not have been eligible as an heir to the throne. Thomas Seymour was later charged with conspiring against his brother the Lord Protector and executed. One of the accusations levelled against him at his trial was his earlier misconduct with Princess Elizabeth, so the story had some foundation.

Earlier, at the age of thirteen, Edward de Vere's right to the earldom of Oxford had been challenged by his half-sister Lady Katherine Vere (twelve years his senior) and her husband Lord Edward Windsor. They claimed that John de Vere's sudden second marriage to Margery Golding, Edward's mother, was illegal because his estranged first wife Dorothy Neville was still living at the time. The suit failed but the rebuttal document gave Edward and his full-sister Mary the same age. Whether intentionally or not this perpetuated the confusion over Edward's exact date of birth and so gave the Prince Tudor myth some added momentum.

A second story citing Queen Elizabeth as a mother also involved Edward de Vere the earl of Oxford. She was now thirty-nine and in the seventeenth year of her reign. The earl was twenty-two and if the Prince Tudor theory applied then the queen was his mother. Implying that she had entered into a sexual relationship with the young earl would have constituted mother-and-son incest if he really was her son by Edward Seymour. Both of de Vere's early twenty-first century biographers, Mark Anderson and Alan Nelson, quote from the letter Mary Stuart, imprisoned in Sheffield Castle, wrote to Queen Elizabeth '… the Earl of Oxford dared not reconcile himself with his wife for fear of losing the favour which he hoped to receive by becoming your lover'.

The child which would have resulted from this second liaison was born in October 1563 and brought up as Henry Wriothesley, the third earl of Southampton. This theory is hard to sustain when portraits of the earl and his mother Mary Browne are compared. Southampton was imprisoned in the Tower after his association with the Essex rebellion of 1601 and painted there by John de Critz in 1603. His facial features closely resemble earlier paintings made of his mother Mary Browne, wife of his father the second earl of Southampton. The portrait of the incarcerated earl now hangs in Boughton House, Northamptonshire. The portrait of his mother Mary Browne, daughter of the 1st Viscount Montagu and painted in 1565, hangs in Welbeck Abbey, Nottinghamshire. It is therefore unlikely that the Queen was the earl of Southampton's mother with the earl of Oxford as his father.

3rd earl of Southampton
1573-1624 born at
Cowdray House in Midhurst

his mother Countess Mary
1552-1607

However, Oxford could still have been his father with his actual mother Mary Browne. This alternative theory cannot be authenticated but as a theory is plausible. At the time in question Oxford was estranged from his wife Anne Cecil, and Mary Browne had separated from her husband the second earl of Southampton. He was suspected of Catholic sympathies which included complicity in the Ridolfi plot to assassinate Queen Elizabeth. He was arrested and still imprisoned in the Tower at a time when his heir the third earl of Southampton would have needed to be conceived. Although there is no record of Oxford having an affair with Mary, the second earl's wife, the circumstances existed which could have made this possible.

This establishes a link to the Shakespeare Sonnets with their enigmatic references to a 'Fair Youth', ostensibly the recipient of homosexual advances from an older man. Henry Wriothesley the third earl of Southampton has always been viewed as the possible object of the writer's affections, mainly by association because the two long narrative poems *Venus and Adonis* and *The Rape of Lucrece* had been addressed to him. There is no recorded evidence that Shakspere of Stratford-upon-Avon ever met the earl of Southampton, still less that they were in a homosexual relationship. The disparity in rank would have made a loving partnership impossible and neither of these two men was known to be homosexual.

Nor was Edward de Vere, if considered as the true author of the Sonnets. He was twice married, had a mistress and fathered at least seven children, so is unlikely to have been the writer of homoerotic poetry. If the reproaches to a younger male in the so-called 'procreation' group of sonnets 1-17 were actually addressed to the earl of Southampton they would not seem so bizarre if the two men were father and son. Awkward phrases such as 'my lovely boy' in Sonnet 126 for example, would fall into place. If viewed as a disabled father addressing a comely young son, some of the earlier sonnets would make more sense than construed as homosexual advances from a middle-aged poet to a much younger man. The first two lines of Sonnet 37 would apply

> As a decrepit father takes delight
> To see his active child do deeds of youth

The number of ennobled persons at Queen Elizabeth's court was very much smaller than in the courts of later monarchs. This small tightly-knit circle of aristocrats serving the Queen all knew one another as a kind of extended family, much-interrelated, and were mindful of the obligations of caste which required infidelity to be kept among themselves. These affectionate lines from the third sonnet suggest at least the writer's fondness and admiration for the earl of Southampton's mother

> Thou art thy mother's glass, and she in thee
> Calls back the lovely April of her prime

A fourth possible scenario is drawn from the poem *Willoughby His Avisa* which hints that the earl of Oxford's poor state of health precluded him from an active sexual relationship with his second wife Elizabeth Trentham. Within the enclosed confines of court life this allowed the twenty year old Henry Wriothesley to form an adulterous relationship with the countess Elizabeth, a liaison which resulted in a pregnancy and the birth of a male child on 24th February 1593. This was Henry de Vere, the future 18th earl of Oxford. Interestingly no other male member of the Vere family had been named 'Henry' so the choice of name is worthy of note. A variant of this theory is that Edward de Vere's desire for a male heir condoned the adultery, indeed that he may have actively sponsored it and contrived the circumstances that made it possible. If Southampton was his natural son the genes passed on would have been very close.

In 1624, twenty years after Edward de Vere's death, an engraving by Thomas Jenner showed side by side in armour, mounted on galloping chargers, two 'Heroes of the Protestant Cause'. It was titled 'The Two Most Noble Henries'. They were Henry de Vere the eighteenth earl of Oxford and Henry Wriothesley the third earl of Southampton. Depending on which version is believed the two heroes could have been father and son, half-brothers or distant cousins. A year later and both had died on active service abroad, in the Protestant cause against Catholic Spain.

A Reclusive Invalid

The letters written by Edward de Vere to his father-in-law Lord Burghley and his brother-in-law Robert Cecil have been preserved in the Hatfield archive and contain information relevant to the authorship, for example his references to being made lame. The nature of the wound de Vere suffered in the feuding with Thomas Knyvet has never been established but in a letter to Burghley dated 25th March 1595 he writes, 'I will attend Your Lordship as well as a lame man may at your house'. In other letters to Lord Burghley, and in later letters to his brother-in-law Sir Robert Cecil, he makes similar references to a disabling condition which impaired his movement in later life. The lameness could have been caused by an injury incurred in one of the martial arts tournaments in which he excelled as a young man or it could have resulted from damage to his knee in a Venetian galley during his travels in Italy. Sonnet 74 mentions 'the coward conquest of a wretch's knife', which would appear to identify the fracas with Thomas Knyvet and his supporters as the most likely source of the disablement. There are references to lameness in Sonnets 37, 66 and 89

So I, made lame by fortune's dearest spite	from Sonnet 37	line 3
So then I am not lame, poor, nor despised	from Sonnet 37	line 9
And strength by limping away disabled	from Sonnet 66	line 8
Speak of my lameness, and I straight will halt	from Sonnet 89	line 3

There is another scholarly consensus that the character of Polonius in *Hamlet* is modelled on William Cecil, Lord Burghley. Polonius is the chief minister of Denmark, Burghley his counterpart in London. It is an unflattering although not a cruel portrait, showing Polonius as tediously fond of the sound of his own voice. In the play he is gently mocked as a 'fishmonger', a reference to his attempts as a Lincolnshire man to revive the flagging east coast fishing industry by encouraging people to eat fish on a Wednesday as well as on Friday.

Hamlet was not shown on the public stage until 1639 although there are some references to earlier versions performed for small private audiences in London, Oxford and Cambridge. In *The First Two Quartos of Hamlet* quoted earlier, Dr Jolly writes, p.186, 'At some point between its composition and its printing *Hamlet* is performed in the two universities of Oxford and Cambridge and in London and elsewhere'. *Hamlet* has always been the play most closely studied for authorship clues. This is because the structure of the play focuses throughout on Hamlet as the main character. It tells Hamlet's story from beginning to end and tells it in such a way that it seems a personal story, leading many to view it as autobiographical.

If Edward de Vere the earl of Oxford was the author this could very well be true. When considered against the other authorship contenders his close and lifelong association with the Cecil family would make him the best qualified to write in intimate detail about his in-laws. Burghley had a daughter, Anne, who died young in unhappy circumstances. Polonius had a daughter, Ophelia, who died young in unhappy circumstances. Burghley had a son, Thomas, who wished to travel to Paris. Polonius had a son, Laertes, who wished to travel to Paris. Burghley briefed his secretary Thomas Windebank to spy on his son Thomas in Paris. Polonius briefed his servant Reynaldo to spy on his son Laertes in Paris (Act 2, Scene 1).

When Thomas Cecil finally set out for Paris on 29th May 1561 he carried with him a travel document from his father. This took the form of a stern Puritan sermon listing the prayers Thomas should say night and morning and the confessions he should make if led astray in Paris by the pleasures of the flesh. These sententious precepts included advice on how to dress and conduct himself.

A Memorial for Thomas Cecil, my son, to peruse and put in use from time to time concerning divers things given to him in charge by me, Wm Cecil, his father. Anno Domini 1561. After morning prayer ... you shall make you ready in your apparel of cleanly sort, doing that for civility and health and not for pride.

A full account can be found in Conyers Read's biography of Sir William Cecil, *Mr Secretary Cecil and Queen Elizabeth*. Ophelia's brother Laertes was the recipient of similar tendentious advice from Polonius when he too set off for Paris. (*Hamlet* 1.3.55-81).

Costly thy habit as thy purse can buy,
But not expressed in fancy, rich not gaudy:
For the apparel oft proclaims the man.

How the author of *Hamlet* was made aware of the advice the humourless Cecil inflicted on his son Thomas will never be known. If written by Edward de Vere, his brother-in-law and fellow sufferer, the close family connection might provide an answer.

On another subject, the impressive level of detailed medical knowledge occurring in the plays adds a further dimension to the Shakespeare enigma. The book *Shakespeare and Medicine* by the Scottish surgeon R. R. Simpson identifies over seven hundred medical references in the plays. The American scholar Professor Stephen Booth (writing from the Stratfordian corner), considers that the published works of the Elizabethan physician George Baker provided the main medical influence on Shakespeare, in particular his 1576 book *The Newe Jewell of Health*.

George Baker wrote several medical works and translated others. He was an advocate of the new Paracelsian approach to health, with medication based on pharmacology. He was also house physician to the Vere family and his famous book *The Newe Jewell of Health* was dedicated to countess Anne, Edward de Vere's first wife: 'To The Right Honourable, Vertuous, and his singular good Lady the Noble Countess of Oxford'. A second edition of this book *The Practice of the New and Old Phisicke* in 1599 was dedicated to Edward de Vere himself. Another committed Paracelsian was the London apothecary John Hester who described himself as a 'Practitioner in the Arte of Distillations'. He translated numerous books on medical matters, one of which, *A Short Discourse on Surgerie* published in 1580 was from the Italian. It was dedicated to Edward de Vere and carried the Oxford coat of arms on the title page.

> From his outlays on drugs and care … nearly one fifth of his total expenses, and from his subsequent patronage of apothecaries, we may infer that Oxford was chronically sickly, hypochondriacal, or both.

This quotation is from *Monstrous Adversary*, Alan Nelson's life of Edward de Vere the earl of Oxford, and it goes some way to answering the question of how the author of Shakespeare may have acquired his medical knowledge. If de Vere was the author then his association with apothecaries, and the books dedicated to him and his wife on medical subjects, could offer an explanation, including his knowledge of plants and their therapeutic applications.

One of the first to employ Paracelsian methods in England was Sir Thomas Smith, de Vere's early tutor and mentor. In November 1574 he provided some herbal medicine for de Vere's first wife Countess Anne to prevent her from miscarrying. Sir Thomas was a Renaissance polymath whose interests included horticulture and gardening which he practised at his manors of Hill Hall in Essex and at Ankerwicke, a former female priory on the north bank of the Thames, not far from Windsor.

Lord Burghley was another keen horticulturalist. He had upgraded his mansion Theobalds House near Cheshunt in Hertfordshire to provide a palace fine enough to accommodate the Queen on her visits. The formal gardens at Theobalds House were modelled after the Château de Fontainebleau in France, the English botanist and herbalist John Gerard acting as their superintendent. In David and Ben Crystal's glossary, *Shakespeare's Words*, the list of botanical references in the plays runs to three and a half pages. These were mostly the shrubs, flowers, herbs and fruits cultivated in the formal gardens of Elizabethan stately homes such as those mentioned above, and where Edward de Vere the earl of Oxford spent most of his life.

The ingredients for the cauldron in *Macbeth* are mostly botanical. 'Tongue of dog' refers to the hounds-tongue plant with its long tapering leaves. This is a member of the Borage family, widely used in herbal medicine until recent times. 'Scale of dragon' refers to the herb estragon, more commonly known as tarragon. 'Eye-of-Newt' was the common name for the small seeds of the mustard plant. Ophelia's distributed flowers in *Hamlet* all had significance, among them Columbine which is traditionally considered a symbol of masculine faithlessness. She gives this to King Claudius. To Queen Gertrude she gives Rue, a symbol of female faithlessness. Rue was also one of the plants traditionally employed to procure abortions.

Edward de Vere had access to some well-stocked libraries and also had the time to read and study matters of interest to him. Even so the depth of knowledge about physical and mental illnesses revealed in the plays is not easily explained. The references to the flow of blood around the body, the regular beating of the heart and pulse for example, display a level of knowledge about the working of the human body long before such matters became accepted by the medical profession. A deranged Hamlet having just slain Polonius with a sword thrust in front of his mother assures her that he is in a sane and normal state of mind.

> My pulse as yours doth temperately keep time,
> And makes as healthful music

Similarly with the abnormal states of mind possessed by characters in the plays, women as well as men. The psychiatrist Sir John Bucknill (1817-1897) wrote three books about the many Shakespeare characters showing symptoms of mental illness. These were *The Psychology of Shakespeare* published in 1859, *The Medical Knowledge of Shakespeare* in 1860 and *The Mad Folk of Shakespeare* in 1867. Sir John was fascinated by the plays and impressed by their forcefulness of language, most of all by the 'extent and exactness' of their psychiatric knowledge.

> That abnormal states of mind were a favourite study of Shakespeare would be evident from the number of characters to which he has attributed them. On no other subject has he written with such mighty power.

In *The Medical Knowledge of Shakespeare* he expresses amazement that the author's descriptions of the 'diseases of the mind' were comparable with 'the most advanced science of the present day'. He writes that Shakespeare used medical terms with 'scientific strictness'. In *The Psychology of Shakespeare* he deals with specific characters in the plays and writes long case-study notes about them, calling them 'psychological essays'. These include studies of Constance, Hamlet, Jaques, King Lear, Macbeth, Malvolio, Ophelia and Timon,

Yet Sir John Bucknill could not explain how the son of a 'wool-comber' (his term for John Shakspere) acquired such extensive medical knowledge. He concluded that Shakespeare must have been 'an insatiable devourer of books', which he says at that time would have needed to include medical treatises written in French. It never seems to have occurred to Sir John that someone other than the son of a 'wool-comber' might have written these extraordinary plays.

Situations and characters in some of the plays could be seen as linked to incidents in the earl of Oxford's own life. The character of Posthumus in *Cymbeline* would apply. He is a young man brought up in the household of Cymbeline the king of Britain who secretly marries his daughter Innogen and is promptly banished. Posthumus travels to Italy where he becomes sympathetic to Imperial Rome. While there he is tricked into believing that his wife Innogen has been unfaithful to him. He arranges for her to be killed but she escapes. On his return Posthumus is imprisoned but eventually released and reconciled to his wife and father-in-law. This sequence of events could be seen as similar to the earl of Oxford's eagerness to visit Catholic Italy, his falsely accused wife Anne Cecil and her politically dominant father Lord Burghley.

A charge of bastardy never quite goes away. Although he survived his sister Katherine's challenge that her son Frederick Windsor should have inherited the earldom it took a year before being resolved in his favour. There is a parallel situation in the play *King Lear*. De Vere had one legitimate son (Henry) and one illegitimate son (Edward). In the play the earl of Gloucester has one has one legitimate son (Edgar) and one illegitimate son (Edmund) . In the same play King Lear has three daughters in need of generous dowries, Goneril, Regan and Cordelia, but his maladroit allocation of territories leads immediately to the darkest of all Shakespeare's great tragedies. Edward de Vere the bankrupt earl of Oxford likewise had three daughters in need of wedding portions, Elizabeth, Bridget and Susan. To provide them he had to sell and parcel out the manor of Hedingham with its castle, the ancestral home of the Vere family for five hundred years. This final humiliation completed his downfall and could be seen as reflected in the plays of *King Lear*, *Hamlet*, *Othello* and *Macbeth* which all end in tragedy and death.

In *All's Well That Ends Well* the count of Roussillon has just died and his young son Bertram is promptly summoned to the French court as a royal ward. He resents this but has to obey the King of France, predicting bitterly that as a ward of court he will be kept 'evermore in subjection'. This resonates with Edward de Vere's unhappy experience of wardship under the thumb of William Cecil, as in his case the subjection did indeed last for 'evermore'. The two main characters in *All's Well* are Helen the daughter of a physician, and Bertram the young count of Roussillon. Helen has grown up in the same house as Bertram just as Edward de Vere had lived in the same house as his future wife Anne Cecil (Hamlet and Ophelia likewise). The King of France has a medical condition resisting treatment but Helen has a remedy learned from her physician father and is able to effect a cure. The king rewards Helen by giving her his ward Bertram in lieu of a fee. Bertram objects strenuously but is married to

Helen at the King's insistence. Edward de Vere's marriage of expedience to his guardian's daughter was equally inauspicious and ill-fated from the start.

The fictional Bertram and the real life Edward de Vere were both eager for active military service, both had their applications refused, and both fled the court in search of battlefield glory. In a defiant letter to his mother Bertram wrote, 'I have wedded her, not bedded her'. Nor does he intend to but Helen is resourceful and determined (3.2.19-27), making use of the 'bed-trick' to consummate her marriage, impregnate herself and force a reconciliation with her absconding husband. Substituting one woman for another in a darkened bedroom to deceive a man is not an edifying practice by the moral standards of the present day but was a popular theatrical device in Shakespeare's time. The bed-trick was also used to steer another Shakespeare play to a conclusion, *Measure for Measure*.

Thomas Looney in *Shakespeare Identified*, (page 234), quotes from a local history source that Anne the countess of Oxford used the bed-trick to be made pregnant by her husband, from whom she had been separated for three years. In *The History and Topography of the County of Essex* published in 1836 the author Thomas Wright claimed, 'He (the earl of Oxford) forsook his lady's bed but the father of Lady Anne by stratagem, contrived that her husband should unknowingly sleep with her, believing her to be another woman, and she bore a son to him as a consequence of this meeting'. (Volume 1 p. 517). The resulting baby born 2nd July 1575 was a daughter rather than a son, which casts doubt on the story, as does implicating Lord Burghley in the subterfuge, but it remains an interesting link between Edward de Vere and plays by Shakespeare.

Timon of Athens is another play which appears to mirror closely the trajectory of Edward de Vere's downfall. Timon in Athens and de Vere in London both maintained a lavish lifestyle but were soon ruined by their reckless extravagance and refusal to heed warnings from their advisers. Generous patronage of the performing arts could be viewed as laudable philanthropy but all too soon the coffers were emptied and the distribution of largesse came to a precipitate and bankrupt end. The fictional Timon and the all too real Edward de Vere were shocked by the equally swift desertion of their friends when news of this reversal of fortune became known. Both realised too late that they had been cheated by those they had trusted, even more so when they sold all their remaining lands and property but could still not reconcile their debts. Humiliated, they withdrew into embittered seclusion and neither died well. With its grisly references to late stage syphilis *Timon* is a harrowing play to read or watch but as an example of the author's obsessive interest in medical matters it synchronises with the authorship profile.

Numerous nautical references indicate close acquaintance with ships and sailing. In *A Midsummer Night's Dream* the fairy queen Titania when speaking to her estranged husband Oberon has some vivid images of observing large trading ships in the open sea

The fairyland buys not the child of me,
His mother was a votaress of my order,
And in the spicèd Indian air by night
Full often hath she gossiped by my side,
And sat with me on Neptune's yellow sands,
Marking th' embarkèd traders on the flood,
When we have laughed to see the sails conceive
And grow big-bellied with the wanton wind.

That a play containing such poetic language could so easily have been lost is hard to imagine but fortunately for all concerned it was safely preserved with many others in the First Folio. The identities of the good people who compiled the Folio are not known but English Literature owes them a debt of gratitude which can never be repaid. Putting it together must have been a daunting task not lightly undertaken, and it remains the least thoroughly researched part of the authorship mystery.

If Edward de Vere was the true Shakespeare then those who conceived the idea of a collected edition of his plays many years after his death, funded it, set the work in motion and guided the project through to completion could have been the close members of his family. These would most likely have been his daughter Susan and her husband Philip Herbert, her brothers-in-law William Herbert and William Stanley, and her mother-in-law Mary Sidney Herbert. These wealthy aristocrats had the means, and between them the range of literary skills, that could cope with the large-scale editing and revising tasks required for such an ambitious undertaking.

All mysteries ultimately have a practical explanation, often the simplest and least contentious, which could apply in the case of the First Folio. The quarto editions of the individual plays appearing in the 1590s were mostly issued anonymously, and after 1598 pseudonymously as by 'William Shakespeare'. Nowhere were the names of 'Edward de Vere' or 'My Lord of Oxenford' associated with writing for the stage, either before his death in 1604, or after the publication of the First Folio in 1623. There was no reason for anyone to ask, or to be told, not even the printers in the Jaggard workshop, that the name of the originating author was different from the name on the title page. Even before the Folio was printed this information had already drifted quietly from view and in the course of time soon became irretrievably lost.

If the compilers of the First Folio were honouring the wishes of the author to remain anonymous after death they were entirely successful. If the suppression of identity was insisted on by the family members, rather than the writer himself, that too was successful. After the Restoration in 1660 a new generation of playwrights and actors came to prominence. The wordy and versified drama of Shakespeare (and most of his Elizabethan

232

counterparts) fell out of fashion until the renewal of interest in them led by David Garrick in the next century. By then the trail had gone cold, nor has subsequent research into the Shakespeare authorship mystery produced a universally acceptable alternative candidate.

Edward de Vere died on 24th June 1604. He was not buried until 6th July which makes plague as the cause of death unlikely, as plague victims were routinely disposed of quickly. No cause of death was given in the parish register but from the decline in his health, as gleaned from his surviving letters, it would seem to have been from natural causes. It is likely that he was interred in the church of St Augustine in Hackney but no memorial exists to confirm this, and it is the absence of a funerary monument for such a high-ranking nobleman that has provoked curiosity ever since.

Dying eight years later his widow countess Elizabeth asks in her will that a suitable monument should be made for herself and her husband, which implies that no monument had been provided after the earl's death in 1604. There is no record that her nineteen-year-old son Henry de Vere the 18th earl of Oxford provided such a monument, nor her brother Francis Trentham, one of the executors of her will.

A distant relative on his mother's side, Percival Golding, left a brief note to the effect that the earl had been buried in Westminster Abbey but this has never been authenticated from the Abbey records. In 1720 the ecclesiastical historian John Strype published a survey of 67 tombs and inscriptions in St Augustine's Church but made no mention of a monument for the Earl and Countess of Oxford. An earlier but less comprehensive survey had been made in 1633 but again no Oxford monument was listed.

For those who believe that Edward de Vere the earl of Oxford was the writer known as William Shakespeare the denial of authorship and the absence of a grave could be seen as an appropriate and inevitable consequence. Anonymous, invisible, incognito in death as in life, the literary earl seemed predestined to live and die in obscurity. If suffering is the midwife of genius then he qualified in heaped measure.

Edward de Vere the 17th earl of Oxford continues to have the most organised support as the author of Shakespeare's works, and would seem to have a strong case, but it falls short from lack of conclusive evidence.

Objections to Edward de Vere as Shakespeare

The point is often made by Oxfordians and other doubters that William Shakspere never put himself forward as the writer of the plays, nor after his death did his few surviving relatives make such a claim on his behalf. The same objection could be raised against Edward de Vere who had ample opportunity if he so wished to leave behind irrefutable evidence that he was the true Shakespeare author. There are some enigmatic clues which could have been planted by him, or by others after his death, but they fall short of full disclosure.

As an example the second of two quarto editions of *Troilus and Cressida* appearing in 1609 contains an address to the reader. It is headed 'A Never writer, to an Ever reader'. This oddly worded construction is seen by some Oxfordians as a cryptic reference to the earl who used the 'Vere' part of his name in several ways. In a letter to Lord Burghley dated 18th May 1591 he concludes, 'Your Lordship's eVer to command, Edward Oxenford'. Another example is drawn from the title of *The Winter's Tale*. There is nothing about 'winter' in the play that would link the title to the contents. Whether or not the title was deliberately chosen as an authorship clue it translates into French as 'Le Conte d'hiver', which sounds suspiciously like 'Count de Vere'.

Shakespeare cryptology produced little of value in the past and the results from modern computer analysis are equally unconvincing. English Literature departments in every school and university solidly maintain their loyalty to the man from Stratford-upon-Avon. Hardly anyone likes the idea of substituting an effete aristocrat for Honest Will, the sturdy man of the people who succeeded by his own efforts, who was patriotically born on 23rd April, St George's Day, and was voted in as their Man of the Millennium.

Although other alternative authors have been proposed none of them are disliked in the same way that Edward de Vere's name is still angrily rejected. The opposition got their retaliation in first and wrote him out of the script as an arrogant hot-tempered dandy who pulled rank to extricate himself from one tight corner after another, such as killing one of his guardian's servants when aged seventeen.

The mistreatment of his teenage wife and the distress it caused to her family is even harder to overlook. It clashes with the positive attitude to women in the plays. One of the many qualities for which the plays of Shakespeare have been critically acclaimed over very many years is the number of good parts for women, both young and old. Masculine domination in a society heavily patriarchal at the time of writing makes this sensitive appreciation and understanding of women a remarkable exception. A cast list of strong-minded, lively and seductive female characters has contributed hugely to the success of Shakespeare as a saleable brand: Adriana, Anne Page, Beatrice, Cleopatra, Helen in *All's*

234

Well, Innogen, Juliet (*Romeo and Juliet*), Katherine the Shrew, Luciana, Lady Macbeth, Marina, Nerissa, Queen Elizabeth (*Richard III*), Queen Margaret, Portia, Paulina, Mistress Quickly, Rosalind, Countess of Roussillon, Titania, Tamora, Viola. It is not easy to see how these spirited, and often courageous women, originated from the mind of Edward de Vere if judged by the misery he inflicted on his pathetically young bride Anne Cecil.

That so many senior academics, men and women, are implacably opposed to the idea of Edward de Vere as the writer of the Shakespeare plays should also be a cause of concern. These distinguished people are the cleverest in their field, with many lifetimes devoted to research, study, debate and scholarly tuition. Their objections have to be taken seriously.

The American scholar Alan H. Nelson, Professor of English at the University of California, Berkeley, wrote a five-hundred-page book with the declared intention of specifically countering the claims made on behalf of the earl of Oxford as the writer of Shakespeare. The title of his book is '*Monstrous Adversary*'. Published in 2003 by the Liverpool University Press it is a masterly treatise based on the transliteration of many Elizabethan handwritten documents. But the author is not sympathetic to his biographical subject. Far from it. Nelson's unrelenting contempt for the earl at every stage of his life is hard to understand. Such vehemence is usually reserved for political hate figures rather than the minor poet he considered Oxford to be. Having trashed his reputation and disparaged his literary pretensions Nelson's concluding sentence contains a playful misquote from *Hamlet*

> No acquaintance or stranger is known to have mourned Oxford's passing. As of 27 June [1604] his name disappeared from lists of peers eligible to attend the House of Lords. The rest was silence.

Another five-hundred page book *The Oxford Companion to Shakespeare* edited by Michael Dobson and Stanley Wells was published by the Oxford University Press in 2011. Under the heading 'Oxfordian theory' the case for Edward de Vere as Shakespeare is scoffed at and demolished in three paragraphs on page 335. Although demeaning for an academic debate the jocular tone is amusing, as can be judged from these short extracts

> De Vere was a notorious figure at Queen Elizabeth's court, violent and irresponsible: he killed a servant when he was only seventeen, and his many subsequent quarrels included a brawl with the family of a lady-in-waiting he had impregnated and a conspiracy against [Philip] Sidney. In between squandering his estate, fighting in Flanders, and feuding, however, he established a reputation as a good dancer and musician.

The view that de Vere supplemented his more public involvement with poetry and the theatre by secretly writing the Shakespeare canon in his spare time was first put forward in 1920 by the unfortunately named J. Thomas Looney in *Shakespeare Identified*. … Looney offered no explanation as to why or how de Vere should have published mediocre work under his own name and masterpieces under Shakespeare's, nor why the deception should have been kept up by the compilers of the First Folio, and he had to argue that the Shakespeare plays visibly written after de Vere's death in 1604 must have been subsequently revised by others.

Edward de Vere supporters were not intimidated by this or similar establishment put-downs and his cause continues to accrue adherents, from north America most numerously. Irritated by the continuing support for other alternative authors as well as Edward de Vere, a caucus of senior academics in 2013 published a collection of essays reaffirming their belief that William Shakspere of Stratford-upon-Avon was the true author of the plays published in London under the name of William Shakespeare. The title of the book was *Shakespeare Beyond Doubt*. It was edited by Paul Edmondson and Stanley Wells and published by the Cambridge University Press.

In it Professor Sir Stanley Wells, the doyen of Shakespeare scholarship, contributes a chapter drawing attention to the number of contemporary allusions to Shakespeare up to the start of the civil war in 1642. Professor Wells concludes his essay on page 87 with a defiant statement of belief. He thunders, 'The evidence that Shakespeare wrote Shakespeare is overwhelming, and to dispute it is to challenge the entire validity of historical research'. So noted.

Only sixty-seven letters and documents in Edward de Vere's distinctive italic handwriting have survived, most of them written to his in-laws, William Cecil Lord Burghley and his second son Sir Robert Cecil. None of them mention matters of a literary nature. It can be supposed that as a well-educated aristocrat with a wide circle of acquaintances de Vere would have written and received many other letters, all now lost. We shall never know whether or not these missing letters contained authorship references but since no positive clues occur in any of the main texts of either prose or poetry, probably not. The decision to withhold the writer's identity seems to have been made at an early stage with the secrecy maintained until the present day.

Eighteen of de Vere's sixty-seven surviving letters are written as appeals for the monopoly of the tin mines in Cornwall and Devon. Tin was mined under licence, purchased in bulk and by the business practice of 'preemption' sold at a controlled price. The first letter in the sequence is dated 20th March 1595 and takes the form of a long application from de Vere to his father-in-law Lord Burghley asking to be appointed as crown agent for the supply of tin. He addressed his letter to 'To the Right Honourable and his very good lord, the Lord Treasurer of England'

I most earnestly and heartily desire your Lordship to have a feeling of mine unfortunate estate, which, although it be far unfit to endure delays, yet have consumed four or five years in a flattering hope of idle words.

He was still writing in the same way in 1599, which added to the 'four or five years' mentioned in the letter implies that almost the whole decade was spent writing begging letters in the hopeless pursuit of a business income at little expense of money or effort from himself. A memorandum from him to the Queen in support of his claim runs to several pages of densely written argument. Addressed 'For the Queen's Majesty', the first two paragraphs are typical of the rest

The tin, which is yearly imported, comes to twelve hundred thousand pound weight and some three-score thousand over, as being cast into blocks doth plainly show. For every block being three hundred and fifty pound weight and three thousand six hundred blocks, it comes to the same number of pound weight which is transported.

The tin which is spent in the realm comes to a fourth part at the least, which is three hundred pound weight. So that the whole quantity of tin is fifteen hundred thousand weight. Thus is tin bought up by the merchant, as shall appear to Your Majesty, by the yearly memorials of the coinages, which I have sent you in a schedule by itself, most commonly at twenty, two and twenty, and three and twenty pounds in money for a thousand pound weight of tin.

Was this dismal missive written by the same hand that wrote *Romeo and Juliet*? It is hard to reconcile the two. The commonplace nature of the subject matter and the uninspired prose are an awkward fit with the lofty humanitarian drama and poetry supposedly being written at the same time. Loyal Oxfordians would surely have hoped and confidently expected that the last decade of the earl's life would have been devoted to writing and revising the great tragic plays with their deep psychological insight into human frailty that made the name of Shakespeare world famous, not wrangling over the price of tin. These stannary negotiations drawn out over many years must have been time consuming, and also counter-productive if it encroached into the time he would otherwise have spent in writing or revising the plays. The tin mining exploits from start to finish are a legitimate cause for doubt and disquiet. They weaken the case that Edward de Vere the earl of Oxford doubled up as William Shakespeare the world-famous poet and playwright.

Whether it was his suspected Catholic sympathies, or the mis-management of his own finances and family affairs as a younger man that caused the distrust, the result was the same. No advancement was provided for the earl by Lord Burghley who died in 1598, or Queen Elizabeth who died in 1603. (He fared better under King James). With equal lack of success he had persevered in his appeals to be granted one of the lucrative sinecures in their gift. Instead he was denied membership of the Privy Council, regularly voted down for a Garter knighthood and offered only token military commands. He lobbied for and failed to obtain the presidency of Wales (awarded to his Hackney neighbour Baron Zouche) , or the governership of Jersey (awarded to Sir Walter Raleigh) . His requests to act as the crown agent for a range of imported commodities other than tin were also refused. Cumulatively these repeated rejections must have been dispiriting. If Edward de Vere was the author they could go some way to account for the bleak closures in many of the Shakespeare plays, retelling in painful detail the downfall of great men and women whose lives also ended in ignominious failure.

Inseparable from any discussion of the authorship is the length of time that would have been needed to write forty plays. Leaving aside their merit it would still have taken many years of concentrated hard work. Writing in ink with a quill pen on vellum during the hours of daylight would have been slow and laborious. Working by candle light in the winter months even more so. Even with secretarial help and adequate funding it would have been a prodigious labour. Did the earl of Oxford, from the little we actually know about him, possess the motivation and strength of character to make the sacrifices inherent in any form of sustained artistic creativity? Many would doubt that he did.

We are now almost a hundred years on from Looney in 1920 and the position is little changed. In any authorship debate the Stratfordians hold a trump card, namely that none of the contending names are supported by direct evidence. This is equally true of Edward de Vere. Although his credentials as the most probable main author are persuasive, some might say compelling, there is no clinching evidence to support such a claim.

10 The Shakespeare Authorship Tragedy

The Shakespeare Authorship Tragedy

Not to know the identity of any great writer would be a matter for concern. For Shakespeare it is a matter of profound regret. The plays and poetry would take on a new significance if viewed as originating from the mind of someone with close ties to Queen Elizabeth and her ruling elite. How much more satisfying would be our interpretation of the plays, and even more so of the sonnets, if they could be matched to real people and actual incidents in the writer's life. Not to be able to give praise where praise is due adds to the frustration that has surrounded the authorship mystery for many years.

The many hundreds (perhaps thousands) of books and articles purporting to tell William Shakespeare's life story are without exception works of fiction. They cannot be otherwise. No documentary evidence exists that would provide source material for an authentic biography, however brief. This lack of documentation has allowed books based entirely on informed guesswork and conjecture to be written with impunity, and published with little fear of challenge or exposure.

All mysteries however seemingly intractable have a practical explanation and in this case it is the distance back into the past, the 18th April 1593 to be precise. This was the day on which the narrative poem *Venus and Adonis* was registered with the Stationers' Company. This launched the name of William Shakespeare and since no living author with that name has ever been traced the only explanation that serves is for it to have been a pen-name devised to conceal the true identity of the writer. Successfully in this case, as no name other than Shakespeare's was subsequently associated with his poetry or with the quarto editions of his plays. This last publishing sequence began in 1598 with the play *Love's Labour's Lost*.

Not knowing the identity of the author means that we do not know the date of his death but the subterfuge over the authorship remained in place up to and including the publication of the collected plays in 1623. In practice the people who knew the identity of the author, or who cared what happened to the plays, could have been few in number. The First Folio dedication suggests that wealthy members of the Herbert family underwrote the project, and chose to stay with the pseudonymous name William Shakespeare. As this was first used in 1593 there exists a span of thirty years until the First Folio of 1623, during which time the identity of the originating author just quietly faded away.

What arrangements the author made for publication after his death will never be known, or the extent to which family alliances influenced the decision. From clues in the sonnets it seems he did not want to be associated with the plays and was reconciled to permanent anonymity after death. These concluding lines from Sonnet 72 would apply

> My name be buried where my body is,
> And live no more to shame nor me nor you.
>> For I am shamed by that which I bring forth,
>> And so should you, to love things nothing worth.

Just why he should write so feelingly about shame and disgrace in his private life, and appear to reject his own work, will also never be known but it elicits our sympathy for what was obviously a distressing set of circumstances for the author. Few would have guessed that the pseudonym would survive and become famous while his real name and identity would be lost for ever. Everyone but the author, that is, who seems to have foreseen that this would happen, and wanted it that way. These few words from Sonnet 81 poignantly express a wish to remain anonymous after death

> I, once gone, to all the world must die

What he cannot have foreseen was that entirely the wrong man would become the recipient of so much misdirected praise and admiration. This is a measure of the tragedy and sorrow which still surrounds the Shakespeare Authorship Mystery and will do so for ever more.

Summary

- Not one page of handwritten manuscript by Shakespeare has survived, either of the plays or the poetry.

- There are no authenticated surviving early works, no 'juvenilia'.

- Not one item of correspondence written by William Shakespeare has ever been found.

- There is no record that anyone named William Shakespeare owned a house in London or moved his family there during the period when the plays would have been written, the late sixteenth and early seventeenth century.

- There is no record of anyone named William Shakespeare receiving payment for any form of writing, either in London or elsewhere.

- No record exists of anyone in London meeting with, speaking with, or having knowledge of, a poet and playwright named William Shakespeare.

- There is no record of anyone named William Shakespeare holding any office in Elizabethan London.

- There is no record that anyone named William Shakespeare ever attended at court.

- No tributes from fellow writers were paid to an author named William Shakespeare on the occasion of his death.

- It is not known when any of the plays of Shakespeare were written.

- It is not known in what order the plays of Shakespeare were written.

- It is not known who revised and edited the plays of Shakespeare for publication in the First Folio in 1623.

- It is not known who underwrote the cost of publishing the First Folio and processed it through to completion.

- It is not known where or by whom the Shakespeare manuscripts were preserved before publication, or what became of them afterwards.

- And finally, we do not know who actually wrote the plays attributed to William Shakespeare.

Bibliography

Anderson, Mark, *Shakespeare by Another Name*, Gotham Books, Penguin Group, New York, 2005.

Anderson, Verily, *The De Veres of Castle Hedingham*, Terence Dalton Limited, Lavenham, Suffolk, 1993.

Barber, Ros, ed, *30-Second Shakespeare*, Ivy Press, 2016.

Bearman, Robert, *Shakespeare in the Stratford Records*, in association with The Shakespeare Birthplace Trust.

Booth, Stephen, *Shakespeare's Sonnets*, Yale University Press, 1977.

Boyce, Charles, *Shakespeare A to Z*, Roundtable Press, New York, 1990.

Brazil, Robert Sean, *Edward de Vere and the Shakespeare Printers*, Cortical Output, LLC, Seattle, WA, USA, 2010.

Bucknill, John Charles, *The Medical Knowledge of Shakespeare*, London, Longman & Co., 1860.

Bucknill, John Charles, *The Psychology of Shakespeare*, London, Longman & Co, 1859.

Bullough, Geoffrey, *Narrative and Dramatic Sources of Shakespeare*, Routledge and Kegan Paul, 1957. In five volumes.

Chamberlin, Frederick, *The Private Character of Queen Elizabeth*, John Lane The Bodley Head, London, 1921.

Chambers, E.K., *Shakespeare : A Study of Facts and Problems*, two volumes, Oxford : Clarendon Press, 1930.

Crystal, David and Crystal, Ben, *Shakespeare's Words : A Glossary and Language Companion,* Penguin Books, 2002.

Dobson, Michael and Wells, Stanley, eds, *The Oxford Companion to Shakespeare*, Oxford University Press, 2001.

Elson, Louis C, *Shakespeare in Music*, London, 1901

Erne, Lukas, *Shakespeare as Literary Dramatist*, Cambridge University Press, 2003.

Fox, Robin, *Shakespeare's Education*, Laugwitz Verlag, Germany, 2012

Gilvary, Kevin, ed., *Dating Shakespeare's Plays : A Critical Review of the Evidence*, Parapress, Tunbridge Wells, 2010.

Gollancz, Sir Israel, *The Sources of Hamlet*, Frank Cass & Co Ltd, London, 1967.

Jolly, Margrethe, *The First Two Quartos of Hamlet : A New View of the Origins and Relationship of the Texts*, McFarland & Company, North Carolina, 2014.

Kail, Aubrey C., *The Medical Mind of Shakespeare*, Williams & Wilkins, Balgowlah, NSW, Australia, 1986.

Looney, J. Thomas, *Shakespeare Identified in Edward de Vere the Seventeenth Earl of Oxford*, Published by Cecil Palmer, Bloomsbury Street, London, 1920.

McGinn, Colin, *Shakespeare's Philosophy : The Meaning Behind the*

Plays. Harper Perennial, New York, 2006.

Magri, Noemi, *Such Fruits Out of Italy: The Italian Renaissance in Shakespeare's Plays and Poems*, Laugwitz Verlag, Buchholz, Germany, 2014.

Mai, François Martin. *Diagnosing Genius*, McGill-Queen's University Press, Montreal, 2007.

Malim, Richard, *The Earl of Oxford and the Making of Shakespeare*, McFarland & Company Inc, North Carolina, 2012.

Malim, Richard, ed., *Great Oxford, Essays on the Life and Work of Edward de Vere 17th Earl of Oxford 1550-1604*, Parapress, Tunbridge Wells, 2004.

Meres, Francis, *Palladis Tamia; Wits Treasury*, Garland Publishing, New York, 1973 with a preface by Arthur Freeman. A facsimile of the 1598 original.

Moore, Peter R., *The Lame Storyteller, Poor and Despised*, Verlag Uwe Laugwitz, Germany, 2009.

Muir, Kenneth, *The Sources of Shakespeare's Plays*, Methuen & Co Ltd, 1977.

Nelson, Alan H., *Monstrous Adversary*, Liverpool University Press, 2003.

Read, Conyers, *Lord Burghley and Queen Elizabeth*, Jonathan Cape, 1960.

Read, Conyers, *Mr. Secretary Cecil and Queen Elizabeth*, Jonathan Cape, 1955.

Roe, Richard Paul, *The Shakespeare Guide to Italy*, Harper Collins, New York, 2011.

Rouse, W.H.D., ed., *Shakespeare's Ovid Being Arthur Golding's Translation of the Metamorphoses*, Centaur Press, London, 1961. A facsimile of the 1567 original.

Schoenbaum, S. *William Shakespeare : A Documentary Life*. The Clarendon Press : Oxford, 1975.

Shakespeare Oxford Society, *Report my Cause Aright*, Fiftieth Birthday Anthology 1957-2007.

Shapiro, James, *Contested Will : Who Wrote Shakespeare*? Faber and Faber, 2010.

Vickers, Brian, *Shakespeare, Co-Author*, Oxford University Press, 2002.

Ward, Bernard. M., *The Seventeenth Earl of Oxford, 1550-1604, From Contemporary Documents*, John Murray, London, 1928.

Wells, Stanley, *Shakespeare, Sex, and Love*, Oxford University Press, 2010.

Wells, Stanley and Taylor, Gary, eds., *William Shakespeare, The Complete Works*, Second Edition, Clarendon Press · Oxford, 2005.

Wells, Stanley and Taylor, Gary, *William Shakespeare : A Textual Companion*, Clarendon Press · Oxford, 1987.

Wilson, J. Dover, *The Essential Shakespeare*, Cambridge University Press, 1964.

Index

Dugdale, William, 1605-86, historian, 64

Duke of Milan, character in *The Two Gentlemen of Verona*, 137

Duke of Venice, the 'Doge', 145

Duke Senior, character in *As You Like It*, 147

Dulwich College, 21

Duncan, character in *Macbeth*, 173

Dutch War of Independence, 1568-1648, 27

Dyer, Sir Edward, 1543-1607, courtier poet, 44, 190

Earl Marshal, Officer of State, 8th in precedence, 25

Earl of Leicester's Men, company of players, 16

Earl of Oxford's Boys, singers and actors, 16, 218

Earl of Oxford's Men, company of players, 155, 192, 211, 218

Earl of Warwick's Men, company of players, 218

Earl of Worcester's Men, company of players, 16

Edgar, character in *King Lear*, 230

Edmondson, Paul, Shakespeare scholar, 129, 236

Edmund Spenser, 1552-1599, English poet, 190, 193, 203, 209, 218

Edmund, character in *King Lear*, 230

Education Act 1870, 5, 72

Edward Bonaventure, a ship, 221

Edward II, play by Christopher Marlowe, 157, 198

Edward III, Shakespeare play, 71, 182

Edward IV, king of England, reigned 1461-1483, 163, 164

Edward V, murdered son of Edward IV, 164

Edward VI, 1537-1553, King of England, 12, 107

Edward, Prince of Wales, character in *3 Henry VI*, 164

Edwards, Richard, ?1523-66, Master of the Children of the Chapel Royal, 44

Egeon, a character in *The Comedy of Errors*, 141

Egeus, a character in *A Midsummer Night's Dream*, 93, 144

Elizabeth I, 1533-1603, Queen, 5, 12, 13, 17, 20, 21, 23, 25, 28, 88, 152, 187, 209, 211, 222

Elizabeth II, Queen, coronation of, 166

Elizabeth, Princess, later Queen Elizabeth I, 166, 222

Elsinore Castle, Denmark, setting for *Hamlet*, 218

Emerson, Ralph Waldo, 1803-1882, writer, 74

Emilia, character in *The Two Noble Kinsmen*, 180

Endimion, court comedy by John Lyly, 142, 143

English Civil War, 1642-51, 5, 62, 236

Ephesus, ancient city in Anatolia, modern day Turkey, 141

Epilepsy, medical condition, 103, 173

Erne, Lukas, *Shakespeare as Literary Dramatist*, 134

Essex Rebellion, February 1601, 18, 28, 199, 202, 223

Essex, earl of, 19, 27, 28, 29, 30, 199

Euphues and his England, John Lyly, 189, 218

Evans, Sir Hugh, character in *The Merry Wives of Windsor*, 94, 138

Fabian, character in *Twelfth Night*, 80

Fair Youth sequence of sonnets, 1-126, 125, 222, 224

Falstaff, Sir John, in 1 and 2 *Henry IV*, 94, 158, 159

Macbeth, Shakespeare play, 36, 91, 102, 173, 204

Mad Folk of Shakespeare, The, Sir John Bucknill, 102, 229

Magri, Dr Noemi, University of Mantua, 145

Malaria, in Shakespeare 'ague', 215

Malone, Edmond, 1741-1812, scholar, 21, 65, 67, 132, 199

Malvolio, character in *Twelfth Night*, 80, 151

Man of the Millennium, William Shakespeare, 5, 164, 234

Manners, Edward, 1549-1587, 3rd earl of Rutland, 24

Manners, Roger, 1576-1612, 5th earl of Rutland, 202

Mantua, Italian city, 92, 152

Margaret of Anjou, 1430-82, character in *Henry VI* trilogy and *Richard III*, 161, 162

Mark Antony, Roman statesman, 86, 171, 172

Marlovians, advocates for a Marlowe authorship, 134, 198

Marlowe, Christopher, 1564-93, dramatist, 21, 22, 109, 129, 133, 198

Marston, John, 1576-1634, poet, 43

Martin Marprelate, pamphlets against religious oppression, 192

Mary Sidney Society, Sante Fe, New Mexico, 194

Mary Stuart, 1542-1587, Queen of Scots, 23, 25, 214, 223

Mary Tudor, 1516-1558, Queen of England, 12, 107, 172

Matthew Bible, 108

Matthew, Thomas, pseudonymous Bible translator, 108

Mauvissière, Michel de Castenau, 1520-92, French ambassador, 216

Mawe, The (The Moor), 21

Measure for Measure, Shakespeare play, 36, 140

Medea, play by Seneca, 89

Medical Mind of Shakespeare, The, Aubrey C. Kail, 100, 101

Medici, Catherine de, 1519-89, mother of French King Charles IX, 90

Mendelssohn, Felix, 1809-47, composer, 91

Menenius, character in *Coriolanus*, 100

Merchant of Venice, The, Shakespeare play, 36, 81, 145, 220

Mercutio, character in *Romeo and Juliet*, 170

Meres, Rev Francis, 1565-1647, compiler of *Palladis Tamia*, 123, 155, 182, 192

Merry Wives of Windsor, The, Shakespeare play, 36, 138

Messina, city in Sicily, 92, 142

Metamorphoses, translation of Ovid, 14, 89, 90, 116, 144, 169, 212

Mexico, 81

Middle Temple, London, 97

Middleton, Thomas, 1580-1627, dramatist, 43, 133, 171

Midsummer Night's Dream, A, Shakespeare play, 36, 92, 144, 196

Milan, duke of, character in *The Two Gentlemen of Verona*, 137

Milan, Italian city, 80

Millington, Thomas, bookseller-publisher, 43

Miranda, character in *The Tempest*, 136

Mirror of Mutability, anthology of poems by Anthony Munday, 192

Mistress Ford, character in *The Merry Wives of Windsor*, 138

Mistress Page, character in *The Merry Wives of Windsor*, 138

Mistress Quickly, character in Falstaff scenes, 138

Oxford University, 172, 203, 212, 226

Padua, Italian city, 92, 122, 148, 202

Page, Anne, character in *The Merry Wives of Windsor*, 90, 138

Page, George, character in *The Merry Wives of Windsor*, 138

Page, William, publisher, 20

Palamon and Arcite, anonymous play based on Chaucer, 180, 212

Palamon, character in *The Two Noble Kinsmen*, 180, 212

Palermo, city in Sicily, 216

Palladis Tamia, compilation by Francis Meres, 123, 155, 182, 192

Pallas Athene, Greek goddess, 113

Pandarus, character in *Troilus and Cressida*, 104, 167

Paracelsus, medical pioneer, 99

Paris, capital city of France, 62, 117, 149, 196, 227

Paris, character in *Troilus and Cressida*, 104

Parma, duke of, 26

Paroles, character in *All's Well That Ends Well*, 94, 151

Parr, Catherine, widow of Henry VIII, 222

Passionate Pilgrim, The, collection of poetry, 124

Paul's Boys, singers from St Paul's Cathedral, 218

Paulina, character in *The Winter's Tale*, 235

Peele, George, 1566-96, writer, 133, 169

Pembroke, earl of, William Herbert, 39, 41, 46, 125, 193, 196, 205, 232

Percy, Thomas, 1528-ex1572, earl of Northumberland, 23, 199

Perdita, character in *The Winter's Tale*, 152

Pericles, Prince of Tyre, Shakespeare play, 37, 179

Persia, now Iran, 80, 81

Perthshire, Scotland, 82, 173

Petruccio, character in *The Taming of the Shrew*, 122, 148

Phelps, Samuel, 1804-1878, theatre manager, 71

Philip II, 1527-98, King of Spain, 116

Philip the Bastard, character in *King John*, 155

Philomel, victim in Ovid's *Metamorphoses*, 169

Phoenix Nest, The, anthology of poems, 1593, 190

Phrynia, character in *Timon of Athens*, 101

Pia Mater, medical definition, 99

Pickering (Pykering) John, writer of *Horestes*, 212

Pistol, character in *Henry V*, 81, 94

Plague, contagious medical condition, 116, 170, 215, 216, 233

Plantagenet, Richard, duke of York, 161, 164

Plantagenet, Sir Richard, character in *King John*, 155

Plautus, early Roman playwright, 90, 141

Plutarch, Greek author of *Parallel Lives*, 86, 90, 92, 168, 171, 172, 177

Polixenes, king of Bohemia, character in *The Winter's Tale*, 152

Polonius, character in *Hamlet*, 88, 94, 103, 226

Pompey, character in *Measure for Measure*, 95

Ponsonby, William, 1546-1604, London publisher, 43

Pontefract Castle, 82

Pontic Sea, now the Black Sea, quoted in *Othello*, 91

265

Printed in Great Britain
by Amazon

42055093R00150